Contents

Socialist Entrepreneurs

Embourgeoisement in Rural Hungary

IVAN SZELENYI

in collaboration with Robert Manchin, Pál Juhász, Bálint Magyar, and Bill Martin

Polity Press

This edition first published in the UK
in 1988 by Polity Press

Editorial Office:
Polity Press, Dales Brewery, Gwydir Street,
Cambridge CB1 2LJ, UK

Basil Blackwell Ltd
108 Cowley Road, Oxford OX4 1JF, UK

British Library Cataloguing in Publication Data
Szelenyi, Ivan
Socialist entrepreneurs: Embourgeoisement in Rural Hungary.
1. Social classes—Europe, Eastern—History—20th century
I. Title II. Manchin, Robert
305.5′0947 HN380.Z9S6
ISBN 0-7456-0460-9
ISBN 0-7456-0461-7 Pbk

Typeset in 10½ on 12pt Baskerville
by Joshua Associates Limited, Oxford
Printed in Great Britain

List of illustrations, figures, and tables

ILLUSTRATIONS

FIGURES

TABLES

Preface

This has been a long project. It started in 1971 when, after a decade of survey research on urban Hungary, I became interested in the countryside, in urban–rural relations.

In that year I wrote an article with my friend George Konrád entitled "Social conflicts of under-urbanization," which was subsequently published at the end of the year in the journal *Valóság* and many years later came out in an English edition (Konrád and Szelényi, 1977). The purpose of this article was to clarify our minds about the social consequences of urbanization under socialism. It was written as a research proposal, an essay, whose main aim was to set an agenda for future research.

There were two features of Hungarian urbanization at that time which struck us as unique and significant for both urban theory and policy formation. First, we figured that the growth of the industrial population was much faster in Hungary during the 1950s and 1960s than the growth of the urban population. This is why we claimed that Hungary had become "underurbanized." Under socialism, extensive industrialization had created an industrial system with a relatively small urban population. Most of the new urban industrial workers stayed in the villages of their birth and began to commute to urban workplaces. Second, we realized that although these peasant-workers are doubly exploited—they spend long hours commuting and are deprived of the somewhat better, government-subsidized urban infrastructure, including government-built housing, better shops, and schools—they often turn their disadvantages into advantages. They maintain semilegal or illegal private enterprises, and in the long run live better and may secure more autonomy for themselves than their fully proletarianized, more highly skilled urban colleagues.

During the early 1970s I was the acting head of the regional research unit at the Institute of Sociology of the Hungarian Academy of Sciences. In this capacity I directed, with funding from the Central Committee of the Hungarian Communist Party, a national rural survey of Hungary, primarily to test my theory of underurbanization and to study the advantages and disadvantages of peasant-worker existence. My essay with Konrád was not very well received by the Party and the academic establishment—we were vehemently attacked in *Társadalmi Szemle*, the theoretical monthly review of the Communist Party, basically for not appreciating Hungary's "socialist achievements"—but I was allowed to continue this project.

In 1972 I joined forces with a then-young research associate of the Institute, Robert Manchin. We designed a national rural sample. Using a stratified random selection method, we chose 100 villages from all over the country and selected more than 2000 households to be interviewed. Over 18 months Manchin and I visited virtually all the villages in preparing the questionnaire for the study and supervising the fieldwork. During two hundred or so days in the field we interviewed local bosses, presidents of kolkhozes and local councils, teachers, priests, shopkeepers, peasants, workers, teenagers, prostitutes, and policemen. We conducted several hundred in-depth interviews, tape-recording many of them.

We were fortunate enough to have an excellent team of advisers, who gave seminars for us, wrote working papers for our project, and gave advice on questionnaire construction. This team of senior researchers from whom I received my first lessons about rural Hungary included Rudolf Andorka, István Bibó, Zsolt Csalogh, Tamás Hoffer, Pál Juhász, Edit Lettrich, István Márkus, Mihály Sárkány, András Vágvölgyi, and others. A large group of young university graduates, mainly my own students from Karl Marx University of Economics, helped us too, in research design and in particular as interviewers and by writing several dozen case studies of individual villages. Let me simply name here the few who probably received their first field training in this project and who later became fine empirical sociologists: Jozsef Hegedüs, Gábor Kertesi, János Ladányi, György Lengyel, Gyula Pártos, and Gábor Vági.

We completed our fieldwork during the winter of 1972–73. During August 1973 I gave a first report about our research at Pécs at the Sociology Conference of the Hungarian Association of Adult Education (TIT). This, probably the best paper I ever gave, was mainly about the misery of declining small villages, which were deprived of all development funds by the 1971 Hungarian Regional Development Plan. But the representative of the Central Committee of the Communist Party who attended the conference was outraged at me for daring to attack the recently adopted Regional Development Plan. This imprudent lecture reinforced the belief of the party officials responsible for cultural affairs that I was a troublemaker, and as a result the project was taken away from me, my passport was revoked (I was on the point of leaving for a one-year research fellowship at the University of Essex—I never made it) and none of my work was published for an entire decade in Hungary. The Institute of Sociology tried to rescue at least the rural project. András Vágvölgyi was appointed to replace me as the principal investigator, and he did his best to bring the project to completion. A team under his direction produced a volume of essays (Vágvölgyi, 1982) based on data from this survey, but given its troubled past no one ever dared to or could produce a coherent theoretical synthesis.

After more conflict with the party and the political police, I left Hungary in 1975. For several years I lived in Australia and tried to forget about my rural project. In 1981 I came to the University of Wisconsin–Madison, and I began to receive hints that the Hungarian regime had begun to reassess the value of my earlier work, particularly my work on rural Hungary. By the early 1980s some of the disastrous consequences of the 1971 Regional Development Plan had become known, so I suppose that it became an appropriate time to rehabilitate my Pécs lecture and the earlier paper on "The social conflicts of under-urbanization." Furthermore, Robert Manchin visited me in Madison during the spring of 1981 and suggested that we could resume the analysis of the 1972 Rural Survey. Most of the collected data were available in machine-readable form, but virtually no analysis had been done on them. Manchin had also collected a similar data set in 1978–79 at the Institute of Sociology; he told me that he could obtain permission from the Central Statistical Office (CSO) to conduct secondary analysis of their income and social mobility surveys, conducted in 1972 and under preparation for 1982. Manchin told me that he would be permitted to bring these data tapes to Madison for scientific use, if I was able to get research funding.

Manchin arrived in Madison in October 1982; he stayed with me, with a few short trips back to Hungary, until March 1986. The initial support for our joint work came from the National Council for Soviet and East European Research (September 1982–August 1983), for analysis of the 1972 and 1978–79 Institute of Sociology surveys, in order to document the changes in part-time family farming in contemporary Hungary. For the 1982–83 academic year I also received a grant from the Graduate School of the University of Wisconsin–Madison to enable me to conduct a study of Wisconsin part-time farmers, in order to have a comparative perspective on the subject in two settings. Finally, for 1985 and 1986 we received a grant from the National Science Foundation (SES-8410136) to complete our study by analyzing the most recent data, the 1982 CSO Income Survey and the Social Mobility and Life History Survey. The Hewett Fund and the Graduate School of the University of Wisconsin–Madison also provided Manchin and myself with salaries for summer 1983. The College of Letters and Sciences of the University of Wisconsin–Madison generously gave Robert Manchin lectureships on several occasions, when bridging funds between grants was necessary. Robert Hauser and Erik O. Wright offered research jobs to Manchin at times when the funding I could find was not adequate. Throughout the whole project we received free computing time and programming assistance from the Center for Demography and Ecology of the University of Wisconsin–Madison.

In 1982 the Hungarian government issued me a Hungarian passport; thus, during the last four years I have been able to go back for visits to Hungary, after seven years of "exile." This gave a big boost to my project. During these summer trips I spent a substantial amount of time in villages, continuing my earlier ethnographic work. Pál Juhász proved to be an excellent guide and a great teacher on such trips. With Juhász, Bálint Magyar, Pál Schiffer, Imre Kovách, and Gábor Havas I spent several important weeks in the field and learned how the peasant-workers I had known a decade earlier were now entering a new economic and social trajectory—a state that we describe hereafter as "embourgeoisement." An important turning point in our project came when, with funds from the Open Society Foundation, Pál Juhász and Bálint Magyar spent a semester at the University of Wisconsin in Madison with me. Words cannot express my gratitude to both of them.

While working on this project I benefited much from my American colleagues too. We received valuable methodological advice from David Grusky, Robert Mare, David Featherman, Robert Hauser, and Hal Winsborough. I had several inspiring conversations about this book with Roger Bartra, Michael Burawoy, Harriet Friedmann, and Erik Wright. Michael Burawoy, David Featherman, and David Stark undertook the arduous task of reading the first, over 600-page manuscript of this book, and they helped me a great deal to reduce it to its current size and to make it, I hope, more enjoyable reading.

I must also express my greatest gratitude to several of my students at the University of Wisconsin who either worked with me as research assistants or commented on parts of the manuscript. My special thanks are due to Bill Martin, with whom I conducted 17 extended interviews with Wisconsin part-time farmers and who is the senior author of our research report upon that subject. Bill Martin was also my research assistant during the summer of 1986 and helped me to tighten up loose ends in the data (we rebuilt several models for the final manuscript and prepared the documentation). Robert Jenkins was my research assistant in the project for the National Council for Soviet and East European Research; Yasuhiro Tanaka worked as a research assistant for me from time to time, and I also received valuable help from Sunghee Nam. Critical comments from Gerardo Otero were always greatly appreciated.

Several of my Hungarian colleagues read and commented upon different drafts of this book. I want to express my thanks to Péter Galasi, Jozsef Hegedüs, Gábor Kertesi, Tamás Kolosi, and János Ladányi for their valuable comments.

The photographs in this book are from an ethnographic film project on Rural Society of Hungarofilms and Hunnio Studio. Director of the film was Pál Schiffer, the photographers were Zsuzsa Burai and Katalin Götze. Subtitles are mine.

This book is about a silent revolution from below, a revolution which is still incomplete but which goes on irresistibly. So much has happened over the last 15 years while I have been a conscious observer of this process. The Hungarian peasants and, half a world away, their Chinese brothers and sisters have over decades patiently educated their new masters, who are not very smart and do not learn very quickly, but slowly seem to be getting the message: agriculture—and, of course, society too—works better if people are allowed to live their lives their own way and produce in work organizations they feel comfortable with. I hope this book is thus the first volume in a series about such silent but successful revolutions from below and about the failures of noisy and aggressive revolutions from above.

Iván Szelényi
New York City
October 1986

Socialist Entrepreneurs

Introduction

Class and social formations: metatheoretical implications of this study

The purpose of this book is to explore the transformation of rural social structure during the epoch of industrialization and collectivization of agriculture in a state socialist society, Hungary. We are particularly interested in understanding the logic of and limits to "socialist proletarianization": how, under the dual pressure of industrialization and collectivization, former peasants and small agricultural entrepreneurs were pushed toward a wage-laborer existence. At the same time, we will also try to identify those mechanisms by which people tried to resist such pressure. Some of them succeeded.

The heroes of our book are rural semiproletarians—people who live in two worlds, who combine work for wages and salaries for the government with part-time family agricultural production. The majority of the rural population in socialist Eastern Europe belongs to this category. Who are these people, where have they come from, and where are they heading?

This is an empirical study, based on years of ethnographic fieldwork in rural Hungary and on statistical analysis of survey data concerning family incomes, social mobility, and life histories. The main body of this book will stay close to empirical evidence, both ethnographic and statistical data. But the introduction is the appropriate place to spell out some of the metatheoretical implications of our investigation, to explain why the Western reader—not only experts on Eastern Europe, but also those who are concerned with socialism, classes and class formations, theory of social formations and social change—should be interested in this book. We call the following set of propositions *metatheoretical*, since the evidence presented here is insufficient to verify or disprove them. This evidence comes from one country at a peculiar historic juncture; the most we can achieve is to cast doubt on some of the widely accepted theoretical wisdom. If in this introduction we succeed in formulating a few questions in a novel way, then we have achieved all that we can aim for at this moment.

This book has implications for class theory, for the theory of social formations, and for the theory of social change. First we summarize our key argument in each of these three areas; we will then elaborate these arguments in some detail.

The theory of class Most study of class stresses the omnipotence of the dominant class and the reproduction of class domination. This book, instead, stresses the countervailing power of peasants and workers, the limits of bureaucratic domination. After three decades of mainly silent, passive resistance, former Hungarian (and Chinese) peasants seem to be winning. They certainly have not "overthrown" the "bureaucratic class," but they have forced them into lasting and strategically important concessions. Gradually, they have reinterpreted the rules of the game of state socialism and have transformed society into a structure complex enough that they can achieve within it living conditions that they find acceptable.

Most class theorists also assume that proleterianization is unilinear and inevitable. The dominant view among class analysts holds that semiproletarians are the worst off: being between two systems of exploitation, they are doubly exploited. In contrast, we believe that many peasant-workers have succeeded in transforming the disadvantages of their semiproletarian position into their own advantage. During the late 1970s or early 1980s, as family entrepreneurial opportunities began to open up, some families even began to enter a "socialist embourgeoisement" trajectory as an alternative to proletarianization.

The theory of social formations The spectre of "capitalist restoration" in the Soviet Union and Eastern Europe has haunted the theorists of the Western Left ever since the October Revolution. Many such theorists would be inclined to interpret the process that we call "embourgeoisement" as the unmistakable sign of such a restoration. But in our view, "embourgeoisement" does not imply the restoration of capitalism. Rather, a new socialist social formation is in the making. This new formation is a mixed economy in which the dominant bureaucratic-redistributive mechanism of coordination (the statist mode of production) is increasingly complemented by market coordination (the petty-commodity mode of production), in which people can break out from the cadre–proletarian axis of social stratification by "embourgeoisement" or "petty-bourgeoisification."

Theorists on the political Left and Right both often presume that systems tend to develop toward their pure forms or ideal types. To formulate it in Marxist language: economies tend to become pure modes of production. Mixed economies will not last too long: a little welfare-state activity in the West is "creeping socialism," a little market activity in the East is "creeping capitalism." In the last instance, countries will have to choose; there are no alternatives to American capitalism or Soviet socialism. The idea of such an alternative, a "Third Road," is often ridiculed as naive or utopian. This book is about the viability of that Third Road. Our story suggests that mixed economies can reproduce themselves, that more complex systems adapt more effectively to economic challenges, and that systems where there are two masters may offer a more balanced distribution of power, with more room to maneuver for the powerless.

The theory of social change Our story is about historic continuity, at both the micro and the macro level. People from middle-peasant families[1] are more likely to reenter the embourgeoisement trajectory, and the emergent new dual stratification system has certain similarities with the prewar social structure. Even if we consider it a Third-Road development, the historical continuity is emphasized: the monolithic statism imposed on Hungary and the rest of Eastern Europe by the Soviet Union as a result of the military status quo after World War II may be loosening, but the region is not merely moving toward a Western trajectory of development; rather, it is returning to its own organic evolutionary path, the Third Road. By emphasizing historical continuity we do not question the possibility of change, but we do doubt the efficiency of "revolution from above." This book shows that such a strategy of social change not only demands a heavy price in human life and suffering, but that in the long run it does not work. At the same time, this book reports a successful "silent revolution from below." Family inheritance matters a great deal, but the "socialist embourgeoisement" now occurring in Hungary is breaking through some of the prewar rigidities, both economic and social, of society.

[1] The terms commonly used to define the economic and social position of the Hungarian peasantry are briefly clarified in Chapter 3.

THEORY OF CLASSES AND CLASS FORMATIONS

Power of the powerless

We are not alone in being astonished at how much countervailing power peasants and workers can after all exercise in a state bureaucratic system in which they are deprived of democratic political institutions. During the last few years two American sociologists—Michael Burawoy and David Stark—conducted fieldwork in Hungarian industrial firms; they both seem to share our amazement.

It is particularly interesting to reconstruct how Michael Burawoy arrived at his more recent position. He became interested in state socialist "factory regimes" after having read an ethnographic study of a Hungarian tractor manufacturing firm by Haraszti (Burawoy, 1985b; Haraszti, 1977). Burawoy had just completed a similar study of an American firm in Chicago (Burawoy, 1979) and he was impressed by how analogous the two stories were. The degree of oppression, the degradation of workers, and the dreadfulness of piecework in the two firms were quite similar, though the mechanisms which produced such outcomes were different. Burawoy in *Manufacturing Consent* (1979) and in the article on Haraszti's book, *Workers in a Worker's State*, pursues a structuralist analysis. He identifies different logics by which the exploitation of the workers is reproduced and appropriation of surplus "obscured and secured," in different forms but with similar results (in competitive capitalism it is "market despotism," in monopoly capitalism, "hegemonic factory regime," and in state socialism, "bureaucratic despotism"). Burawoy's workers are in a no-win situation. Although in advanced capitalism the internal "state" within the industrial firm does manufacture consent, so that the workers may believe that they are not coerced to produce, in reality they have become their own prison guards. "Manufacturing consent" is basically just a mechanism to obscure surplus appropriation; it does not significantly alter the balance of power among classes.

In 1983–85 Burawoy went to Hungary to find out more, this time firsthand, about work under state socialism. In the two articles about his field experiences (Burawoy, 1985a; Burawoy and Lukács, 1986) he reports an unanticipatedly high degree of "workers' power" in state socialist firms:

> uncertainty . . . in a state socialist enterprise, provides the foundation of considerable worker power and potential resistance to managerial dictatorship. . . . key workers are able to pose considerable countervailing

> power by virtue of their position in the labor process. . . . Management is forced to rely on such workers, so that they are able to extract concessions in defense of their interests.
>
> [Burawoy and Lukács, 1986, p. 733]

But Burawoy may not depart radically from his earlier structuralist framework. He still emphasizes that management gives concessions primarily to core workers; thus, he could always revert to the idea that in the last instance, the workers' power he is writing about only fragments the working class and maximizes managerial power. Still, in his earlier writings Burawoy emphasized the ability of the factory to "contain struggles" (Burawoy, 1979, p. 202) and the effects of collective bargaining, which "guarantee[s] management the support of the union . . . and . . . [contributes] to a reduction in the level of militancy on the shop floor" (p. 188). Now, he writes about the "considerable countervailing power" of the workers and attributes such workers' power to the inherent characteristics of a bureaucratically organized labor process.

This argument is consistent with the findings of Hungarian industrial sociologists and economists about the limitations of managers and even of central planners and redistributors. Industrial sociologists had during the late 1960s and early 1970s documented workers' success in developing "transactive" relationships with management (Héthy and Mako, 1972). Economists had also attacked the myth of the omnipotence of central planners, arguing that the reality is "plan-bargaining" (Bauer, 1981, pp. 492–95, 520; Bauer, 1978; Kornai, 1980; Fehér et al., 1983, pp. 77–83). In plan bargaining, bureaucratic subcenters can effectively block the will of central redistributors, but even workers on the shop floor can gain substantial bargaining power (Köllő, 1981).

David Stark is another Western commentator on the state socialist industrial system. In his earliest article on the subject (Sabel and Stark, 1982) he developed the theme of the shop-floor power of state socialist workers very much along the lines of Burawoy, Héthy, and Mako. According to Sabel and Stark (p. 440):

> the planned economy by its very nature creates the precondition for shop floor power. . . . struggles within the party became entwined with more limited workplace struggles . . . allowing workers an indirect, but not insignificant voice in the choice of national economic strategy . . . and allowing workers a veto over important decisions.

In 1985 and 1986 Stark also became engaged in fieldwork in Hungary (Stark, 1985, 1986), and his research began to move beyond Burawoy's work to explore the genesis of this countervailing proletarian power. Stark discovered that its foundation is the "second economy" or, in our terminology, the survival of semiproletarian positions (Stark, 1985, p. 248; for the concept of the "second economy," see Gábor, 1979a, b; Galasi and Gábor, 1981; Kemény, 1982; Galasi and Sziráczki, 1985, pp. 122–79; Grossmann, 1977; Duchêne, 1981). In analyzing the new internal subcontracting system in Hungarian industry, Stark notes that it developed as a response of the bureaucracy to the strengthening of the second economy. Semiproletarians, mostly unskilled and semiskilled workers who occupy only a peripheral position in industrial firms, were generating high incomes for themselves in the emergent, marketlike "second economy," particularly in family agricultural production. Industrial bureaucracies, in order to keep "core workers," the highly qualified urban industrial proletariat, had to develop "internal markets" within the firms; they were forced to break redistributive regulations governing wage levels. In the emerging new system, management now subcontracts jobs at "market prices" to "private" work collectives, formed, typically, by the core workers of the firms, who perform these tasks after hours and are paid at several times the official rates. (For internal subcontracting as a mechanism which compensates "core workers" for the privileges "peripheral workers" can gain through family agricultural production, see also Mako, 1985; Kövári and Sziráczki, 1985.)

We believe that Stark has a more complex understanding of the countervailing power of workers in a state socialist economy than does Burawoy. We agree with Stark that the genesis of this countervailing power lies in the second economy. First, unskilled or semiskilled peasant-workers through part-time family agricultural production began to gain some autonomy and reasonable living standards for themselves, though increased labor fluctuation pushed their wage levels up in the bureaucratically controlled industrial plant. Core workers responded to this with frustration. Some left industry to join kolkhozes and forced management to begin to give concessions to them too. Thus Burawoy's idea about the fragmentation of the working class is not all that persuasive. Yes, the working class is fragmented, but this is hardly masterminded by the bureaucracy, and the success of one group of workers may help other groups to gain concessions. Furthermore, the ultimate and real source of countervailing popular power is self-employment, petty commodity production. Classes struggle to achieve compromises, to alter the distribution of power between the classes at the point of production and by establishing an alternative economic system (paradoxically, in Eastern Europe it is the public-political sphere where the least action occurs!).

So if this book—reinforced by the findings of Burawoy, Stark, or Hungarian industrial sociologists—reports that peasants and workers under state socialism have greater countervailing power than anticipated, does that mean that we are offering an apologia for state socialism? Do we conclude that, after all, state socialism, though it may have its shortcomings, is in the last instance a better system than capitalism—that it offers the worker more power than a system of private ownership? Burawoy sometimes sounds a bit like it (see Burawoy and Lukács, 1986). Comparing his Chicago firm, Allied, with his Hungarian firm, Bánki, he argues that in the Hungarian firm productivity is higher, the quality of production is better, there is less waste, and norms fit performance better; all these, he states, can be attributed to the socialist organization of production.

We are reluctant to offer such an apologia for the system of state socialism. Our purpose is to invite our fellow class analysts who study "class reproduction" in capitalist countries to rethink the way they view class struggles and class formation. Our inspiration comes from the work of Adam Przeworski (see his *Capitalism and Social Democracy* (1986), particularly Chapters 4 and 5; see also Wright, 1985, pp. 123–26). For Przeworski, class struggle is not a zero-sum game: the subordinated classes may quite conceivably make genuine and lasting gains without any revolutionary break in the social structure. Orthodox Marxist structuralists argue that when "market despotism" gives way to a "hegemonic factory regime," capitalism is simply reproduced in a new form. Thus the opening up of family entrepreneurship and the introduction of internal subcontracting in the Hungarian economy merely reproduce bureaucratic domination. Not much has happened; the evil machine perpetuates itself. We disagree with this view on two counts. First, in both cases—since power is not a zero-sum game—workers can make important and lasting gains, even if capitalists or bureaucrats lose little or nothing. Second, instead of the politics of class compromise, orthodox Marxists advocate the "big bang," the elimination of the old dominant class altogether. But how much will workers gain from this? They may gain little or nothing; they may even lose. The new masters who replace the old may, at least for a while, be even cruder, greedier, and less willing to make concessions. Those subordinated to domination will need time to figure out what the new masters are up to and how to teach them the wisdom of political compromise.

The advantages of semiproletarian status: alternatives to proletarianization

It should now be clear that assessing the strengths and weaknesses, advantages and disadvantages of the semiproletarian position under socialism is of major significance for this book. Our heroes are semiproletarians. We think that in recent history, East European semiproletarians have been particularly successful in forcing their new masters to make substantial concessions.

Immanuel Wallerstein is one who sees the historic advantages of full-scale proletarianization and who defines semiproletarians as doubly exploited. He regards full proletarianization as the result of successful class struggle. For him, the existence of large semiproletarian masses is advantageous for capitalism. The size of the semiproletariat shows the weakness of the subordinated classes (Wallerstein, 1984). According to Wallerstein, capitalists are primarily interested in how much they can appropriate; therefore they prefer semiproletarians, or even slave labor. Fully proletarianized workers are more likely to be unionized and can more effectively bargain for higher wages. Full proletarianization is likely to reduce profit rates; thus workers will fight for proletarianization and capitalists will resist it.

Wallerstein's argument that proletarianization is the result of successful class struggle is applicable to "socialist" countries as well. A world-system theorist would presumably argue that the exceptionally large semiproletarian masses in "socialist" countries are good both for accelerated accumulation and the interests of the dominant bureaucracies.

We view semiproletarian status somewhat differently. We regard its persistence in state socialist societies as an indication of the success of the "struggle of subordinated classes."

True, semiproletarians were in a sense "doubly exploited." They had to work harder and contributed even more to meet the costs of accelerated industrialization than those who were only wage laborers. But at they same time they were also better placed to force their bureaucratic rulers into substantial concessions. They achieved some autonomy and reasonable living standards, not only for themselves, but indirectly for all workers (Konrád and Szelényi, 1977).

Furthermore, the incompleteness of the proletarianization has a second positive consequence for those subordinated to authority. The failure of state socialism to complete the proletarianization process shows that this system of domination has remained unstable. The survival of large semiproletarian masses keeps a "window open for the future." It indicates that society is not yet irreversibly frozen into a bureaucratic state socialist system but may develop in other directions.

Although we are certain that this argument is correct for socialist Eastern Europe, we are not sure of its implications for Third World countries.

Neo-Marxist theorizing about the Third World, particularly dependency theory, emphasizes that the maintenance of masses of people in a semiproletarian state is one mechanism by which the dependency of the Third World is being reproduced. The *proletarianistas*, or Leninist theorists in Mexico, for instance, argue that full proletarianization is necessary, inevitable, and progressive. In their view, progressive change will be possible in the Third World only when semiproletarian status is eliminated, or at least when semiproletarians begin to behave like wage laborers. (For a description of the *proletarianista* position, see Otero, 1986; Bennholdt-Thomsen, 1982, pp. 12–30.) Third World friends who read earlier versions of this manuscript tried to persuade us that although our analysis may be true for Eastern Europe, we should not generalize it to the Third World.[2] They hinted that our emphasis on the positive features of semiproletarian existence can be used to justify the poverty of the semiproletarian masses in peripheral societies, and that our approval of Hungarian peasant-workers could be interpreted as an apologia for the condition of migrant workers in South Africa.[3]

We hope this book will have readers from the Third World, and we would be delighted if we could in one way or another contribute to the ongoing *proletarianista–campesinista*, Leninist–Chayanovist debate. We are suspicious of the *proletarianista*–Leninist view because the historical equivalent of that ideology, the official theory of agriculture and the peasantry promulgated by the East European Communist parties, was used in Eastern Europe to substitute socialist proletarianization for capitalist proletarianization. Communist parties suppressed tendencies toward embourgeoisement and worked against the evolution of family farming, particularly following the radical land reforms after 1945. This book casts doubt on the wisdom and efficiency of these East European *proletarianista*–Leninist policies. Replacing capitalist or feudal landlords with state bureaucratic landlords was not such a wonderful idea. It created crippled economies, which had—and after several decades of operation still have—elementary difficulties in feeding people. These Leninist measures were also resisted by the former semiproletarians and

[2] We would like to express our thanks to Roger Bartra and Gerardo Otero for critical comments on earlier versions of this manuscript.

[3] Michael Burawoy suggested that we should make a distinction between peasant-workers and migrant workers, presenting the migrant workers as net losers.

peasants, who wanted to hold on to their land. Many of them—often the best of them—were killed, jailed, or tortured. Fortunately, the Hungarian and Chinese peasants at least were smart enough to survive the years of forced collectivism, and as their bureaucratic rulers began to abandon their ideological obsessions, the peasant-workers once more quietly started doing what they had always wanted to do: produce in their family enterprises, cheaply, effectively, and with self-respect, without being bossed around by usually ignorant and aggressive cadres.

These statements should not be taken as full-fledged support for a Chayanovist position. *Campesinistas*–Chayanovists, just like some of the pre-World War II Hungarian populists (*népiesek*, about whom more in Chapter 2) had romantic illusions about the peasantry. Undoubtedly the transition from a semifeudal, semicapitalist agrarian system like the present one in Mexico or the prewar one in Hungary requires the proletarianization of some of the semiproletarian masses, the maintenance and creation of large, wage-labor-operated agricultural enterprises, and a general reduction in the agrarian population. But all rationally organized agricultural systems have room—indeed, a fair amount of room—for family farming. Although some semiproletarians following a radical land reform will become wage laborers, others will succeed in establishing themselves as small family agricultural entrepreneurs, family farmers; in effect, they achieve petty-bourgeois status. Our major objection to the *proletarianista*–Leninist position is that it blocks embourgeoisement as an alternative to proletarianization. It helps to create a more monolithic economic system, with a single hierarchy of bureaucratic domination.

Thus we ask our readers whose main interests are agrarian reform in peripheral capitalist countries to keep an open mind about what we say here about the "advantages" of a semiproletarian position, about embourgeoisement as an alternative to full proletarianization.

THEORY OF SOCIAL FORMATIONS

A socialist mixed economy

In the early 1970s some of the rural semiproletarians in Hungary began to exploit the liberalism of the regime, to intensify and orient toward the market production on their family minifarms. They have ceased to be peasant-workers; instead, they are now becoming "bourgeois." According to our calculations, by the early 1980s somewhere between 5 and 15 percent of rural households were running highly specialized, primarily market-oriented, family agricultural enterprises. Gaining a significant proportion of their cash incomes (at least a third or one-half of total family income) from agricultural production, they could be regarded as "entrepreneurs."

Such embourgeoisement produces changes in the system of rural stratification. During the years of forced collectivization, rural social structure was transformed into a single hierarchy, in which power and privilege were determined exclusively by rank in the bureaucratic order. Now, a new dual system of rural stratification is emerging, and the still dominant bureaucratic order is being complemented by a market-based system of inequalities.

At this point our friends on the Western Left will ask: "Are you talking about the restoration of capitalism?" During the last decades Western Marxists have warned repeatedly about the "dangers of capitalist restoration," "creeping capitalism." (See, for instance, Cliff, 1979, or Bettelheim, 1976. For reviews of the relevant literature, see Dupay and Truchil, 1979; Jerome and Buick, 1967; Fehér et al., 1983, pp. 22–37.) We basically agree with Fehér and his colleagues: all these theories are fundamentally flawed. The Soviet Union or the East European societies cannot be called "capitalist" or "state capitalist" in any meaningful sense of the term (at least, not yet). We also sympathize with the irritation of our East European colleagues at Western Marxist theorizing about capitalist restoration. Reform-inclined East European intellectuals typically refuse to enter into this discourse at all. They know all too well that "capitalist restoration" is often the slogan used by party hawks to block pragmatic social and economic reforms. Party conservatives thus paradoxically find allies in Western Marxists—though this may be the last thing these Western Marxists want—for their Stalinist restoration projects.

More concretely: the kind of embourgeoisement we are describing here—at least until now—has not led to "capitalism." Rather, a new, state socialist type of mixed economy is emerging, with a uniquely new dual system of social stratification. It is as different from laissez-faire or welfare state capitalism as it is from the Soviet style of monolithic, redistributive, state socialism.

The emergent new family agricultural entrepreneurs are not "capitalist" in any meaningful sense of the term. Most of them are just part-time farmers; they work for themselves and do not use wage labor, or use it only seasonally. They distrust the regime and do not dare to become full-time private farmers. They remember how short-lived past liberalizations—"let the hundred flowers bloom"—usually were. Leaving aside the possibility, the motivation to become a full-time entrepreneur is also limited. The dual existence these peasant-workers have established for themselves has many advantages: state employment guarantees a permanent flow of cash income into the household and insures against the uncertainties of the climate and the market. Why should they give it up? Furthermore, it is a long way from their highly intensive, productive and profitable, but tiny family minifarms to a viable full-time family farm. Without a proper commercial credit system and with legal restraints on land ownership, our new entrepreneurs would find their opportunities to become full-time family farmers very restricted indeed, even if they wanted to.

Our new family agricultural entrepreneurs are also integrated into an economy which is basically redistributive and a stratification system which is predominantly based on bureaucratic rank. They have learned how to live with this; it is the only system in which they know how to operate. In fact, they live so well on their tiny farms precisely because they operate in a redistributive economy and a not too competitive environment. In a market system proper, most of them would go bankrupt immediately; the rest would starve on their one-acre farms. So they themselves have little interest in letting loose the "anarchic forces of the market." They may after all, despite their complaints, prefer the warmth of state socialist paternalism. They are "entrepreneurs" who operate in the "market" sector of an integrated economic system that is primarily redistributive.

There are two important theoretical implications to the above argument.

First, the transition from self-employed, "petty bourgeois" commodity producer to capitalist entrepreneur (or pure proletarian) may not be so easy and inevitable as Marx himself believed and as later Marxists, particularly Leninists, warned us it might be. Marx in his debate with Proudhon (Marx, 1847), was already expressing his doubts about the long-term viability of self-employment. He dismissed as "petty bourgeois utopianism," Proudhon's vision of socialism, which was based on a universalized petty commodity production and self-employment. Marx believed that the forces of bureaucratization and industrialization would inevitably lead to large-scale capitalist or socialist forms of work organization. Petty commodity production or self-employment was not a form which could reproduce itself in the long run. Later, in the chapter on commodity fetishism in the first volume of *Capital*, Marx argued on theoretical grounds that commodity production, even in its "petty" form, was the breeding ground of capitalist, exploitative relations (Marx, 1867).

In the same vein, Lenin in 1919 stated unambiguously: "The

economic system of Russia in the era of the dictatorship of the proletariat represents . . . the struggle against petty commodity production and against capitalism . . . which is newly arising on the basis of petty commodity production." Later in the same article he wrote: "Peasant farming continues to be petty commodity production. Here we have an extremely broad and very sound, deep-rooted basis for capitalism, a basis on which capitalism persists or arises anew in a bitter struggle against communism." (Lenin, 1919 [1971], pp. 290–91).

We will not defend Proudhon against Marx here. In that debate Marx was probably right: a modern economy cannot be based on a universalized system of petty commodity production. But Marx may have underestimated the extent to which, under both capitalism and state socialism, self-employment can survive and reproduce its own "subsystem." The idea that "small is beautiful" is still with us. Technological change sometimes enables or even favors the decentralization of production (think of the computer revolution, for instance). The proportion of self-employed, very small businessmen and farmers has declined radically since the last century, but it is now stable and may even be on the increase.

Even more important: Lenin is wrong when he claims that petty commodity production is the "basis on which capitalism persists and arises anew." A capitalist type of development in Eastern Europe is far from unimaginable or undesirable. If the Soviet Union would loosen its control over this region, it could be a reasonable strategy for countries like Hungary, under the pressures of the world market, to move closer toward the Western model, import functioning capital, and try to attract multinational companies. But we see no signs whatsoever that this type of capitalist development could ever come from family entrepreneurship, and particularly from capital accumulation on our market-oriented family minifarms. Family entrepreneurship and petty commodity production are not inevitably a breeding ground for capitalism!

Second, we must carefully reinterpret concepts borrowed from capitalist market economies proper for the study of this new state socialist mixed economy, in which redistributive power has until now retained its hegemony. *Market* is articulated through the dominant redistributive mechanism, market-based inequalities; *entrepreneurship* is articulated through the dominant bureaucratic order. Concepts and theoretical propositions worked out for capitalist societies must be "converted" before they can be applied to the study of the newly emerging phenomena. Neo-Marxists studying the Third World have begun to develop a theory of articulations which explains how, for instance, precapitalist forms or forces are transformed if they operate within a social formation in which the "capitalist mode of production" has become dominant. (A. Foster-Carter [1978, pp. 47–77] offers a good summary of this literature.) Our book is a first step toward a theory of articulation of a state socialist mixed economy.

Third Road?

Polish, Prussian, and Hungarian intellectuals have been fascinated by the idea of a "Third Road" for a century now. Eastern—they preferred to call themselves *Central*—European intellectuals saw themselves as sandwiched between the greedy and anarchistic capitalism of the West and the traditionalism and despotism of the Orient (Russian or, even worse, Mongol or Turkish). They disliked both and dreamed of a Third Road, which would merge Western ideas of democracy and citizenship with Oriental notions of community.

During the 1930s Hungarian populists were inspired by these ideas in their critique of the large feudal estate. They wanted to make sure that their attacks on the semifeudal latifundia were not misunderstood either as support for collectivization or as a surrender to commercialized capitalist farming. They advocated, rather, radical land reform; they argued that small family farms, particularly if they were oriented toward market gardening, were socially and economically viable and desirable alternatives. László Németh, the talented novelist and a major populist ideologue of the 1930s and '40s, advocated transformation of the country into "Garden Hungary," built on the agricultural and peasant or peasant-burgher traditions of the nation. Industrialization for industrialization's sake should be resisted (Németh, 1943). Peasant-burghers, peasants who had become bourgeoisified and had moved from clientelism to citizenship, from subsistence farming to family entrepreneurship, are the heroes of the most powerful sociological theorist of the epoch, Ferenc Erdei. Embourgeoisement rather than the proletarianization of the peasantry was to be the foundation for "Garden Hungary," which was neither Soviet-style state collectivist nor Western-style greedy capitalist.

"Garden Hungary" projected a vision of a future society primarily based on self-employment, family farming, and individual small businesses, rather than upon wage labor delivered either to the kolkhoz or on commercialized large estates. Erdei was the least "utopian" among these populists. He had a keen interest in the cooperative movement in the West, and probably even before 1945 was less opposed to the idea of the kolkhoz than his comrades. It is a sad irony of history—though not totally an accident—that during the Stalinist years Erdei, the advocate of peasant embourgeoisement, served for a time as minister of agriculture. In 1960 he became the main architect of Hungarian collectivization and thus was more responsible than anyone else for the proletarianization of his beloved Hungarian peasants. But other populists of this epoch were attracted more to the Proudhon's than to Marx's vision of socialism. They hoped to find a solution to the injustices of private ownership not by its elimination but by its universalization, by making everyone the owner of his or her means of production.

There was a second, short-lived wave of Third Road theorizing after 1945. István Bibó, the most able political theorist of the epoch and a former associate of Ferenc Erdei, again repeatedly warned his fellow East Europeans that they should keep searching for a third alternative. Bibó refused to accept the claims of the Communist Party, which presented Soviet-type socialism as the only alternative to greedy capitalism or to the prewar ancien regime (Bibó, 1945; 1946a, b; 1948).

For a while it appeared that the sovietization of Eastern Euorpe in 1949 and the forced collectivization of agriculture had irreversibly closed off the possibility of a Third Road. But in different ways the idea is returning to the political and theoretical agenda in this part of the world. In Poland, most theorists of the Solidarity movement have emphasized that they seek an alternative to Soviet-style socialism which is also different from Western socioeconomic systems. In Hungary particularly, the resurgence of family entrepreneurship, the reemergence of an embourgeoisement process that was earlier interrupted, can be interpreted as proof that a uniquely East European, Third Road development may be, not just a theoretical fantasy, but a stubborn trend in history.

Our book was inspired by the work of the populists, particularly the young Erdei and Bibó, and by the populists' criticism of the latifundia, their advocacy of the embourgeoisement of the peasantry, and their belief in the possibility of a Third Road. We hope that it will be read as belonging to this tradition, as continuing this heritage. But we use the concept of a "Third Road" with somewhat different, more ironic overtones than the Hungarian populists of the 1930s. For them, even for Bibó, the Third Road meant the "good society." In this book we show that Hungary is moving toward a new mixed economy and a dual system of social stratification which is distinguishable from both Western capitalism and Soviet-style socialism and more in the Hungarian or East European tradition of social organization. But we refrain from value judgments; we do not recommend this as the *desirable* future for Eastern Europe, even less so for the rest of the world. All we suggest is that without superpower interference this may be the most obvious, most likely future for the region.

By emphasizing that Hungary is now (mid-1980s) returning to the trajectory she was following in 1945–49—by regarding the last 30 years as a "side-track" in Hungarian history—we do not wish to leave the impression that the whole episode of collectivization has been without lasting impact. Society and the economy in Hungary are certainly not returning to their *state* as of 1949 even less as of 1945. They are reentering the same *trajectory* but at a more advanced stage of development. More concretely: by all indications, the kolkhoz is here to stay as a dominant form of agricultural organization. Collectivization did contribute to the modernization of the land tenure system. In a more rational, less ideological, more pragmatic system, market-oriented family farms, part-time and full-time, will play a greater role, but the most likely future scenario is that they will remain "integrated" by the socialist latifundia, subordinated to the kolkhoz.

Our most general, metatheoretical point is this: in a world divided into two camps by superpower rivalry in the spirit of the Yalta agreement and Cold War politics, it is useful and refreshing to think about a Third, a Fourth, a Fifth Road. Both superpowers try to persuade us, East Europeans and the people in the Third World, that the only alternatives open to us are Soviet Communism or American capitalism. We believe in the diversity of historical destinations and structures, and the viability of mixed economies. Paradoxically, those social scientists who think only in pure types, who believe in the inevitability of structures becoming pure types (often contrary to the political intentions of the theorists) serve superpower interests. The superpowers want us to believe that a little larger market, a little entrepreneurship in Eastern Europe, is "creeping capitalism," a little more welfare redistribution in the West is "creeping socialism." We believe this is nonsense. Pragmatic structural mixes are viable, and can reproduce themselves without inevitably being converted into one or the other pure type.

THEORY OF SOCIAL CHANGE

Historical continuity of microstructures

One of the main tasks of this book is to explain why nine out of ten rural families accept the proletarian or peasant-worker existence and one out of ten seizes upon the reopening entrepreneurial opportunities. Who are these people? What motivates them, makes them entrepreneurial? In exploring these questions we found a strong correlation between family entrepreneurship in 1944–49, before the socialist transformation of Hungarian society, and the current market orientation of family agricultural producers. This is somewhat mysterious. Why on earth should people today produce more for the market if their parents, sometimes even their grandparents, were middle or rich peasants before World War II?

Family inheritance of entrepreneurship is surprising given that the "normal" mechanism of passing it on from one generation to the next, inheritance of land and capital, has not been operative. This fact supports a Weberian, "culturalist" explanation of the origins of entrepreneurship. We are sympathetic to historical materialist explanations, and where private property is inherited, Marx's explanation of entrepreneurship may be sufficient. But we find the Weberian inspiration enlightening in exploring the early origins of entrepreneurship when, as in contemporary Hungary or China, we must account for the initial impetus toward entrepreneurship.

In exploring the mechanisms by which entrepreneurship may be passed on from one generation to the next, we focus upon life histories, both occupational and educational histories of individuals. This way we hope to find ways to measure how values, particularly those related to autonomy, and education are socialized. Our main hypothesis is that among people from the "right" social background, that is, those from entrepreneurial families, only those individuals will achieve "bourgeois" status who chose the "right" occupational trajectories and pursued the "correct" educational path. In investigating the work and educational histories of individuals, we attempt to define those "hiding places" or "parking orbits" where, during the years of the command economy and forced collectivization, people with entrepreneurial aspirations could resist the pressure to become fully proletarian or the temptation to become a cadre. Thus they preserved the will and the capacity to reenter the embourgeoisement trajectory when opportunities reopened.

Historical continuity of macrostructures

We also look beyond the individual level of analysis, beyond the phenomenon of family inheritance. Those of our readers who are interested in the philosophy of history may also discover a similar historical continuity in social structure. The recent development of entrepreneurship in rural Hungary can be interpreted as the resurgence of a long historical trend toward embourgeoisement, which was interrupted temporarily but not for the first time in 1949.

The creation of a rural bourgeois, the transition from peasantry to market-oriented family farming, was delayed in Eastern Europe in general and in Hungary in particular for centuries. Some historians and sociologists argue that the first setback to rural bourgeoisification probably dates back to the seventeenth or eighteenth—or even the sixteenth centuries.[4] Economic historians see a second phase of feudalism beginning in Hungary after the reconquest of the country from the Turks, at the end of the seventeenth century. During the 150 years of Turkish occupation, serfs had begun to act like the private owners of their land, as free peasants; some even began to behave like peasant-burghers, "entrepreneurs," or farmers. Now they were forced back into "second serfdom": their land was taken away and they were required to perform labor services on the reestablished manorial estates. By the mid-eighteenth century the system of Junker estates, or what Lenin called the "Prussian Road of agricultural development" (Lenin, 1907 [1962], pp. 238–42) was in place, and earlier embourgeoisement of the Hungarian peasants was blocked.

During the nineteenth and early twentieth centuries the Junker estate gradually lost its grip upon society. Even though the serfs in Hungary and in fact in the whole region were emancipated in a way that maintained the dominant role of the large estates, by the beginning of the twentieth century and during the interwar years the entrepreneurially oriented family farms had begun to gain ground (Orbán, 1972, pp. 16–22). The idea that large estates were superior was challenged, and in light of the success of small farms and market gardens it was questioned if indeed large estates were more efficient. Thus land reform was demanded, in the name not only of social justice but also of economic efficiency (Kerék, 1939). Land reform, which in its radical shape came only after World War II, opened the gates wide for rural embourgeoisement. Indeed, between 1945 and 1949 rural Hungary experienced development which was extraordinary in its speed and revolutionary in its character.

Socialist collectivization of agriculture could be interpreted as a second setback to rural embourgeoisement. Officially, collectivization is called the "second agrarian revolution" (the first being the epoch that began with the land reform of 1945; see Orbán, 1972). But to the extent that it represents a return to an earlier form of economic organization, it

[4] For a comprehensive comparison of the development in feudalism in Western and Eastern Europe see Brenner, 1976; and for the "second feudalism" in Hungary see Pach, 1963; Szücs, 1981; Gunszt, 1974.

may be more appropriate to label it as a counter-revolution, a "third feudalism."

Indeed, several commentators noted the astonishing parallels between the kolkhoz system and the Junker estate (Juhász, 1973; T. Toth, 1981; Szabó, 1968; Szelényi, 1981). As peasants were forced to join the kolkhozes in Hungary they were allowed to keep one hold, slightly more than one acre, of land under family cultivation. This was exactly the amount of land to which manorial laborers on the large estates before World War II were entitled. There were many other parallels. For instance, the newly formed kolkhozes in socialist Hungary prohibited family enterprises from owning horses (they were encouraged to keep hogs and were allowed to have one or two cows). Centuries ago, feudal estates forbade their servants to own horses; the new kolkhoz rule, therefore, was merely copied from the statutes of the Junker estates.

The similarities in the regulations governing relationships between the minifundia and latifundia are not so surprising. Both the kolkhoz and the Junker estate used the minifundia as the main mechanism for binding poorly paid agricultural workers to the latifundium. At the same time, it was imperative to prevent laborers from spending too much time on their family plots, so the minifundia were limited to subsistence production. Limits on the size of family plots and on means of transportation (such as horse ownership) achieved this goal.

The continuity between the Junker estate and the kolkhoz was not limited to such "symbiotic" relations between minifundia and latifundia, but extended in many respects to work organization (Juhász, 1973; Szabó, 1968). During our ethnographic field trips we found several kolkhozes which occupied exactly the land of the former estate. On one occasion, the kolkhoz president in 1972 had been the manager of the same estate before 1945. From this perspective, the collectivization of agriculture indeed opened up a "third feudalism," forcing peasants into a "third serfdom."

This historical continuity did not escape the attention of former peasants either. During a field trip in 1973 to the village of Nagygéc, one of our respondents told us about his experiences in the kolkhoz: "We are manorial laborers on extended service" ("Továbbszolgálo cselédek vagyunk"). He knew what he was talking about. Before the war, as a young man, he had been the carriage driver for local landlords, the Szomjas family; later, he drove wagons for the kolkhoz.

Thus the resurgence of family agricultural entrepreneurship during the late 1970s and early 1980s could be interpreted as a return to the embourgeoisement trajectory which had been interrupted for the second time in 1949. Hungary is recoiling to its "organic trajectory" of development, reentering an evolutionary pattern deeply rooted in its history. On this organic trajectory, family farms and large estates, market competition and bureaucratic paternalism, citizenship and officials' powers are carefully balanced in order to avoid both the anarchic individualism of its Western and the untrammeled state power of its Eastern neighbors. The last 40 years should probably be seen as a rather unfortunate, socially costly sidetrack, which pushed Hungary and perhaps the rest of the region backward in time and eastward in geography. During these postwar years the Soviet Union tried to force on its western neighbors a monolithically statist, bureaucratic, and clientelist form of internal social and economic organization that was alien to them. It may make sense to suggest, that Hungary (and probably Poland?) are once again searching for a social identity that will distinguish this society both from the Soviet model and from Western capitalism. The question of the "Third Road" again returns to the intellectual agenda of Eastern Europe.

This book is about historical continuity, but it is also about social change. Our story shows how difficult it is to impose social change from above. Our empirical study will indicate that people learn how to adapt to changing structures, how to live their lives basically the way they wanted to anyway, regardless of what their rulers want. As opportunities reopen, they will bounce back to old, familiar ways. We are skeptical about the efficiency of revolutionary change implemented from above by modernizing elites. A "silent revolution," structural change from below, is being carried out by the everyday practices of Hungarian semiproletarians. Commentators upon Hungarian politics have frequently pointed out that 1956 was, paradoxically, a *successful* revolution. Although Russian tanks crushed it, most of the revolutionaries' demands were met by the mid or late 1970s. The success of this "second," post-1956 revolution is often attributed to János Kádár and his enlightened cadre elite, or to the wisdom of Hungarian reform intellectuals or the dissenting intelligentsia. They probably all played a role. But this book emphasizes the vital contribution of rural semiproletarians in resisting pressures toward proletarianization and in pursuing their old goals of economic autonomy and citizenship. The humble task of the sociologist is not to elaborate the ideology of this transformation, but to act as a witness to history, to record the events of this new wave of "silent revolution."

How unique is the Hungarian experience?

Our ambition is to contribute to the theory of "socialist proletarianization," but our analysis is based on empirical evidence from one rather exceptional socialist country, Hungary. Thus our findings cannot be widely generalized.

Except for China, the Hungarian regime has pursued during the last decade the most liberal, pragmatic policies toward family agricultural production and small family business in general.[5]

Hungary differs from other East European countries in several respects:

1. In Hungary, a greater proportion of agricultural production comes from family enterprises than in any other East European country with collectivized agriculture.

   At the same time, one should not exaggerate the uniqueness of the Hungarian situation. Family production is important everywhere in the region, particularly in the Soviet Union, where, according to Soviet sources, 50 years after collectivization more than a quarter of agricultural production still comes from personal household plots (see Shmelev, 1981, p. 44; Wadekin, 1973, pp. 55–68). Even in East Germany, where rural proletarianization has progressed further than anywhere else under state socialism, family minifundia still produce 40–50 percent of the national output in certain key products, for instance eggs and poultry (Münch and Nau, 1983, p. 668).
2. In Hungary the share of total production that comes from family agricultural production has remained quite stable over the last decade, whereas in most countries it has declined. Other countries have advanced along the road to socialist proletarianization at a much faster rate (Schinke, 1983).
3. Most important, from the perspective of our embourgeoisement theory, the reemergence of family entrepreneurship seems to be limited in Eastern Europe to Hungary.

Thus our Hungarian case study may not reveal too much about the current circumstances of other East European countries. At the same time, we hope that those who wish to explore the directions in which this region and state socialist countries in general may move in the future will find our analysis of interest. Genuine theory, after all, may not be limited to "being," but may be more interested in "becoming"

[5] For discussions of the extent of family production and agricultural policies in other socialist countries see Wadekin, 1973, 1982, pp. 94–100; Grossmann, 1977; Shmelev, 1981; Eckart, 1983; Münch and Nau, 1983; Schmeljow and Steksow, 1983; Fischer, 1984.

(Mannheim, 1925 [1971], pp. 104–15; Horkheimer, 1972, pp. 188–243). If Hungary's pioneering experiment with a mixed economy and dual system of social stratification is successful, other European countries (and to some extent even the Soviet Union) may follow suit.

There are economic and historical reasons to believe that the experiment we are reporting has a good chance of success, not only in Hungary but eventually in the whole of East Europe.

First, the more complex task of managing an intensively growing economy may require movement toward a mixed economy. Even in the West, after the Great Depression, when there emerged an intensively growing economy in which the driving force behind economic growth was increased productivity rather than an expanded work force, the economic system became increasingly mixed. The dysfunctionalities of the dominant market mechanism had to be corrected with growing, though still subordinated, government redistributive sector. Analogously, using Stark's approach of "mirrored comparisons" (Stark, 1986, p. 493) one could argue that socialist societies may have to learn how to use the market to correct the dysfunctionalities of their dominant redistributive mechanisms, if they wish to adapt to the rapid changes of a mass consumption society and to the world economy (Manchin and Szelényi, 1987).

Second, as we discussed in more detail in the section on the Third Road, the purely statist form of economy was always somewhat alien to Hungary and other East European societies. The resurgence of the market, the reconstitution of a relatively autonomous civil society, are indications that Hungary is recoiling to a more "organic" developmental trajectory. Is it not reasonable that other countries which, before World War II, already had reasonably developed civil societies, particularly Poland, Czechoslovakia, and Germany, would also feel more comfortable under a mixed economy and a system of dual stratification? Indeed, the Hungarian experiment seems to fascinate reformers elsewhere in Eastern Europe. It may be overoptimistic but it is far from absurd to assume that the pattern emerging in Hungary is not just a "Hungarian model" but may represent the first materialization of a Third Road, an East or Central European model.

RESEARCH DESIGN AND PLAN OF THE BOOK

We are now ready to begin the task of empirical analysis. In this section, we briefly describe our strategy of analysis and how, accordingly, this book is structured.

This empirical analysis is based in part on ethnographic observations we made first during 1972–73 while organizing a national rural survey for the Institute of Sociology of the Hungarian Academy of Sciences, and then during other field trips to Hungarian villages during the summers of 1983 and 1984. The statistical data for this book are from the Income Survey and the Social Mobility and Life History Survey of the Hungarian Central Statistical Office, both conducted in 1982–83. (For a more detailed description of the data base, see Appendix A.)

Chapter 1, using the Income Survey and other published official statistics, summarizes what we know about family agricultural production and its changes during the last decade in Hungary. We document the relative stability of family production and the extent to which entrepreneurial orientations gained ground.

Chapters 2 and 3 review three alternative theories about the character of family agricultural producers.

1. Until recently the common view held that family production in collectivized socialist economies is a necessary, but temporary phenomenon. As the kolkhozes become stabilized and incomes from wages and salaries achieve an acceptable level, family producers will give up production on their allotments and will become fully proletarianized.
2. By the late 1960s and early 1970s another theory—we label it the "peasant-worker" or "new working class" theory—suggested that single-family agricultural production is a lasting phenomenon, even after collectivization. The rural population has learned how to delay proletarianization for a whole generation; it uses family production to complement incomes from bureaucratic employment and to strengthen its bargaining position toward employers.
3. The most recent theory suggests that the increasing market orientation of family minifundia is an indication that embourgeoisement, which was interrupted by collectivization, is now resurgent. Some family agricultural producers will never turn proletarian; instead, they are becoming entrepreneurs.

Synthesizing these theories, we argue that the three processes, proletarianization, formation of the new working class, and embourgeoisement, took place simultaneously; they should be understood as different "destinations." The task of empirical research is to define which families are heading toward which destination. We hypothesize that differences in family background and life history may affect family chances of becoming entrepreneurial.

Chapters 4–7 present our empirical findings. Chapter 4 offers a systematic theoretical discussion and an ethnographic account of the four destinations—cadre, proletarian, peasant-worker, and entrepreneurial—which can be distinguished in rural Hungary today. Chapter 5 is an attempt to develop a sample selection model to assess the relative explanatory power of each theory discussed in Chapters 2 and 3 and to show that our own "interrupted embourgeoisement" theory is superior to the others, particularly when, as our dependent variable, we use the value of commodity production instead of the aggregate value of family agricultural production or the value of subsistence production. Chapter 6 discusses family background and the differences in the social background of families who have reached different destinations. Chapter 7 offers a similar analysis of the life histories of heads of households. Chapters 6 and 7 are introduced by a theoretically informed ethnographic analysis. In each chapter we return to the sample selection model we developed in Chapter 5, add new variables and fine-tune old ones, and assess how much the explanatory power of the models is improved.

In the sample selection model that is at the core of our statistical analysis, our dependent variable is the monetary value of family production. We have built a nested model. In the baseline model, the independent variables describe the demographic characteristics of the families, such as age and current agricultural occupation of the head of the household and labor supply within the household. Next, we enter mobility variables (size of family landholding in 1944, land received during the land reform) into the model, and last we add life history variables (number of years in different types of jobs; characteristics of the education of the head of the household). In each chapter our dependent and independent variables are specified in different ways.

In Chapter 5 we begin to build our sample selection model with the crudest possible measure of the value of family agricultural production as our dependent variable. The measure we use is the aggregate net monetary value of all production, including both self-consumption and market sale. By so specifying the dependent variable, we create the most unfavorable conditions for the embourgeoisement theory (after all, our theory is specifically about *commodity production*, and not about subsistence!). If our model works, then, there will be good reason to believe that we can proceed with our analysis.

In Chapter 5, the way in which we specify the demographic and occupational variable corresponds to the proletarianization theory. Because this theory predicts that older, agricultural manual laborers with larger families are the most likely to keep producing agricultural goods in their family enterprises, we define our demographic and occupational variables with such dummies. We are very generous toward the proletarianization theory; we first use its specifications to let it explain as much as it can from the variance in the value of production.

In our next two steps we define mobility and life history variables according to the embourgeoisement theory, which predicts that people from a middle- and rich-peasant background, with a history of autonomous employment and an emphasis upon education, will be likely to be the bigger producers. Chapter 5 proves that, even under conditions most unfavorable for the embourgeoisement theory, the mobility and life history variables improve the explanatory power of the model. Furthermore, the sample selection model consists of two equations. The first gives probit scores for the probability of becoming a producer at all, the second estimates the probability that families will produce more. Including the specified mobility and life history variables improves the explanatory power of the model even in the first equation, but as one might anticipate from our theory, the improvement is greater in the second equation.

In the last section of Chapter 5 we disaggregate our dependent variable to create a better fit with the embourgeoisement theory. Redefining our dependent variable as the monetary value of agricultural goods sold in the market, we show that our model, with the same specifications for the independent variables as in an earlier section of Chapter 5 produces a better fit. As expected, the mobility and life history variables have the least to contribute to the explanation of family production when such production is measured as the monetary value of food consumed within the family.

In Chapter 6, we keep the new independent variable (monetary value of agricultural goods sold in the market), but we add more family background variables and fine-tune our existing variables. We prove that, indeed those family background variables which, according to our ethnographic description, characterize the proletarian or cadre families have negative parameters in our sample selection model.

In Chapter 7, we go through the same exercise with the life history variables. We prove that life trajectories which, from the ethnographic evidence presented in this chapter, lead to proletarian or cadre status have negative values in the sample selection models.

1

Family agricultural production

The Hungarian case

In this chapter, we first show that although Hungary had by the mid-1980s completed industrialization and was entering the postindustrial age, it still had a surprisingly large rural population, and an astonishingly high proportion of its population was engaged in food production. We argue that both these phenomena are linked to the socialist character of the society and its industrialization policies. Second, we compare the extent of family agricultural production in Hungary in 1972 and 1982. Family production remained quite stable: declines in some respects were compensated by growth in others. Third, we analyze trends toward commodity production and the concentration or specialization of family production between 1972 and 1982. There has been some growth among the largest, most market-oriented producers; in fact, the single most important event in recent agricultural history has been the birth of small agricultural entrepreneurs.

SOCIALIST COUNTRIES IN THE POSTINDUSTRIAL EPOCH

In 1971 we suggested that during the epoch of accelerated, extensive industrialization under the socialists, Hungary, and presumably most of Eastern Europe, became "underurbanized"—a term we coined on the analogy of "overurbanization" (Konrád and Szelényi, 1977).[1] Demographers studying Third World urbanization during the 1950s had noted that in some developing countries the growth of the urban

[1] The concept of overurbanization was first proposed by Davis and Golden (1954) and was tested in a UNESCO investigation (UNESCO, 1957). The theory was savagely criticized by Sovani and others (Sovani, 1964), but Gugler has attempted at least partly to rehabilitate it (Gugler, 1982; Gilbert and Gugler, 1982, pp. 163–64).

population was significantly faster than the growth of the urban economy, of jobs, and more specifically of urban industrial jobs. People move to cities although the urban economy is not yet ready to absorb them. Such countries become overurbanized: their urban population growth is "too fast," and this creates social problems like the growth of slums and massive, long-term unemployment or underemployment.

In preparing our first rural project during the early 1970s we began to analyze aggregate data on urban–rural population distribution and were surprised at how slowly the rural population in Hungary declined during a period of extensive socialist industrialization.

The relative slowness of urbanization is even more obvious when one compares the dynamics of the urban–rural distribution with the changing occupational composition of the population. After 1949, the accelerated industrialization policy of the socialists was spectacularly successful in increasing the proportion of the population that was employed full-time outside agriculture, primarily in urban industry. For instance—to use the simplest and crudest measure available—in 1930 the nonagricultural population was only 10 percent greater than the urban population; in 1949, the proportion grew to 12.3, in 1960 to 23.6 and in 1970 to 32.2 percent (K. Kulcsár, 1982, p. 27). Thus a "gap" was created between a relatively small "urban" and a relatively large "nonagricultural" population. But as people under the dual pressure of industrialization and collectivization gave up their full-time agricultural occupations and took industrial jobs, many did not or could not move to cities permanently. They remained rural residents, commuting to urban workplaces. In 1949 76 percent of the rural population was still agriculturalist, but by the mid-1970s the majority of village dwellers worked outside agriculture, and a third of them commuted to an urban industrial workplace (Andorka and Harcsa, 1982, pp. 193, 200; Andorka, 1979; Márkus, 1980, pp. 14–15). If, then, overurbanization described a situation in which the urban population was growing faster than urban industrial jobs, Hungary could be considered underurbanized, since urban industrial jobs were growing faster than the urban population.[2]

We linked the concept of underurbanization to accelerated socialist industrialization—some theorists called it primitive socialist accumulation. We believed that the relative delay in urban growth was the inevitable though presumably unintended result of the push for the fastest possible industrialization. Planners achieved quite extraordinary

[2] Our "underurbanization" is very similar to Golachowski's (1967) concept of "semiurbanization," developed to describe the peculiar features of urbanization in post-World War II Poland.

rates of industrial investment by drastically reducing personal consumption and infrastructural expenditures; they were particularly successful in cutting back government expenditure on urban housing development. The logic of socialist accelerated industrialization was to create as many industrial jobs as quickly as possible and to provide the newly proletarianized rural workers with public transportation, bringing them daily to urban industrial workplaces but leaving them as village residents. Thus one did not have to build new houses, schools, shops, and other facilities for them. In a 1973 article in *Szociológia* Jiri Musil tested our hypothesis against data from all East and West European countries; he confirmed that indeed most East European countries (particularly Czechoslovakia, East Germany, Poland, and to some extent Rumania) experienced a degree of underurbanization during their extensive industrialization under socialism.

Planners often justified the strategy of depressed personal consumption, delayed infrastructural investments, and delayed urbanization with the conventional wisdom of not eating the goose that lays the golden egg. They promised rapid growth in consumption and infrastructural development after the industrial base had been successfully created.

Interestingly enough, as these countries have entered upon intensive economic growth, the relative decentralization of their population seems to be preserved. For urbanization at least there has been no "golden egg": urbanization is far from catching up on the growth that was postponed during accelerated industrialization. In Hungary, for instance, by the mid- or late 1970s, infrastructural investments had begun to rise but the growth of cities had slowed further.

Slowing of the decline in rural populations is, of course, not unknown. The United States has also experienced a "demographic turnaround" since 1968—a century-long trend toward metropolitan growth and nonmetropolitan decline has been suddenly reversed. But it would be totally misleading to think that these are similar phenomena. In the United States and other developed countries, the demographic turnaround began after the metropolitan population had reached 70–80 percent and the agricultural population was reduced to 4–5 percent. Hungary and the other East European countries, in contrast, never experienced a true "flight from the land." Their rural populations stabilized when at least half of the population still lived in traditional villages.

Thus Hungary and several other state socialist countries not only completed extensive industrialization with astonishingly high rural populations but are also likely to maintain those large rural populations well into their postindustrial phase. How is this possible? We believe that the key to underurbanization and also to this uniquely "socialist" pattern of urbanization in a stage of intensive growth lies in the survival of part-time family agricultural production and of a substantial rural semiproletariat. That is why our project, which began as a study of underurbanization, finally became an investigation of proletarianization and the resistance to it.

Underurbanization was possible because the first generation of industrial workers, those who were forced by collectivization to leave agriculture for urban industry, were able in "compensation" to retain their family minifundia. Thus they generated reasonable living standards for themselves and even some autonomy from their employers in industry. Rural revitalization, which occurs in the transition to intensive growth and which, in comparison with development patterns in Western countries, is "premature," is the result of further consolidation of family agricultural production. During the decade of the 1970s people ceased to leave Hungarian villages, and some even started to move back, because greater entrepreneurial opportunities were opening up there than in cities. Part-time family agricultural production and its reorientation toward commodity production are our keys to understanding both underurbanization and the current phase of "socialist urbanization" as the Hungarian economy enters upon a period of intensive growth.

Two decades after collectivization, family agricultural production still plays an important role. Six out of ten Hungarian families are engaged in food production. Almost 90 percent of the rural and 30 percent of the urban population grew agricultural products in 1982. In this country of 10 million inhabitants, there are some 1.5 million minifarms which are large enough to qualify as "enterprises" in government agricultural surveys. These 1.5 million small farmers cultivate slightly more than 12 percent of the arable land and produce 34 percent of the gross farm product. After deducting expenses, an average rural family earns 1765 Forint (Ft) a month (this figure, also includes the more than 10 percent of rural families that do not grow food). That is a handsome sum, if one considers that the average wage in industry in 1981 was 4332 Ft a month. One word of caution: a significant proportion of this income is the estimated value of the agricultural goods consumed by the families themselves. In 1981, small producers still consumed 38 percent of their own products (Oros, 1984, p. 83). Although they were responsible for 34 percent of the gross farm product, they produced only 25 percent of all agricultural commodities (Table 1.1).

Hungary leads the socialist countries in the significance of its family

TABLE 1.1 *Extent of family agricultural production in Hungary, 1981–82*

Number of family "enterprises"	1,500,000
Arable land under family cultivation	
Hectares	810,000
%	12.2
Proportion of families producing agricultural goods (%)	
All families	60.6
Rural families	88.3
Net value of monthly production among rural families (Ft)	1,765
Per capita monthly wage in state industry (Ft)	4,332
Share of family "enterprises" in	
Gross agricultural production (%)	34.0
Agricultural commodity production (%)	25.3

Source: CSO (1982), Oros (1984), and our calculations from the 1982 CSO Income Survey. The CSO's definition of "enterprises" is discussed in Appendix A.

agricultural production, but it is by no means exceptional. In Rumania, the U.S.S.R., and Bulgaria, family production is also sizeable, and even the most rigidly state socialist countries, Czechoslovakia and East Germany, could not live without their small semiprivate sectors.[3] These other socialist countries have a higher semiproletarian, part-time population and one might expect at their level of economic growth and in comparison with Western market economies; they also have disproportionately high rural populations.

CHANGES IN THE EXTENT OF FAMILY PRODUCTION, 1972–82

What are the prospects for family agricultural production under state socialism?

[3] In 1980 the share of family production from total production, for selected agricultural goods, was as follows (percentage shares are given in parentheses after the name of the country):

Vegetables: Hungary (46.6), Rumania (41.7), U.S.S.R. (32.9), Bulgaria (27.7), Czechoslovakia (39.3), German Democratic Republic (28.3).

Fruits: Hungary (51.0), Rumania (49.5), U.S.S.R. (42.1), Bulgaria (39.8), Czechoslovakia (59.6), German Democratic Republic (59.7).

Eggs: Hungary (62.0), Rumania (60.0), U.S.S.R. (32.2), Bulgaria (54.2), Czechoslovakia (40.6), no data for GDR.

See Oros, 1984, p. 85; Eckhart, 1983, p. 416; Münch and Nau, 1983, p. 668; Wadekin, 1973, pp. 43–80.

When the farms were collectivized, peasants were allowed to keep their houseplots, but the advocates of collectivization saw this as a temporary, though presumably long-term concession. Soviet and East European agricultural planners envisioned the future of agriculture as large-scale units of production organized according to industrial principles. Production on houseplots they saw as archaic, a concession to the backwardness of rural folks and their peasant consciousness (Vágvölgyi, 1976, p. 270). The houseplot made it easier for peasants to swallow the bitter pill of collectivization (Fazekas et al., 1985, p. 155; Biró et al., 1980, pp. 34–36). And family production made up for the relative inefficiency of the new kolkhozes, which were not yet up to their tasks (Fazekas et al., 1985, pp. 157–58).

This vision is still predominant; even Western observers find it difficult to resist its technocratic agricultural utopia. Peter Bell is one of the most prominent American commentators on rural Hungary. In his fine and in detail authentic study of the transformation of a Hungarian village during collectivization, he accepts that the industrialization of agriculture is inevitable and that family production is transitory. Says Bell: "Traditional peasant agriculture . . . has given way to large-scale modern collective enterprises." (1984, p. 297). About the future he remarks that the new, better-trained employees of kolkhozes "will place greater emphasis on leisure time . . . and will not be willing to maintain significant houseplot enterprises. Although these houseplots will continue to be an important element in Hungarian agriculture . . . it may be that the houseplot . . . will no longer form a focal point" (p. 302).

In the *very long run* this may well be true (though remember: social scientists have in the past been notoriously poor prophets, fortune tellers, or forecasters!), but the experience of the last decades instead demonstrates the stubborn resistance of family production.

This stubborn resistance is reflected in the data which describe changes in Hungarian agriculture. In certain respects family producers lost ground to the kolkhozes: the number of family minifarms which met the CSO criteria for an "enterprise" (see Appendix A) declined, as did the amount of land cultivated in those enterprises. But those kolkhoz members who gave up family production—and there were many, as Bell predicted—were more than offset by those who were not kolkhoz members but who took up family production. Some of these cultivated very small plots that did not even appear as "enterprises" in official statistics; others were quite big, market-oriented producers. Furthermore, those fewer families who remained producers began to spend more time on their family businesses and less on their jobs. If they were indeed interested in leisure they were apparently more likely to filch it from their bureaucratic employers, not from their family business! Finally, although the share of the gross farm product represented by family production declined, its share of agricultural commodity production remained stable; in other words, family production, rather than decaying, seemed to be adapting to the changing requirements of the time, and probably doing so more effectively and rapidly than the kolkhozes themselves. To those, then, who speak of family production as "still" with us, may we not respond, with equal precision, that kolkhozes are "still" with us? One phenomenon appears as permanent as the other.

Fewer "enterprises"; less land under family cultivation

Let us first consider whether the family farm is decaying. There is indeed solid evidence that family production is retreating, just as predicted by Soviet and East European agricultural experts, and that socialist, industrialized, bureaucratically organized, large-scale enterprises are on the rise.

Both the number of "enterprises" and the amount of land under their cultivation has declined significantly (by 11 and 23 percent, respectively) during the last decade. Both types of family enterprises declined, but houseplots declined more rapidly than auxiliary farms (14 as opposed to 8 percent).[4] In terms of the amount of land under cultivation, the opposite seems to be true, but only at first glance. In fact, the amount of land effectively cultivated in houseplots declined even more rapidly than the land under cultivation in auxiliary farms.

Changes in family production on the houseplots and auxiliary farms have different causes. Houseplot production began to decline primarily because kolkhoz policy toward family production changed. During the 1970s kolkhozes offered cash or animal feed to those who did not claim houseplots. Many kolkhoz families were interested in such arrangements, although for different reasons. Some wanted, as Bell suggests, to free themselves from the time-consuming tasks of the houseplots; others, probably the majority, decided to intensify their production, to give up growing hay or corn, which was inefficient and unprofitable, and to concentrate their efforts on stock raising. Thus in a single decade the effectively cultivated land in houseplots declined by 55 percent, whereas the number of houseplots declined by only 14 percent. Only a

[4] A houseplot is the land allocated to a family that is a kolkhoz member; auxiliary farms are other minifarms under the cultivation of nonkolkhoz families. For a more detailed definition, see Appendix A.

minority of families actually gave up agricultural production, and at least for some families cultivation of less land opened up opportunities to expand agricultural production.

The decay of auxiliary farms is mostly attributable to the decline of larger units of production, particularly farms of 5 acres or more (CSO, 1982, p. 22). This reflects the continuing disappearance of full-time private farms. During the main push for collectivization in 1960, a very few, very stubborn peasants, typically old people, stayed outside the kolkhozes. In 1960 these peasants were running rather traditional economic units and were gradually dying off; thus their number was steadily declining. Their disappearance from the scene was not necessarily proof that family agricultural production as such was on the retreat; it only showed that the old, peasant farming was on its way out in Hungarian villages. Very interestingly, the number of the smallest "enterprises," those with an acre or less, actually increased between 1972 and 1981 (CSO, 1982, p. 22). While the old-style peasants were disappearing, a new type of small agricultural producer was emerging.

New people enter production; more time is spent in the family enterprise

That there was no unidirectional decline in family agricultural production is even more obvious if we do not limit our analysis to "enterprises," but consider all family agricultural producers.

The number of "enterprises" declined, but the number of families who were producing food increased, both in urban and rural areas. Larger holdings declined, private farmers died or retired, and kolkhoz peasants cultivating their houseplots in traditional ways gave up family production, but more people began to produce food on small pieces of land. Some were hobby farmers who produced very little, but some were quite significant producers.

Thus decay is merely a surface phenomenon for houseplots and auxiliary farms both. And below the surface one can begin to detect a structural change.

The most dramatic change over the last decade has been the reduction in the proportion of agricultural manual laborers among agricultural family producers. In 1972, 21 percent of all families with agricultural enterprises were agricultural manual laborers or kolkhoz "peasants"; by 1981 these were reduced to a bare 11 percent. The proportion of retirees among family producers grew, but not sufficiently to explain the decline among active kolkhoz "peasants." Even in 1972 one could argue that family agricultural production was not a peasant phenomenon, did not simply represent the survival of a peasant mentality: only 55 percent of all producers were agricultural manual laborers, retirees (most of them presumably former peasants), or members of families with both agricultural and industrial incomes. But by 1981, exactly half of the family producers were industrial or white collar workers. Most spectacularly, the percentage of family agricultural producers who were not manual laborers doubled from 1972 to 1982. How on earth could these figures be made to jibe with a view that family agricultural production was "still" around merely because there had not been enough time yet for the old "peasant mentality" to wither away?

Furthermore, while the number of "enterprises" and the amount of land under their cultivation declined, people who maintained such "enterprises" increased their efforts within family production. They were spending more time in family businesses and less on their jobs.

From this we can draw several important conclusions. First, in every single occupational category, time spent on the job declined and time spent in family business increased. This is hardly an indication of the irresistible advance of the "socialist" sector. On the contrary, during the decade from 1972 to 1982 Hungarian workers were reorienting themselves, paying less attention to their jobs and their state employers and spending more of their lives in the family work organization. Second, differences among occupational groups in amount of time spent in family "enterprises" were disappearing. In 1972 kolkhoz "peasants" spent 50 percent more time on their houseplots than white-collar workers in their auxiliary farms; by 1981 the figure was reduced to some 20 percent. Third, probably as a result of this last, the difference between auxiliary farms and houseplots was also disappearing. On the auxiliary farms, intensification of production occurred at a faster rate than on houseplots. It is increasingly unconvincing to argue that only the houseplots are the "real thing," that auxiliary farms are merely a working-class "hobby." Over the last decade auxiliary farms have become less of a pastime and more a serious productive venture in the second economy. Finally, time spent on productive activities on the minifarms increased even though the area of land under cultivation declined. Thus by 1981 people were spending more time cultivating smaller plots; they were increasing labor intensity, per acre productivity, and possibly also profitability. (CSO, 1984, pp. 12, 32.)

But the growth of small family producers, the shift away from the more traditional peasant type of production, and the increase in labor intensity were not enough to compensate for the decline in the family "enterprises" and in the amount of land under their cultivation. In the final accounting, the share of gross farm product generated by family "enterprises" declined from 1972 to 1981.

Family agricultural production lost real ground to the kolkhozes even in Hungary, and even during the liberal 1970s. In 1970, small producers still accounted for an impressive 40 percent of the total aggregate value of agricultural output; by 1981 this had declined to 34 percent. The decline was particularly swift in crop production; in animal husbandry, family producers by and large kept their position in the national economy.

The declining share of small producers is attributable to the dynamic expansion of production in the collective sector, not to the decline of family production, whose value in 1981 was about 10 percent greater than in 1970. Small producers increased their production particularly rapidly in animal husbandry, but could not keep up with the growth of kolkhoz production.

The growth of production in the collectivized sector may, however, have been unusually high during the 1970s, and it is not certain that such growth rates can be sustained during the 1980s. Those who cite the declining share of family production as proof of the inevitable, long-term decay of part-time farming should be cautious. During the 1970s, the Hungarian regime made a major effort to beef up the collective sector. A new generation of young, dynamic, technocratically oriented agricultural engineers entered the kolkhozes (Swain, 1985, pp. 114–29; Juhász, 1983a; Hann, 1983, pp. 89–90; Sárkány, 1983, pp. 51–52). Investment funds were made available to them (Swain, 1981, p. 234), and the combination of the expertise of young technocrats and up-to-date technology had results. Crop yields per acre rose swiftly, and in several areas Hungary achieved an internationally respectable position. Semiproletarian small farmers simply could not compete with corporate giants who were receiving major transfusions of government money.

But this strategy of kolkhoz development was not without its price. Capital costs rose very rapidly in Hungarian agriculture, negatively affecting its competitiveness on the world market. Hungarian kolkhozes have impressively high yields per acre for most crops, but they do so at higher capital costs. For instance, production of corn per hectare in Hungarian kolkhozes in 1970–73 was 3.8 metric tons; and it was 6.3 tons by 1980–83. The same figures for wheat were 2.9 and 4.4, and for potatoes, 3.8 and 6.3 (Fazekas et al., 1985, pp. 202, 204, 297). But fixed capital assets also grew qucikly. If we set the 1968 level at 100, capital assets rose to 169.3 in 1975 and 246.8 in 1983 (Fazekas et al., 1985, p. 187; Swain, 1981, p. 238). Ferenc Donáth attempted to measure efficiency, particularly capital efficiency, in Hungarian agriculture. One of his measures was "new value per 100 Ft of gross agricultural production value" ("gross value" includes capital costs; "new value" excludes them). If this indicator is defined as 100 in 1961–65, the first years of collectivization, in the kolkhozes it declined to 87 in 1966–70, and to 77 in 1971–75 (Donáth, 1982–83, p. 165; see also Donáth, 1977, p. 259). The net production value for 100 Ft of capital assets declined even more sharply. This indicator stood at 1678 Ft in 1960, but dropped to 543 Ft in 1965, 302 Ft in 1970, and 298 Ft in 1975 (Donáth, 1982, p. 167; see also J. Juhász, 1980, p. 18). In 1984, the World Bank also noted the increasing efficiency problems, throughout the 1980s, of Hungarian agriculture (World Bank, 1984, pp. 75–79). Under such circumstances we would anticipate that growth would slow in the collective sector, so in the 1980s family production may lose no more ground to the kolkhozes or may even reverse the trend of the last two decades.

Some signs point in this direction. For instance, during the early 1970s kolkhozes invested huge sums of money in technologically superb, complex breeding plants for hogs and cattle. By the early 1980s the capital expenses of running these complexes had proved to be prohibitive, and many kolkhozes were beginning to "put out" stock to individual families. Often the animals ended up in nineteenth-century farm buildings, while several of the complex breeding plants now stand empty.

We are therefore not too pessimistic about the prospects for family production in the 1980s!

True, production costs were also increasing and profits declining for family producers, without the lucrative investments the kolkhozes were making. The cost of chemicals, fertilizers, and fuel inflated rapidly, while the price of food remained relatively stable. But in comparison with the kolkhozes, the semiproletarian minifarms maintained their capital efficiency. According to Donáth, new value per 100 Ft of gross agricultural production value declined by 23 percent in the kolkhozes over the 15 years after 1960, but by only 9 percent for the houseplots (Donáth, 1982–83, p. 165).

AGRICULTURAL COMMODITY PRODUCTION WITHIN THE FAMILY ENTERPRISE: CONCENTRATION OF PRODUCTION

The most striking change in rural Hungary during the last decade has been a movement toward entrepreneurship. In 1970, family agricultural production was still overwhelmingly traditional, a new version of the peasant economy. With few exceptions, people used their houseplots to grow enough corn to feed the one or two hogs they wanted to slaughter for themselves. In addition, they tried to grow their own vegetables and run a few dozen chickens for meat and eggs. This model still exists during the 1980s, and the smallest producers have even increased, as we pointed out earlier. But the novel feature of the agricultural system is the reappearance of the market-oriented entrepreneurial minifarms. These farms are run not by peasants, but by entrepreneurs; they primarily produce for the market, do not necessarily want to grow their own food, and are likely to run specialized enterprises.

Family agricultural production has lost ground to the kolkhoz in total volume of production mainly because of the proletarianization of traditional peasant-workers. Many family producers who were running subsistence minifarms gave up production or reduced it to hobby farming, and thus became fully proletarianized. But those who maintained family production shifted quite dramatically toward commodity production. The total volume of production on the minifarms increased by only about 10 percent during the 1970s, but their commodity production almost doubled. In 1970 family minifarms were primarily subsistence-oriented: only 40 percent of their products were sold on the market. In 1980 the figure was 62 percent. So if our semiproletarian minifarmers lost ground to the kolkhozes in one area they kept or to some extent improved their share of total agricultural commodity production from 24 percent in 1970 to 25 percent in 1981.

The increase in the value of production shows a bipolar distribution, being significantly above average in the top 5–10 percent and in the bottom 10 percent. For our present analysis the increase at the very top of the income hierarchy is of major significance. In 1982 the top 10 percent of producers earned as much as or more (over 47,000 Ft a year) than manual wage laborers in the kolkhozes or in state industry. In 1981 the average industrial manual wage was 52,000 Ft per year; manual workers in kolkhozes earned only 46,000 Ft per year (Oros, 1984, p. 87). Thus the "biggest" family entrepreneurs earned the equivalent of 1–3 industrial wages (the top 1 percent of family producers earned more than 125,000 Ft a year). They had clearly increased their autonomy since 1972 and were becoming less dependent on wages, even if they were still employed full time.

To summarize the major features of family agricultural production in the early 1980s and the directions of change since 1970:

1. Hungary and probably most, if not all, other East European state socialist countries had completed industrialization with a higher

rural and part-time farmer population than one could anticipate from comparisons with market capitalist economies at a similar stage of economic growth.

2. The number of "enterprises" and the amount of land under cultivation had declined, but family agricultural production had generally proved to be stable. In fewer "enterprises" and on smaller plots of land, people spent more time in family production and sold a larger part of their produce in the market. Despite a major drive to beef up the collective sector, the share of family "enterprises" in total agricultural commodity production remained unchanged.
3. There has also been a tendency toward the emergence of relatively large, exclusively market-oriented enterprises. About 5 per cent of the rural population earned from their family enterprises about as much as or more than the head of household did from his or her job. Some families, rather than gradually sliding from semi-proletarian status toward full proletarianization, are changing course; they are by now on their way toward a new family entrepreneurship. The reality of family agricultural production is shaped by several trends, which exist simultaneously and often cross-cut and counteract each other. Among former subsistence producers, only a few become entrepreneurs; the majority either reduce their operations to hobby farms or leave family production altogether. But the former peasant-workers who are now fully proletarianized are offset by workers, white-collar and even cadre, who have entered family agricultural production during the last decade. Mainly they go in for hobby farming, but some venture beyond and experiment with family entrepreneurship.

In this book we will argue against both *under*- and *over*-estimating the significance of family agricultural production and the second economy in general. In the past, commentators on Hungarian society have been more likely to underestimate it, and in Chapter 1 we have, therefore, focused our attention on criticizing the view of family production as transitory, "still" existing, and possibly unimportant. But during the last few years there has emerged an opposing myth, that family production or the second economy are the universal cure for the ills of state socialism.

Indeed, the relative success of the Hungarian economy during the late 1970s and early 1980s can be attributed in no small part to the tolerance of the Hungarian regime toward small business. There is some indication that Hungarian central planners did not perform so much better than their Polish colleagues where the state-run sector of the economy is concerned. Hungarian redistributors wasted most of the hard currency they borrowed on international markets during the second half of the 1970s on the reconstruction of the steel industry and the creation of a Hungarian petrochemical industry. Hungary averted economic collapse not primarily because it invested the borrowed hard currency more wisely than the Poles or Rumanians, but because Hungarian planners invested less and used more to purchase consumer goods and keep spirits in the second economy high. Most important, higher incomes from family agricultural production and other private economic activities fragmented the Hungarian working class and distracted its attention from problems at the "point of production." Hungarian workers, who knew very well that life begins after working hours and that they must earn their real living on the houseplots or in moonlighting jobs after they leave the factories, could not quite understand the obsession of their Polish comrades with trade unions, plant meetings, and the like. Thus the second economy was, generally speaking, a big success, economically, socially, and politically: it kept the Hungarian economy afloat, the political system legitimate, and society content.

Although we believe that family agricultural production is viable and is here to stay, we must emphasize that incomes from such activities are typically quite small. Room for genuine entrepreneurship is not so great; not more than 5–15 percent of the rural population in Hungary can be called entrepreneurs. Entrepreneurs remain a small minority, and not only because most people do not have the entrepreneurial spirit. There is, after all, only limited room for entrepreneurship. Though family agricultural production and the second economy in general do have an equalizing effect on income distribution in a dominantly redistributive economy (Manchin and Szelényi, 1987) the emergent market sector not only counteracts but also generates inequalities and can be the source of new types of social conflicts. We are basically sympathetic to family agricultural production, regarding the new agricultural family entrepreneurs as our "heroes," but the second economy cannot be a substitute for reform of the first economy. Thus in this book we will "fight on two fronts," both repeatedly criticizing those who regard family production as transitory, backward, "still" existent, and also distancing ourselves from those who regard emergent petty commodity production as a universal remedy.

2

Alternative theories of family production

There exist three different theories to describe the sociological character of family production in collectivized socialist agriculture: the proletarianization theory, the peasant-worker theory, and the "interrupted embourgeoisement" theory. Each generates different hypotheses about the demographic characteristics, current occupations, and family background of the family producers.

THE PROLETARIANIZATION THEORY

Advocated for decades by the official theorists of Soviet-type agriculture, this theory is generally expressed by Soviet or East European textbooks on socialist agriculture, but it is also shared today by the majority of sociologists, even in a liberal country like Hungary. (For an exposition of such views, see Böhm and Pál, 1985, p. 77; Kulcsár and Szijjárto, 1980, pp. 80–88, 193–214; Vágvölgyi, 1976, p. 270.) According to this view, family agricultural production is a temporary phenomenon, reflecting the survival of a backward peasant consciousness and the insufficient technical and organizational development of the kolkhoz sector. Socialist agriculture gradually but inevitably develops toward an "industrial factory type of regime," and the former peasants advance toward full proletarian existence.

Vágvölgyi (1976), for instance, sees family agricultural producers as a *stratum in transition*:

> This stratum in many respects has a dual character. Members in this stratum are *still* tied in several ways to the peasantry: their way of life is

> more of peasant character; in their value system, the peasant *past* also plays an important role. The members of this *transitory stratum* are neither workers *yet*, nor peasants *any more*. Their characteristics will gradually become proletarian as they proceed along their trajectory from peasantry to proletarian existence.
>
> [p. 270; emphasis by I.S.]

Böhm and Pál go one step further. During the 1950s there were indeed semiproletarian, semipeasant families, who, they think, were accurately called peasant-workers, but during the 1970s proletarianization was completed. By the early 1980s "The mass process of depeasantization . . . has ended; . . . there is no doubt in our mind about the proletarian character of the rural-resident commuting workers." A single, internally stratified working class has been created, a "rapprochement among the fundamental classes has occurred" (Böhm and Pál, 1985, pp. 77, 78). They concede that the rural working class, commuters, and family agricultural producers are different from the established urban proletariat, but they suggest it is sufficient to call them a stratum *within* the working class.

Using a somewhat different terminology, Vágvölgyi, Böhm and Pál, and many other East European commentators on rural social structure agree that former peasants are either already members of the proletariat or, if not there yet, certainly heading inevitably in that direction.

Böhm and Pál's view of the future of family agricultural producers in general and part-time farmers in particular is cast in Marxist language favorable to the Hungarian Communist regime, but it is not uniquely East European. Many sociologists in the United States and Western Europe do not think very differently about part-time farmers either. They also believe that most people who become part-time farmers could not support their families from their farm, had to take a job, and most likely at some point or other will realize they are better off giving up the farm altogether. The driving force behind this is economies of scale, the superiority of large agricultural enterprises organized according to principles of industrial firms and relying on wage labor. One does not have to believe in a communist, classless future to accept the proletarianization theory; it can equally well be argued in terms of the "logic of industrialism."

The final test of the validity of the proletarianization theory comes, of course, from history itself. But meanwhile, one can derive from it hypotheses to guide empirical investigations. We were unable to locate in the literature any systematic attempt to test empirically the assumptions of this theory. Thus the hypotheses below are our own reconstruction, but we hope they will sound reasonable to proletarianization theorists.

1. Proletarianization theorists would anticipate that family agricultural producers are likely to be agricultural manual workers, particularly kolkhoz "peasants." When peasants become industrial or white-collar workers, they may for a while continue family production, but as they absorb working-class values and adapt to working-class ways of life they will abandon such activities. Thus among industrial workers, particularly those who commute to urban workplaces, the proportion of producers will be smaller.
2. Families with older heads of household are more likely to be minifarm operators. Older people absorbed peasant values, so they will keep up the old ways. As time passes, as the peasant past becomes more and more distant, the average age of family producers will also rise.
3. Since the main purpose of family production in collectivized agriculture is subsistence, the volume of production will vary according to the demographic composition of households. Hypotheses 1 and 2 predict who, among all rural people, are likely to produce any agricultural goods; hypothesis 3 explains who among the producers will produce more. We can think of two further refinements: (a) Families with greater consumption needs will produce more; thus families with larger numbers of dependants are likely to be bigger producers; (b) because the amount produced within a family also depends on the availability of labor, families where the wife is not employed or the number of adults is greater are likely to produce more. Extended, three-generational families are expected to be the biggest producers; the older generation will guarantee that traditional values are respected, and the younger generation will provide labor. Finally, within the confines of this hypothesis, we must anticipate that the number of small children will be negatively related to production. They may increase consumption needs, but they reduce labor time available for agricultural production.
4. The proletarianization theory offers no hypothesis about social mobility. Family agricultural production is regarded as a one-generational phenomenon which will disappear as people who were brought up in peasant families retire or die. Within this single generation, family production is subsistence-oriented and quite universal: thus it is not reasonable to assume that parents'

occupation or size of parents' landholdings will have much to do with current agricultural production.

By the late 1960s new evidence began to shed doubt on the validity of the proletarianization theory; such doubts are reinforced by the facts presented in Chapter 1. First family agricultural production under socialism did not appear to be so transitory or temporary as the theory would suggest. Family production remained formidably stable: 20, 30, or 40 years after collectivization family minifarms produced more goods than ever before. Second, the proletarianization theory did not seem to predict accurately the social and demographic composition of family producers. As the first generation of collective farmers, those who had begun as private peasants, grew older and began to give up work on their houseplots, younger, working-class, or even white-collar families took up production. Finally, as early as the late 1960s observers had begun to notice that rural families not only were not giving up family production, but were beginning to sell larger proportions of their produce on the market. Such a trend, irrespective of how limited it may then have been, would not jibe with the thinking of proletarianization theorists.

THE PEASANT-WORKER THEORY

István Márkus was probably the first to offer a coherent alternative to the proletarianization theory.[1] During the early 1970s Márkus conducted fieldwork in the Galga Valley, in market gardening villages northeast of Budapest (Márkus, 1973). Márkus observed that some rural families, many with industrial-worker heads of households, were engaged in rather innovative family agricultural production. Exploiting the closeness of their villages to the large Budapest consumer market, they began to intensify production in their gardens and to behave more like minifarmers than peasants. To describe this new phenomenon, Márkus adopted the concept of "postpeasantry" from Henri Mendras (1967).

Márkus uses the term "postpeasantry" to describe a qualitatively new phenomenon, not just a mixture of "peasants" and "workers." He tries to encompass a relatively stable, lasting, new cultural and economic pattern of behavior by a social group which lives between two worlds

[1] For earlier attempts to describe the dual, proletarian-peasant character of rural households, which in a way foreshadow Márkus's work, see Hegedűs, 1970, and Gyenes, 1968.

(urban–rural; agriculture–industry) and tries to make the most of both.

At the same time, István Kemény studied the social stratification of the Hungarian working class (Kemény, 1972). Kemény noted that about half of the industrial workers were first-generation proletarians (Kemény, 1972, pp. 40–41) of peasant origin, or were formerly farmers themselves. He emphasized that this "new working class" is quite distinct from the older urban proletariat; many of them continued to live in the country and were still involved in family agricultural production. The ideas of the "postpeasantry" and the "new working class" complement each other; they both challenge the earlier proletarianization theory.[2]

In one important respect, both Márkus and Kemény remained firmly within the proletarianization theory: they both regarded the "new working class" or the "postpeasantry" as a transitory stage on the road to proletarianization, assuming that full proletarianization was merely delayed by one generation. In our first publications on the subject, we were strongly influenced by Márkus and Kemény (see Konrád and Szelényi, 1977; Szelényi, 1981). Basically, we tried to synthesize their work, but in one respect we extended their criticism of the proletarianization theory: we began to wonder about the transitoriness of family agricultural production as well.

In our synthesis of Márkus and Kemény we emphasized family agricultural production as an innovative and successful working-class strategy. One consequence was that the new industrial worker, the peasant-worker, might be better off than the traditional urban proletariat. Workers who maintain rural residence can complement their incomes from increasingly market-oriented, effective, and intensive minifarms. Though, typically, peasant-workers are less skilled than the established "old urban proletariat," they may end up earning higher total incomes. By the mid-1970s, this had become a source of some social tension. The most highly skilled urban workers, particularly in heavy industry like steel or machine-tool manufacturing, were quite privileged during the 1950s or early 1960s and earned significantly higher incomes than the average unskilled and semiskilled worker. With the emergence of the "postpeasant" phenomenon, these income differentials began to wither away. By the mid-1970s some of the more senior workers or

[2] The term "new working class" was adapted by Kemény from S. M. Miller and of course not from Serge Mallet. For Miller, migrant workers, particularly Puerto Ricans, were replacing the "old working class" in the United States during the 1960s. Thus they represented a "new working class." Mallet, on the other hand, used the term very differently to label the most highly skilled employees in industry—technicians or even some engineers; see Miller, 1964, pp. 81–85.

foremen found that unskilled worker subordinates, who commuted from neighboring villages and took their industrial jobs rather easily, might be living in larger houses and, counting the value of their family production, might have higher total incomes than they did. Some party and trade union conservatives opposed to the second economy—the "ouvrierist opposition"—tried on these grounds to stir up political trouble for the Party reformers, to shore up urban working-class support for policies that would limit "unreasonably high peasant incomes." These attempts failed in the end, but the very existence of this movement indicated that the division between the "new working class" and the "old proletariat" that Kemény had for the first time depicted was real.

Thus, by emphasizing how much the rural semiproletariat gained by becoming postpeasants, by retaining and redefining their peasant-worker, semiproletarian status, we began to posit the possibility of a long-term reproduction of part-time farming under socialism. If indeed peasant-workers were better off than the established proletariat, if the family minifarm guaranteed higher incomes and was an effective way to resist "socialist exploitation" and improve workers' bargaining positions in labor markets, why would it pass away in just one more generation?

During the 1970s some new theories of socialist agriculture also supported the idea that peasant-workers were there to stay. The proletarianization theory of agriculture assumed that the large-enterprise, factory-type organization would entirely replace family work organizations. But agricultural economists were beginning to emphasize that large-scale and small-scale enterprises coexist in socialist agriculture—indeed, they presuppose each other in the long run. If the cooperative sector "integrates" the minifarms, if the two forms "symbiotically" coexist in a rational division of labor, then part-time farming may not in principle be doomed to extinction, and certainly not in the foreseeable future. In harmony with this new perspective, the "new working class"/postpeasantry theory emphasizes that family agricultural production is not a survival of peasant traditions but a qualitatively new phenomenon, beyond peasantry.

In 1980 Márkus added another important building block to his theory: a hypothesis concerning the social origin of family agricultural producers (Márkus, 1980). In this very influential paper, Márkus identified the poor peasants as the major driving force beind Hungarian history after World War II (his proposition could be generalized to most of Eastern Europe). According to Márkus, in 1945 the poor peasantry

> genuinely found itself. . . . The poor peasantry was the major driving force behind every single important economic and social event of the last

> three and a half decades. . . . Without them the agricultural cooperatives . . . (at least in their present form, with their present system of incentives) would have been unimaginable. The sons and daughters of the poor peasants were the first to provide the labor force for the most important new factories.
>
> [Márkus, 1980, p. 24]

Land reform and socialist transformation led to an outburst of social energies—poor peasant ambitions and aspirations for better living, social mobility, and respectability, suppressed for centuries, were suddenly liberated. "The historically new combination of a large-scale agricultural production within the part-time family minifarm also utilized these energies" (Márkus, 1980, p. 28). Poor peasants were behind the land reform, founded the first cooperatives, became the first functionaries in villages and kolkhozes, pioneered in socialist industrialization, and formed the core of the postpeasantry. The commodity-producing, part-time, family minifarm was also their innovation.[3]

We are now ready to summarize the empirically testable hypotheses that can be derived from the new wave of theorizing about family agricultural production. So far we have interchangeably used the labels "postpeasantry," "new working class," or "peasant-workers," always attempting to stay close to the terminology of the author we were discussing. Authors use these terms in slightly different ways, but here we will treat them as synonyms and, for the sake of simplicity, we will mainly use the term "peasant-workers." Our concept will, of course, try to synthesize all the insights we gained from the theories of the postpeasantry and the new working class.

1. Although the majority of family agricultural producers may be agricultural manual workers, an increasing proportion of them are industrial workers. After all, the main reason for the cultivation of the minifarm is not the survival of peasant values, but a new strategy by workers to improve both their level of consumption and their labor market position.
2. The correlation between age and family production will be weaker than anticipated by the proletarianization theory. Nor should we anticipate that, over time, the average age of family producers will

[3] Despite his emphasis that the combination of large-scale agricultural production with the part-time family minifarm was historically novel, Márkus remains skeptical about the prospects of family agricultural production. It must wither away; there cannot be another generation of rural Hungarians who are ready to accept this extraordinary degree of self-exploitation. (Márkus, 1980, p. 29).

increase; for quite some time young families too will join the ranks of minifarm operators.

3. Since the peasant-worker theory presumes that peasant-worker households will at least partially be oriented toward commodity production, the demographic composition of the family will not be the good predictor of the quantity of production that the proletarianization theory implied. Current occupation and labor market position may be equally if not more significant predictors of the extent of family production.
4. Márkus believes that poor peasants play a predominant role in the development of the postpeasantry. It may be implicit in his position that people from social strata below the poor peasantry became fully proletarianized, whereas those from social strata above the poor peasants entered the middle classes.

Undoubtedly, the peasant-worker theory was a major step toward an adequate sociological interpretation of family agricultural production in collectivized state-socialist agricultural systems. But the most recent evidence regarding the dynamics of production on minifarms is beginning to show the limitations of this approach also. Our data in Chapter 1 indicated that between 1972 and 1982 family production, especially commodity production among the "bigger" producers, tended to become concentrated. Somewhere among the top 5–15 percent of family producers, the market orientation is becoming dominant. A qualitatively new phenomenon seems to be appearing on the scene: small agricultural family *enterprises*. These enterprises show signs that they are becoming (1) the primary source of family income; (2) full-time businesses—although most husbands until now have kept their jobs, over the last five or so years some wives have quit state employment and become full-time managers; (3) highly specialized—they sell most of their products in the market. These producers compete with each other in the marketplace, and such competition is beginning to force accumulation on them. The minifarm operators are thus beginning to behave like genuine entrepreneurs who accumulate capital and not "wage laborers" who maximize consumption. For the new entrepreneurs the personal motivation may at first have been consumption, but they have begun to move beyond consumption considerations. Typically, the capital thus accumulated is still rather small, about 1–2 million Ft ($20,000–40,000, or about 20–40 years' income for an average industrial worker!), but the rate of accumulation is quite impressive. Gross income generated with an investment of 1 million Ft can be around 1 million Ft a year. Finally, some entrepreneurs are beginning to employ wage labor, though usually only in the peak growing season (picking fruit or tomatoes) or in a cooperative manner (several cattle farmers hiring one cowboy). Nonetheless, the trend is unmistakably in the direction of "enterprise proper."

There are probably very few farms—perhaps as few as 1 or 2 percent of all family agricultural producers—that meet all the above conditions, but quite a few that meet one or several of them. And none of these conditions can be understood merely as a sign of innovative working-class strategy. They are, rather, signs of the emergence of an entrepreneurial mentality, of entrepreneurship. The embourgeoisement theory of Pál Juhász is an attempt to come to terms with this new phenomenon.

THE "INTERRUPTED EMBOURGEOISEMENT" THEORY

Juhász was the first theorist to notice that some operators of market-oriented minifarms were no longer following "working-class strategies." Jobs, incomes from jobs, improvement of their bargaining position in labor markets, and levels of consumption are not their primary considerations. They run their farms as enterprises, think about returns on investments, and begin to economize both with labor and capital. They are not wage laborers, workers, or even permanent semi-proletarians; they are entrepreneurs, "burghers," or "bourgeois," as some Hungarian sociologists like to call them. Instead of "proletarianization," or the "formation of a new working class," the social process thus described should therefore be called "embourgeoisement."

Embourgeoisement, or *polgárosodás*: a semantic analysis

Over the last few years, the idea of embourgeoisement has captured the imagination of many Hungarian social scientists, particularly, though not exclusively, the critically inclined. In 1984, George Konrád, the noted novelist and leading dissident, was interviewed for a Swedish newspaper. Questioned about the single most important event in recent Hungarian history, he replied: "socialist embourgeoisement." This concept seems to play a role in the thinking of Hungarian dissidents comparable to the role of "society" or "civil society" in Polish opposition ideology.

Here we will attempt to reconstruct what Hungarian critical theorists mean by "embourgeoisement." This is no small task. The subject is much talked about, but precious little has been written on it. We must proceed in a rather unusual manner by the standards and conventions of Western scholarship, relying more on conversations we have conducted with dozens of critically minded or dissident intellectuals during the last three years than on quotes from scholarly publications for our "data."[4]

We start this exercise with a little semantic analysis. In the Hungarian language the terms *polgár* (burgher or bourgeois) and *polgárosodás* (embourgeoisement) are used. The term *polgár* has about the same meaning as the German *Bürger*; thus it combines the meanings of the French *citoyen* and *bourgeois*. *Polgár* and *Bürger* describe a concept that in English, as in French, we can express only with two words: "burgher" or "citizen" on the one hand, and "entrepreneur," "capitalist," or "bourgeois" on the other. Thus the terms *polgár* and *polgárosodás* can be used with a comfortable vagueness: when I call somebody *polgár* I don't necessarily imply that this person is a capitalist, or a bourgeois, or even an entrepreneur. No economic content is necessarily attached to the concept. Thus even "socialist embourgeoisement" may not be a contradiction in terms. *Polgár* may mean capitalist; after all, if I explicitly wanted to exclude this possibility, I could use the word *állampolgár* in Hungarian, the proper translation of "citizen." But in the word *állampolgár* the term "state"—*állam*—is substituted for the "city" in the English word "citizenship." One reason that Hungarian dissidents, with strong antistatist feelings, are uneasy about the more unambiguous *állampolgár* is precisely its link to the concept of "state."[5]

This comfortable vagueness or ambiguity in the term *polgárosodás* makes it particularly suitable for encompassing rather diverse phenomena; if necessary, it can even shift its meaning slightly over time. When the term first entered the vocabulary of critical analysis in the late 1970s, mainly its cultural and political connotations were emphasized. People with autonomy, both cultural and political-social, were called *polgár*; they were thus distinguished from "state subjects." During the 1980s, as the private sector strengthened and the second economy expanded, the economic dimension was added. At least for some, *polgár*, now began to mean entrepreneur, though it still did not mean "capitalist," and elements of the earlier cultural and political content were retained. Juhász's (1983) use of *polgárosodás* to describe the increasing entrepreneurial orientation of family agricultural production was an important step toward such a reinterpretation of the concept of *polgár*. But this more economic and, as we will argue, more "populist"

[4] For one of the few sophisticated, though primarily historically oriented, discussions of burgherhood and embourgeoisement in Hungary, see Losonczi, 1977, pp. 129–84.

[5] For an early analysis of these concepts, see Bibó, 1947 [1983], pp. 812–15.

definition of *polgár* does not replace the earlier, more cultural-political notion. That notion described urban phenomena: it expressed the life experience of humanistic intellectuals, and still retains its popularity among the dissenting urban intelligentsia. Thus the meaning of *polgár* varies over time and across different groups of critical intellectuals.

Changes in the meaning of *polgár* and *polgárosodás*

During the Stalinist period the term *polgár* was a negative label. The dual meaning of the term was ignored, it was simply equated with "bourgeois," "petty bourgeois," or "capitalist," and it was treated as antagonistic to "socialism." Some 10 or 15 years ago in Hungary reevaluation of the notion of *polgár* began, and the term once again began to carry a positive meaning.

This occurred first in the cities: urban "burgher" values of the presocialist period were rediscovered: the beautiful homes of "bourgeois intellectuals," where people sipped afternoon tea from fine china in living rooms full of antique furniture, conversing about Proust or Mahler. "Burgher" values and ways of behavior were also rediscovered and revalued. In contrast to the collectivist values promoted by Communism, the autonomy of presocialist burgher intellectuals was emphasized, their sense of irony and humor (so badly lacking among party intellectuals), their loyalty to friends (in contrast to the party loyalty of Communists, who, in principle, should always have been ready to betray personal friends for the "cause"), their unshakable good aesthetic sense (in contrast to the horrors of socialist realism) and so on and so forth.

One young writer, Pál Granasztoi, Jr., the son of a respected "burgher" architect and city planner, has given a vivid, colorful, nostalgic description of such a "burgher" environment in his parents' house, in the monthly literature review, *Kortárs*. Granasztoi emphasized how this "burgher" lifestyle (and value system) survived even Communism; despite the public Stalinist facades of his 1950s childhood, the "burgher" existence continued in the remains of the old bourgeois apartments of Budapest, as in his father's apartment.

Granasztoi's article was received with delight and enthusiasm by critical intellectuals, who realized that he was describing values and ways of life they also shared and to which they aspired. For Granasztoi, the term "burghers" or *polgár* had positive connotations. Several critical intellectuals we interviewed in Hungary during 1982–84 had liked Granasztoi's memoir particularly because it depicted a change in contemporary Hungarian society that they regarded as most interesting and from their point of view most promising: the resurfacing of "embourgeoisement," interrupted and forced below ground after 1949.

In Granasztoi's memoir lifestyles and cultural preferences play a prominent role, but what made the concept so appealing was the perceived political characteristics of the *polgár*. The stubborn survival of the *bürgerliche* ways of life and refined cultural taste was seen as an indication of the strength and unshakable autonomy of this class. It had successfully resisted statism, had been able to stop the state at the front door of the house even during the worst times of Stalinism. Burgher homes remained their castles, islands of proud individual autonomy in an ocean of totalitarianism. In a social system which tries to force everybody to become a state subject—modern state serfs—the idealized *polgár* is seen as the symbol of silent, nonviolent resistance, the Gandhi of state socialism. The civic and civil consciousness of the *polgár* contrasts sharply with the clientelism and deference of state subjects.

The rural "interrupted embourgeoisement" theory of Juhász is an exciting extension of this cultural-political and probably rather elitist conception of *polgárosodás*. Juhász develops a more "populist" version of "embourgeoisement," in which the essence is not the autonomy of ideas among elite intellectuals and the refinement of their lifestyles, but the autonomy of producers, particularly petty commodity producers, from the social order based on bureaucratic rank.[6] Suddenly the market gardener or the hog and cattle farmer becomes the hero of embourgeoisement, replacing or at least complementing the critical or dissenting urban intellectual.

Much to our surprise, this shift in emphasis met with no resentment from many critical intellectuals; some even welcomed it. During the summer of 1983 I participated in a so-called "flying university" seminar on the question of embourgeoisement, in a private home in Buda. The seminar was attended by some 40 young people, also by several dissidents, among them two important figures of the Hungarian social movement that labels itself the Democratic Opposition and therefore of the dissenting urban intelligentsia, Lászlo Rajk and Bálint Nagy. Our opening discussion was guided by the "culturalist" concept of embourgeoisement, which led us to consider the possibility of embourgeoisement among the statist or cadre intelligentsia. We could think of several establishment figures in academe, who were unconditional apologists for the regime but whose lifestyles, tastes, and personal values were always, or had recently become quite bourgeois. Several of us

[6] See, for instance, the commentary of Juhász on "Medve Alfonz," a new agricultural entrepreneur, a "peasant-burgher" from the documentary film "Ne Sápadj," directed by the Gulyás brothers: Juhász, 1983b.

quite liked that idea: the process of embourgeoisement, in the beginning linked to dissent, turns into a silent revolution, moves almost unnoticeably into the very fortress of power, and erodes it internally. But Bálint Nagy strongly objected to such a line of reasoning. His notion of embourgeoisement was much more like the one developed by Pál Juhász. Nagy argued that the core of embourgeoisement is economic transformation, its central agent not the intellectual, but rather the "peasant-burgher" or "worker-burgher," those peasants and workers who create autonomy for themselves through family entrepreneurship. Thus for Nagy the main arena of embourgeoisement is the second economy.

The growth of family agricultural entrepreneurship as embourgeoisement

The origins of the theory of rural embourgeoisement expressed by Juhász and Nagy can be explored through their links to Ferenc Erdei's ideas about "peasant-burghers."

The "interrupted embourgeoisement theory" was foreshadowed by the work of Erdei during and shortly before World War II. Erdei, the most powerful sociological theorist of the presocialist epoch, also identified embourgeoisement tendencies in Hungarian villages and "agricultural cities" (see below for a definition). The central figure in the sociological oeuvre of the young Erdei, writing during the late 1930s and early 1940s, is the "peasant-burgher" (*paraszt polgár*), the peasantry undergoing "embourgeoisement." Erdei's heroes, these peasant-burghers, are counterposed both to the rural gentry and to the urban capitalist bourgeoisie (which in Erdei's view also happens to be "alien," thus German or Jewish). For the young Erdei these "peasant-burghers" in Hungary and in Eastern Europe in general represented a unique, and for him highly desirable, force for modernization.

Erdei, in his fascinating book, *A Magyar Város* [The Hungarian City] (1939), argued that Hungarian peasants had been on an embourgeoisement trajectory for centuries. Gradually orienting their farms toward market production, they had simultaneously developed civil institutions and local self-government. Their most lasting and spectacular achievement was the Hungarian agricultural city. During the sixteenth and seventeenth centuries, under the Turkish occupation, the Hungarian peasantry was left to itself by its feudal lords and priests, who fled from the conquering Turkish army. The Turks did not want to impose their social order, so long as they could collect taxes. Under such circumstances the peasants left their villages and, so as to be better placed to negotiate with the Turks from a position of power, moved to quite large agricultural cities. Here, on a relatively backward economic-technological basis, they created a market-oriented economy and fine civic, cultural institutions. In Erdei's view, these civic institutions were second to none; they were comparable to institutions in the most advanced countries of Western Europe.

Within a generation, the former serfs learned how to govern themselves and how to produce for markets, even for the world market. They became "bourgeois": as producers they acted like "entrepreneurs," and as city dwellers they became "citizens" or "burghers."

Erdei's analysis has fascinating implications for the Weberian theory of embourgeoisement, and in particular for his thesis of the Protestant Ethic. The peasant-burghers of the newly formed agricultural cities during the sixteenth century were also looking for a new religious ideology. The Roman Catholic Church had left them at the mercy of the Turks, and they also sought a religion in which laymen had a greater say. Calvinist presbyterianism proved to be exactly such a religion. In Hungary it did indeed function as a precondition for the evolution of civic institutions and a market economy, although the development of the forces of production did not yet justify such an evolution. Thus Erdei, with very little knowledge of Weber, rediscovered the Protestant Ethic in a Hungarian context.

According to Erdei, the tragedy of Hungarian history was that the further evolution of "peasant burgherhood" was later blocked. With the defeat of the Turks the feudal order was restored to Hungary (and generally to Eastern Europe). The first wave of embourgeoisement ended and turned into a second feudalism. From the eighteenth century on, the gentry limited peasant embourgeoisement. Strongly opposed to the gentry, Erdei believed that this had been a major disaster, particularly because the interruption of peasant embourgeoisement carried with it the danger that modernization of the economy would be accomplished by the "alien," capitalist element. The long rule of the gentry deformed Hungarian society, destroying its "defense mechanism" against "greed." By uncontrolled pursuit of greed the "alien" urban capitalist elements could produce the most uncivilized form of capitalism (Erdei, 1976).

In his early works—*Futóhomok* [Drifting Sand], *Magyar Falu* [The Hungarian Village], and *Parasztok* [Peasants]—Erdei repeatedly emphasized that resumption of the already interrupted embourgeoisement of the peasantry might be a way out of a dilemma in which there were two unsatisfactory choices: a gentrified present and a greedy capitalist future that was alien to Hungarian society.[7] His main conclusion is that although "it is not possible to build a nation of peasants . . . one can build a nation with [bourgeoisified] peasants" (from *Parasztok*, *fide* Bibó, 1940 [1982], p. 332).

Later Erdei's views changed; from being the first of embourgeoisement theorists, he became, in a way, a proletarianization theorist. In his second major theoretical statement about the peasantry, *A magyar paraszttársadalom* [Hungarian Peasant Society], written in 1942, he began to put the word "embourgeoisement" in quotation marks (Erdei, 1942, [1980], p. 163) and to emphasize the prospects for proletarianization. In his important lecture at the Szárszó conference of anti-Nazi, leftist Hungarian intellectuals in 1943, he accepted both an orthodox Marxist view about the inevitability of proletarianization and the political reality of Russian occupation of Hungary after World War II (Erdei, 1943 [1983], p. 209). After 1945, he shelved the idea of embourgeoisement altogether, seeming to accept that socialist proletarianization was an inescapable requirement of the times.

The interrupted embourgeoisement thesis should be understood against this background, as a genuine adaptation and extension of the work of the young Erdei. In extrapolating Erdei's pre-1945 analyses it may be argued that after 1945, following the collapse of gentry rule in the countryside and the coming of land reform, a new wave of embourgeoisement took off. It was interrupted and forced underground again in 1948–49 by Stalinism.[8] The key idea of the interrupted embourgeoisement theory is that the market-oriented family agricultural production of the late 1970s and early 1980s should be understood as a reemergence of the same process.

Juhász also shares with the young Erdei the idea that rural embourgeoisement does not necessarily imply capitalist greed but may instead be the best cure for it. In the dual meaning of the concept *polgár* he emphasizes the citizen and deemphasizes the bourgeois. One of the most important indicators of embourgeoisement is that family production ceases to be a privilege given in exchange for labor services and becomes a citizen's right (Juhász and Magyar, 1984, p. 189). The new entrepreneurs are not state subjects any more. Instead, they enter a

[7] István Bibó, a major Hungarian Third Road theorist, was understandably open to such reasoning and assessed Erdei's early work positively; see Bibó, 1940 [1982], p. 329. For Bibó's own theory of embourgeoisement and the Third Road see Bibó, 1945, 1946a, b, 1947, 1948, 1971–72. For an interesting critique of Bibó's concept of the Third Road, see Lukács, 1945.

[8] Sadly enough, Erdei not only provided theoretical ammunition for full-scale collectivization but played an active political role in interrupting the "second wave" of rural embourgeoisement that had been the dream of his youth.

contractual relationship with the state and will develop a civic consciousness that will prevent a capitalist type of development.[9]

Embourgeoisement versus civil society: Hungarian and Polish dissenting theories

"Embourgeoisement" in Hungarian critical thought plays a role like that of "society" or "civil society" in Polish dissident thought. The initial Hungarian interpretation of *polgárosodás* was not in fact so very different from the Polish conception of the evolution of society versus powers. But with the recent Hungarian emphasis on entrepreneurship this has changed, and the two theoretical approaches are beginning to express two different social realities, two different strategies of emancipation, in the search for a non-Soviet road under state socialism.

Recent Hungarian dissident thought emphasizes entrepreneurship, individualism, and individual autonomy. The Polish dissident theorists, by fostering the idea of the autonomous development of society from powers, have more of a collectivist accent. This difference may not have much to do with national cultures and traditions or past history, but may reflect instead a contrast between the most recent Hungarian and Polish strategies for breaking free of the straightjacket of Soviet-style state socialism. While the Hungarians during the last decade worked their way toward greater autonomy by expanding the second economy (following, in a sense, an individualist strategy) the Poles confronted the power structure directly in the political sphere, through trade unions, the Workers' Defense Committee (KOR—an organization of dissenting intellectuals formed during the 1970s), political organizations, and collective action.

Common to dissent in both countries is that with rare exception it explicitly seeks a "Third Road": the stated goal is not to move toward capitalism, but to move away from totalitarian state socialism, toward political and economic autonomy, freedom, and democracy in a third system which is like neither U.S. capitalism nor Soviet socialism. Recent history seems to teach that Soviet socialism tolerates the Polish type of challenge, based on collective action, less readily than the more individualist Hungarian strategy for emancipation. One may even

[9] When in interviews we pressed Juhász to explain why he thought embourgeoisement was not the restoration of capitalism, he repeatedly returned to the "sense of community" and "civic duty" of these new entrepreneurs. Even the most successful entrepreneurs would not want to become particularly wealthy, he argued, because embourgeoisement was breaking down the caste-like divisions within the villages and egalitarianism becoming the dominant norm.

suggest that, if democracy is the goal, the Hungarians are following the historically known road. Even in the West, entrepreneurship came first, and democracy followed. The Poles have tried the impossible: to start the change at the political level. Indeed, the "Hungarian road" may deserve more theoretical interest with the collapse of the Polish experiment (though it may be a little premature to talk about "collapse": by the summer of 1987, five years after martial law was imposed, Polish social dissent had not yet been broken). Is the "Hungarian road" of "embourgeoisement" more viable than earlier attempts to break out of state socialism? If it is indeed viable, does it lead to a "third destination"?[10]

Empirically testable hypotheses of interrupted embourgeoisement

Now, after all these fascinating metatheoretical questions, we must return to research, try to define our terms in empirically measurable ways, and develop empirically testable hypotheses.

We must first take a stand on what we mean by "embourgeoisement" —not an easy task because of the "comfortable ambiguity" of the term *polgár*. Here we will use "embourgeoisement" as a synonym for "entrepreneurship," without assuming that the evolution of entrepreneurship coincides with the development of citizenship. It may or it may not; we are somewhat skeptical, for we can think of entrepreneurs with little civic consciousness, individuals who are more bourgeois than citizen. Our task here is not to test citizenship; we will focus on entrepreneurship.

With this specification of the interrupted embourgeoisement theory, we can identify a few empirically testable hypotheses. The key question, of course, is this: how is it possible that entrepreneurship should reemerge three decades after the socialist transformation of Hungarian society? Who are these new entrepreneurs; where were they "hiding" during the last decades? We can develop the following hypotheses from the embourgeoisement theory:

1. There is no reason to believe that the agricultural occupation of the head of household has much to do with family agricultural entrepreneurship. If we seek to explain why certain families produce more goods for the market, rather than why families produce at all or produce only for subsistence, then the current

[10] See, for a more detailed analysis of a Hungarian–Polish comparison, Manchin and Szelényi, 1985.

TABLE 2.1 *Who are the family agricultural producers? alternative hypotheses*

Variable	*Proletarianization theory*	*Peasant-worker theory*	*Interrupted embourgeoisement theory*
Current occupation of producers	Agricultural manual laborers	Industrial workers	No hypothesis
Age	Older individuals	Younger individuals also	No strong correlation expected
Demographic composition	Families with more labor power and greater consumer needs	Same, but weaker correlation	No correlation with consumer needs, weak correlation with labor supply
Family background	No hypothesis	Poor peasants	Middle and rich peasants
Nature of production	Subsistence	Subsistence, with some market production	Primarily market production

agricultural occupation of the head of household is likely to lose its explanatory power.

2. Age will be irrelevant for predicting increases in commodity production. Young people will become entrepreneurs as well.
3. Because the primary goal of family production is commodity production, the demographic characteristics of the family will play a decreasing role in predicting increases in commodity production. Labor supply will still matter, but consumption needs will be irrelevant.
4. The "interrupted embourgeoisement" theory offers a hypothesis which challenges the mobility hypothesis of the peasant-worker theory. Márkus claimed that the new type of family agricultural production was another historical innovation of the poor peasantry; Juhász, however, implies that former middle or rich peasants (former peasant-burghers) or their children are more likely to develop new patterns of family production.

Table 2.1 summarizes the hypotheses formulated by the different theories of family agricultural production.

3

The "interrupted embourgeoisement" theory reformulated

Some hypotheses

The "interrupted embourgeoisement" theory is one that the authors incline toward, and it is our guide in beginning our analysis. In two important respects, however, we modify it.

1. We wish to integrate the "interrupted embourgeoisement," "peasant-worker," and "proletarianization" theories. Entrepreneurship, we posit, is only one possible destination in the transformation of class structure currently occurring in Eastern Europe, and we distinguish several other destinations.
2. We ask: how is entrepreneurship passed on from one generation to the next, particularly when the obvious and usually operative mechanism, inheritance of private wealth, is absent? Here, we will explore the importance of life history for the genesis of entrepreneurship.

THE CHANGING CLASS MAP OF STATE SOCIALISM: HOW MANY DESTINATIONS?

In Chapter 2 we presented three theories of family production as "alternative" sets of hypotheses, but they can be viewed as complementary explanations. We believe that in the state socialist societies of Eastern Europe rural social structure is undergoing a complex transformation in which several processes are operating, some complementary, others contradictory.

Thus the hypotheses advanced by István Márkus and Pál Juhász are not mutually exclusive, but may be complementary. A postpeasantry or new working class may well be forming and an entrepreneurial class reemerging at one and the same time.

This is all the more conceivable, because embourgeoisement may be quite limited in scope. The proportion of rural families which, by all our criteria, could be regarded as "entrepreneurial" may be as small as 5–10 percent of all rural households. Even by the loosest and most generous definition, it is unlikely that the "pool" of all rural families which may enter the ranks of the new "bourgeoisie" would be more than 20 or 25 percent of all households. From Table 1.1, in 1982 the average net yearly value of family agricultural production was only 21,000 Ft, or about half the income of an average industrial worker. The majority of rural households then, are in all likelihood peasant-worker households, consisting primarily of wage laborers who produce agricultural goods merely to supplement their incomes and whose lives are basically determined by their state jobs. Most of these peasant-workers are indeed simply "postpeasants." They wish to maximize rather than delay consumption and do not want to work long hours, unless they have an immediate consumption goal. Even if they wished to become entrepreneurs, were willing to run the inherent risks, most could not—entrepreneurial openings in agriculture are highly limited. Under the socialist system of land ownership, scarcity of land doees not, as it usually does, control the number of entrepreneurs: minifarms can become very profitable on very small plots of land. But the size of the consumer market for agricultural products sets strict limits to the expansion of agricultural entrepreneurship.

This was clearly demonstrated in vegetable gardening during the 1970s. Vegetable production, particularly under plastic tunnels, exploded following 1975. By 1983–84 a small crisis had begun to hit these private market gardeners.[1] Urban markets became saturated, and increased production resulted in price stagnation while inflation was pushing production costs up. Bankruptcy threatened some of the new entrepreneurs. Late arrivals, who had started their businesses three to five years after the pioneers, complained that they had missed the really good times when profits were high and it was easy to accumulate. They, the late starters, had had to borrow money on the black market to get

[1] Pál Schiffer made an excellent documentary film about this crisis. In his "Földi Paradicsom" [Paradise on Earth] he interviewed a small tomato producer in the city of Szentes. The following account of the crisis relies heavily on evidence from this documentary film.

started and as their profit margins decreased were now suffocating under their excessive debt.

For the first time in "socialist" agricultural entrepreneurship, bankruptcy became a reality. For a while, it had appeared that under socialism small businesses could only be successful, that there was no possibility of failure. Now this had proved to be a myth.

Thus, the number of positions open for entrepreneurship is limited; entrepreneurship is only one of the possible destinations for rural families. It is, furthermore a destination at which only a minority—and possibly a rather small minority—will arrive. If we acknowledge that entrepreneurship and the new peasant-worker existence are two different destinations, then of course both Juhász and Márkus can be right: people from a poor-peasant background may end up as peasant-workers, while those from middle- and rich-peasant families may move toward entrepreneurial positions.[2]

To begin with, let us draw up a map of all "destinations" in rural state socialist societies, particularly in order to do justice to the proletarianization theory, which we have until now only criticized, primarily to point out that it is not so universal and inevitable a process as it was for some time presumed to be. Proletarianization of course has also occurred in state socialist rural societies, but there are counteracting tendencies. Rural society is not so defenseless against the pressures of socialist proletarianization as early theorists of Soviet-type societies believed.

Some of the rural population has, however, been thoroughly proletarianized. How large is this fragment of the rural society? Family production figures suggest that about 10–30 percent of rural society lives exclusively or overwhelmingly from wages and salaries. It is also quite possible that proletarianization is irreversible; a possibility we investigate in Chapter 7 is that those who have become fully proletarianized may be indefinitely "lost for the cause of embourgeoisement."

[2] The rural stratification system in Hungary around 1944 can be briefly summarized as follows (in % of all rural households): agricultural proletarians (landless or cultivating only tiny plots), over 30%; semiproletarians (industrial and other wage laborers, who cultivate less than 1 hold of land, 10%; poor peasants (primary source of income is the landholding, which is less than 5 holds), over 20%; small peasants (5–10 holds), 10%; middle peasants (11–25 holds), 10%; kulaks and gentry or commercial landowners (over 25 holds), 5%.

The rural genteel "middle class," petty bourgeoisie, established industrial workers with no land, constituted less than 15%.

Sources: Donáth, 1977, p. 22; Andorka, 1982, pp. 32–54; Berend and Ránki, 1972, p. 150, Andorka and Harcsa, 1982, pp. 213–17; Hanák, 1982, pp. 250–56.

Furthermore, proletarianization is not the only process which "irreversibly" (there is, of course, nothing ever completely irreversible in history) diverts people from embourgeoisement. It has its "twin process," which we call "cadrefication." We can indeed assume that those who commit to a lifelong career as party or state officials are unlikely to enter an embourgeoisement trajectory. These individuals, in the perception of the average village dweller, have "never worked," but have spent their careers in positions of power and administration, rotating from party secretary, to chairman or secretary of the local council, to president of the cooperative.[3]

Thus we can distinguish at least four different "destinations" on the map of the social structure of state socialist societies—cadres, proletarians, peasant-workers, and entrepreneurs—and we can identify the routes leading to these destinations.

The fundamental division in state socialist rural structure is the cadre/proletarian axis. Here, following Weberian conventions (Weber, 1921 [1978], pp. 302–7, 926–39) we call this dominant system of social stratification a "rank order," distinguishing it from an emergent, but still subordinated market-based system of social stratification, which could be called a "class order."

In our investigation of family agricultural production we try to identify the defense mechanisms that people can employ to resist pressures to fit into the fundamental rank order. Peasant-workers remain within the dominant bureaucratic order, but they carve out for themselves "hiding places"—activities in the second economy, jobs where some autonomy is possible—which are tolerated or not noticed by the cadres. From time to time they withdraw to these hiding places to try to heal wounds they suffer in the world of state-controlled work. Entrepreneurship is a more active strategy of resistance. It creates a new hierarchy and if successful transforms rural social structure from a single hierarchy based on a bureaucratic rank order into a dual structure where a competing hierarchy, structured according to the principles of the market, can emerge.

During our field trips to Hungarian villages and agricultural cities in the summers of 1983 and 1984 we were particularly impressed by the visible signs of this dual hierarchy (Manchin and Szelényi, 1987). One ethnographic illustration: during the last decade a new, two-storey family house has appeared in the Hungarian countryside (the tradi-

[3] Peter Bell confirms this: "from the . . . workers' point of view, most vezető-s [bosses] do not do any hard work. As one women stated, 'Oh, they don't work; they're just this sort of brigade leaders.' . . . [For the rural workers] the only true work is physical labor" (Bell, 1984; p. 170).

tional rural house was only one story). These prestigious new two-storey buildings tower above the traditional village. When, during our field trips, we picked the most impressive houses and asked our local informants who the lucky owners were, we systematically received two lists: on one, we found most of the local cadre elite, from the president of the kolkhoz to the veterinarian; on the other were the successful entrepreneurs (both agricultural and industrial), like the TV repairman, car mechanic, "big" hog farmer, or market gardener.

By the early 1980s there were clearly two ways to get ahead in a Hungarian village: one could climb the rank order of the bureaucratic hierarchy, or one could try the market. (China experts have reported a similar dual hierarchy in rural China since 1979 or 1980; see Unger, 1983, and Whyte, 1985.)

LIFE HISTORY AS MEDIATOR OF FAMILY BACKGROUND

As a second modification or extension of the "interrupted embourgeoisement" theory we introduce into our analysis the investigation of individual life histories. In so doing we hope to explain why and how family background in 1945–48 can have a significant effect on entrepreneurship in the late 1970s and early 1980s, after three or four decades of socialism. Absent inherited material wealth, we are inclined to subscribe to a Weberian "culturalist" explanation of the genesis of entrepreneurship: the "entrepreneurial spirit" is preserved and passed on to the next generation by selection of the type and level of schooling and nature of employment, all guided by values internalized during early socialization in the family. Values and ideals, particularly those related to autonomy and risk taking, resistance to being subordinated to the bureaucratic order and to accepting ascribed ranks in a hierarchy, desire to be one's own boss, value attached to hard work, and willingness to delay consumption may be decisive in the formation of an entrepreneurial class. Note that a more straightforward Marxist approach may be sufficient when an entrepreneurial system is already in operation, the entrepreneurial class has already been formed, and private wealth is inherited.

By bringing life history to the center of our analysis of social structure, we express our epistemological sympathies with the class analysis theories of E. P. Thompson. Thompson, a critic of Marxist structuralism, rejects the concept of class as an "empty box"; for him, "class is an event" (Thompson, 1963). For Thompson, struggle, the process of class formation, and individual experiences of such struggles and processes are central in the analysis of social structures. Such an "activist" or "praxis-centered" conception of class seems particularly appropriate to recent East European history, where the last four decades have been a history of unmaking, making, and remaking of classes. Change, the struggle to "stay on course," to learn the ever-changing requirements for maintaining autonomy, have constituted an individual's ultimate experience of social structure.

The interrupted and now resurgent embourgeoisement process is a case in point. To use the language of missile science to describe it: the years between 1945 and 1949 saw an early liftoff, soon aborted. Those already on an embourgeoisement trajectory were subjected to pressures to fit into the emergent bureaucratic order, to become either proletarian or cadre. Only around the mid-1970s did reentry to the interrupted embourgeoisement trajectory become possible. The question is, who will now be able to use this reentry opportunity?

To a significant extent, we believe this will depend upon the life strategy followed by candidates for embourgeoisement during those four decades. Those who could not resist the double pressures toward becoming proletarian or cadre are by now conceivably "lost" to embourgeoisement; those who successfully located themselves in "parking orbits" under the command economy will be able to take up again their journey toward entrepreneurship. Those "parking orbits" are "hiding places," sequences of jobs in which people can maintain a certain degree of autonomy, can wait for the better times, and resist subordination.

So, for instance, some of the more entrepreneurial characters in rural Hungary, as the prospects for entrepreneurial activity closed down, might have taken cadre positions; many actually did. To take a position of power in the bureaucratic order, to become the president of the newly formed kolkhoz or chairman of the local council, may have been a rational strategy for resisting proletarianization. The choice was clear: either you became the boss, or somebody else would boss you. At the same time, one had to know when to quit this cadre trajectory. Those who stayed for too long internalized a different value system; they became too dependent on bureaucratic promotions and networks, and could not recoil to the entrepreneurial trajectory as the opportunity reopened. To have been a boss for a while but not for too long may be a good indicator that somebody was in a "parking orbit."

Another example: the decision to join the cooperatives. The fact that somebody held out for a while as self-employed, did not give in too early to the pressures of collectivization, is likely to be a good measure of commitment to entrepreneurship.

Typically, we anticipate, those who have most successfully remained on the embourgeoisement trajectory are individuals who were self-employed until 1960, the joined the kolkhoz but let their wives do the actual kolkhoz work. They themselves took industrial jobs, preferably local or in neighboring cities, achieved some—but not too high—qualifications there, and returned to the village or even to the kolkhoz a couple of years later. Our ethnographic fieldwork suggests that such returning migrants may have played a strategically important role in bringing newer urban industrial skills back to the villages and in setting patterns of new entrepreneurship.

Our own theory, then, can be called "reentry to the interrupted embourgeoisement trajectory" as a way of emphasizing that life history, strategies adopted during the years of the command economy, crucially modify initial family impetus. We suggest that people from the "right" family background (from families on an embourgeoisement trajectory by 1949) may have entered the "wrong" life history, become too early or too deeply proletarianized, or stayed for too long in cadre positions. In either case, they are unlikely to be able to take advantage of reopening entrepreneurial opportunities today.

It is also imaginable that people from the "wrong" background (for instance, former poor peasants, or even agrarian proletarians) may have found themselves in the "right" type of job, picked up useful skills, and become relatively autonomous. They may, in essence, have moved into a "parking orbit," and can now join the ranks of the burghers. If Márkus is right in emphasizing the very high social expectations of former poor peasants, their commitment to hard work and upward mobility, then we may find more former poor peasants in entrepreneurial locations than we at first allowed for.

Measuring the possible trajectories and identifying the sequence of jobs that should qualify as "parking orbits" is a formidable task. So as better to interpret the character of life trajectories people might have followed since 1945, it may be useful to identify the changes in rural social structure in Eastern Europe and to define the most typical structural pressures and processes in each of the major postwar epochs. We will take three snapshots of the "road" rural folks had to traverse over the last half century—one in, say, 1944, one in the early 1960s, and one in 1984–85.

In the first such snapshot (Figure. 3.1), we rely heavily on Ferenc Erdei's characterization of rural social structure in Hungary. Before land reform in 1945, Erdei describes a dual system of social stratification

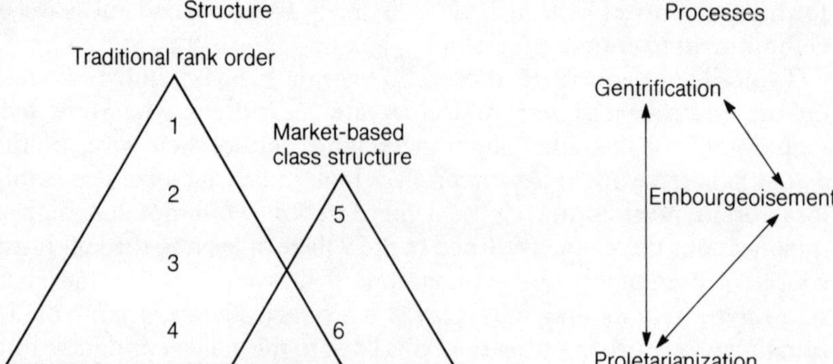

Structural positions: (1) landlords; (2) genteel middle class; (3) landed peasants; (4) landless agrarian semiproletarians, manorial laborers; (5) burghers, entrepreneurs peasant burghers; (6) wage laborers in the entrepreneurial sector.

FIGURE 3.1 *Rural social structure and processes around 1944 and earlier*

in the Hungarian village and agricultural city. The dominant social hierarchy was the one between the "gentleman" (*úr*) and the "peasant" (*paraszt*). Distinctions were based upon rank in the traditional social order of the village. At the top was the landlord, one or just a few for each village; below the landlord, a couple of families belonging to the "genteel middle class" (teachers, the doctor, priests, the lawyer, officials of the local administration—town clerks, etc.), followed by the land-holding peasants with differing family fortunes and finally by the landless seasonal workers or manorial laborers.

The burghers, the local small industrial entrepreneurs, shopkeepers, artisans, owners of the mill, and owner-managers of market-oriented agricultural enterprises, were at the top of the second system of stratification. They were followed by the peasant-burghers, those peasant families which had entered the road toward bourgeois status and were running their family enterprises increasingly like family farmers or market producers, rather than peasants or subsistence producers. At the bottom of the hierarchy were wage laborers working for the entrepreneurs and burghers of the village or agricultural city. The main processes which shaped this structure were gentrification, proletarianization, and embourgeoisement.

As we saw earlier, according to Erdei the major shortcoming of the system was the dominant role of the traditional rank hierarchy and the subdued nature of the embourgeoisement process. As Erdei repeatedly noted, even the entrepreneurial class was tempted by gentrification; they were linked by marriage to the local gentry, often aspired to their lifestyle, and therefore did not really perform a "civilizing" or "modernizing" role (Erdei, 1942 [1980], p. 164). Those on embourgeoisement trajectories were threatened by both proletarianization and gentrification; these two pressures could divert them from their course.

The second snapshot (Figure 3.2) is taken after agriculture has been fully collectivized—in Hungary, the early 1960s. During the previous 15 years the dominant hierarchy had been radically transformed. The landlords and a significant fraction of the genteel middle class had been eliminated, and the rest of the middle class had become either cadre or proletarian. With collectivization, the landholding peasantry was to a significant degree proletarianized, though most succeeded in "hiding" in a part-time farming, peasant-worker position. Former agrarian semiproletarians were also fully proletarianized except for the few who became cadres, and most joined the former peasants in a peasant-worker existence.

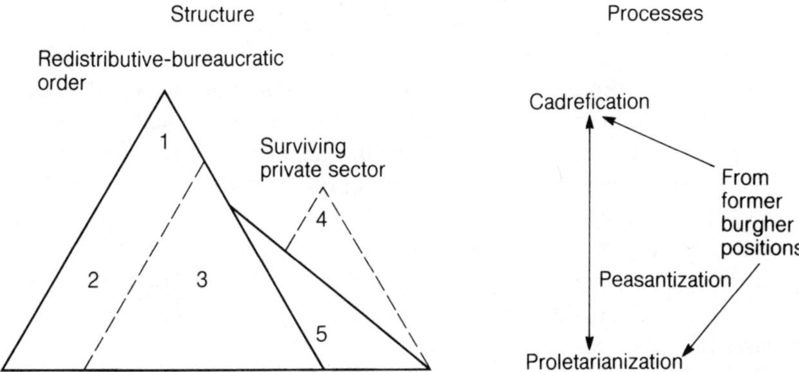

Structural positions: (1) cadre elite; (2) workers (industrial and agricultural); (3) peasant-workers (people between the first and second economies); (4) "truncated area" from which former burghers and peasant-burghers were pushed into the redistributive-bureaucratic order; (5) pauperized private peasants.

FIGURE 3.2 *Rural social structure and processes immediately after collectivization (early 1960s)*

The formerly dominant gentleman-peasant axis has now been transformed into the cadre-proletarian axis, a significant change not only in the personnel of the elite, but to some extent in the quality of social relationships. The replacement of a traditional rank order with a redistributive, bureaucratic rank order is a step in the direction of rationality; positions in the system become somewhat more "open," selection to the positions somewhat less "ascriptive." At the same time, the experience of the underdogs in the two systems may be strikingly similar; in both cases, they are forced to fit into the bottom of a rank order.

As the system becomes consolidated, the cadre becomes somewhat gentrified in its patterns of everyday behavior. Like the gentlemen of the village in the old days, today's village cadres go hunting and entertain their superiors from county headquarters in hunting cabins especially reserved for the "comrades" on whom so much in the life of the village depends. The ironic, popular term *elvtárs-úr* "comrade-gentleman" picturesquely expresses this continuity. Of course, the redistributive-bureaucratic order of state socialism is not identical with the traditional prewar order; new people rule, and somewhat differently. But both are rank orders, and in addition to their differences we must acknowledge their continuity.

The real novelty of the new rural social structure is the monopoly of the rank order. As Figure 3.2 shows, the second system of social hierarchy has been truncated. The rural private sector did not completely disappear in most East European countries, but it was suppressed. In those countries where collectivization occurred (Yugoslavia and Poland never massively collectivized their agriculture; for their rural stratification system see Franklin, 1969, pp. 180–217), about 2–3 percent of the villagers still remained "private" peasants. These were usually individuals so stubborn that they became outcasts in one way or another. You had to be a little crazy to resist the extraordinary pressure put on people to join the cooperatives, and, indeed, the few who remained outside the collective sector were usually rather odd fellows.

Right after collectivization, the private sector was in no position to compete with the collectives as an alternative source of wealth or prestige. Private peasants were pushed into marginal economic positions, into poverty. Consequently, the surviving private sector was really not a "parking orbit" where one could hide to await the reappearance of entrepreneurial opportunities; it was, instead, a sort of "asylum," where the "socially and mentally handicapped" were allowed refuge. (See, for the same argument, Bell [1984], who reports that in the village he investigated only about a half-dozen people attempted to continue to farm privately after collectivization and that they were "more objects of pity than of admiration" [p. 138]).

Most of the former burghers did not accept this "asylum"; rather, they allowed themselves to be pushed into the redistributive-bureaucratic order. Many did indeed become peasant-workers, clearly taking a step backward historically. A step backward indeed; people who previously were running commodity-producing enterprises, who had complex agricultural and marketing skills, now settled into a pattern of rather traditional, subsistence-oriented family agricultural production and often took unskilled or semiskilled jobs in industry. The luckier and more ambitious ones, particularly in Hungary after 1960, when the collectivization policy was rather tolerant, became bosses. During the 1950s (in the Soviet Union during the 1930s) antikulak hysteria pushed the former entrepreneurial element out of the villages altogether. By the collectivization drive of 1960 many of the former successful peasant-entrepreneurs were offered posts as presidents of the newly formed kolkhozes, and there were indeed several "kulaks" or "burghers" who took such jobs.[4] Thus it seems that those who survived these difficult years did so by strategies that allowed them to be in part cadre, in part peasant, in part proletarian.

The third snapshot is taken during the early 1980s (Figure 3.3). As we have already noted, the most striking development is the resurgence of the "second hierarchy," the system of inequalities based on market transactions rather than position in the bureaucratic order. Social structure seems to be returning to its "normal" state: the second, market-based, burgher hierarchy which was temporarily forced into the dominant rank order regains its relative autonomy, although it remains more subordinated than it was before 1945.

The most important single event is the reappearance of an entrepreneurial, burgher class, the resurfacing of temporarily suppressed

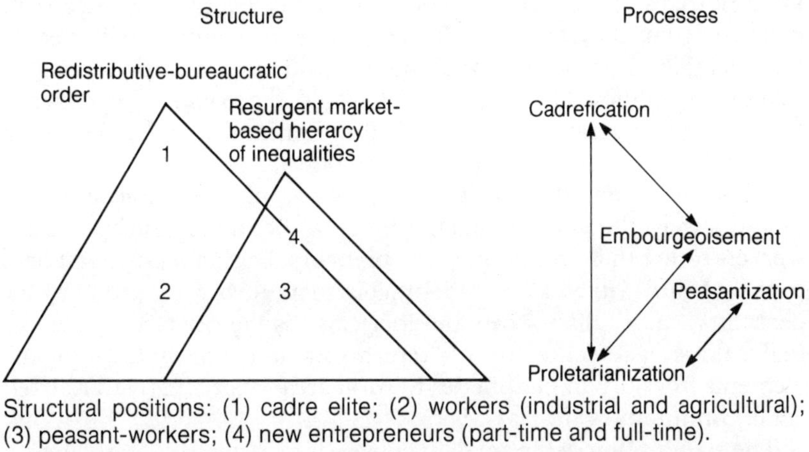

Structural positions: (1) cadre elite; (2) workers (industrial and agricultural); (3) peasant-workers; (4) new entrepreneurs (part-time and full-time).

FIGURE 3.3 *Rural social structure and processes during the early 1980s*

[4] Bell (1984, pp. 132, 238, 240) also notes the importance of wealthier peasants, even some former kulaks, in the formation and leadership of kolkhozes in the 1960 collectivization drive .

embourgeoisement. The domination of the redistributive-bureaucratic hierarchy is still unchallenged, and most of these new entrepreneurs still "play safe": they keep their state jobs. But for the new entrepreneurial class, even for those who are only "part-time entrepreneurs," income from state employment is not of primary significance. The job is downgraded into "security" against unpredictable political fortunes, ill health, or old age (pension and health benefits are superior in the bureaucratic sector; in this respect, full-time entrepreneurs are still penalized).

Who is able to reenter the embourgeoisement trajectory? As our schemes below attempt to illustrate, they are those who could resist the pressures to become proletarian or cadre, who succeeded during the years of the command economy in locating themselves midway between the two. Former burghers, who maintained a "parking orbit" in the middle distance between pure proletarian and pure cadre positions, are now becoming bourgeoisified.

A new wave of "peasantization" may also be under way. During the 1950s and early 1960s the former small agricultural entrepreneurs were sliding down into a semipeasant, semiworker existence, sometimes probably even to a purely peasant status. Just as after the mid-1970s, some families began to reenter the embourgeoisement trajectory, some former agricultural proletarians or members of the urban lumpen-proletariat were possibly forming a new peasantry. The pattern or the aspirations to embourgeoisement may be set by the few successful entrepreneurs; they are being followed in greater numbers by people from families with lower social status, without production skills or marketing abilities. These families too would like to gain independence from the bureaucratic structures; if they cannot do so by becoming bourgeois, they may do so by becoming peasants.

There is a paradox in this new wave of embourgeoisement: quantitatively, the most dominant trend may be an increase in peasant-workers rather than in genuine entrepreneurs. During our two last field trips we heard critics of the embourgeoisement theory argue that a new peasantry, rather than a new burgher class, is the net result. Interestingly, there has been a sort of "return migration" of quite "lumpen" elements from urban peripheries to rural areas, particularly to isolated small communities (Juhász, 1985).

The stabilization of the smallest villages is a fascinating story. During the summer of 1984, for instance, I visited the village of Ibafa in southern Hungary. This area was rapidly being depopulated during the late 1960s and early 1970s, but the process had stopped thereafter. In 1984, I met several families in Ibafa and neighboring villages who were recent outmigrants from cities. They were typically young, unskilled proletarian families, who had moved to this isolated district in the hope that they could share the good fortune of rural folks and become successful agricultural businessmen. Indeed, several of these families had been among the first to apply for cattle that the kolkhoz was "putting out" from the collective enterprise for raising. Some of them had acquired 10–15 or even 20 head of cattle (by Hungarian standards, that represents a sizeable farm). It was most astonishing to see how they coped with this new challenge. Needless to say, most had no skills whatsoever in cattle raising, so they were suffocating under their new burden. They were not really entrepreneurs, and it was unlikely that they could become so. They were in the process of becoming "new peasants."

At the lower end of the hierarchy, along with the new peasantry, there is also appearing a new group of private-sector workers. These are typically part-time employees from fully proletarianized families who have neither the knowhow nor the willingness to take risks. They take advantage of the "second economy" not by becoming part-time, self-employed peasant-workers or entrepreneurs, but by taking wage-laboring jobs with the new entrepreneurs. There are still very few such workers, but the phenomenon is theoretically interesting because it indicates that the "second economy" can produce its own layer (or class?) of economically dependent (and exploited) people. Furthermore, embourgeoisement for some may mean further proletarianization for others. How could an entrepreneurial class "proper" exist without a proletarianian class "proper"? If embourgeoisement is allowed to proceed it is difficult to avoid the conclusion that the working class will be divided into two fractions, "state workers" versus "private-sector workers."

To conclude our third snapshot: if the resurgence of the "second hierarchy", the gradual making of a new entrepreneurial class, was the most spectacular process of the last 5–10 years, nonetheless processes other than embourgeoisement were also under way: the peasantization of former proletarians, the proletarianization of former peasant-workers, and the cadrefication of all sorts of groups.

IDENTIFYING "PARKING ORBITS"

We hope that our three snapshots vividly illustrate how much in flux was the world that the subjects of our investigation were traversing and how complex, therefore, is the sociologist's task of working out who stayed "on course," who moved up, and who slid down in this ever-changing social space. Armed with these insights, we will make a first attempt to identify those positions that may qualify as "parking orbits" in people's life histories within the dominant proletarian/cadre rank order.

The positions along the cadre/proletarian axis can be measured in three dimensions: authority, autonomy, and skills. The cadre are people in positions of authority, who are bosses now and who have been bosses for a long time. The cadre values authority more than autonomy. Many cadres are professionals who could have been their own bosses and controlled their own work processes, but at the cost of authority over other people. Cadres are dissatisfied with such jobs; they are ready to give up their autonomy in exchange for authority.

Cadres are usually highly skilled. They are particularly likely to have what Bourdieu (1979) or Gouldner (1979) call "cultural capital" rather than just "human capital" (see also Martin and Szelényi, 1987). It is usually not sufficient for cadres to have only technical competence (or human capital); they also need skills of social domination, they need the knowhow and often the credentials to boss other people.

In state socialist societies a good indication that such skills are being acquired is attendance at different levels of party schools. Take, for instance, an agrarian engineer who has a fair amount of "human capital": if he or she wants to become the president of a kolkhoz, he or she will probably be expected to go to the Evening University of Marxism–Leninism or even to a full-time one- or two-year course at the Political Academy of the Communist Party. Sometimes such "ideological education" is a precondition for an appointment to a *nomenklatura* job (Voslensky, 1984); at other times people go to party schools after they have first been appointed to positions of authority.

The same logic seems to operate at lower levels also. Workers who aspire to become cadres, who would like to give up physical work, become supervisors, or get some desk job with promotion schedules or possibilities of achieving more powerful positions, first attend evening high schools of Marxism–Leninism. Such credentials and the skills thus acquired are attributes of cadre existence; they are "convertible currencies." Like money for the capitalists, they guarantee that cadres can move from one position of authority to the next.

Cadres can, therefore, be defined as people in a position of authority who may potentially be autonomous but who are ready to trade that autonomy for authority. They are highly skilled people; at their disposal is "cultural capital," credentials acquired in order to receive or maintain positions of authority.

Proletarians are at the other end of the scale. Those who are fully proletarianized are not only subject to authority, but were unable to maintain much autonomy. Under pressure to join the collective they quite easily surrendered self-employment and could not find jobs in which they could control their own work processes or the speed of their work. Proletarianization usually went along with deskilling. Following collectivization, many former peasants, particularly peasant-burghers, were deprived of their earlier, complex, agrarian or commercial managerial skills and were reduced to unskilled laboring jobs. The degree of deskilling Braverman (1974) described is modest compared with the depth and extent of deskilling which occurred in rural Eastern Europe.

We define as "parking orbits" those positions which are between these two extremes. The people most likely to retain their ability to reenter the embourgeoisement trajectory are those who succeed in maintaining a "contradictory position" (Erik Wright's [1978] term may be quite approprite to capture the nature of this location) between the cadres and the fully proletarianized.

Those in "parking orbits" between the time of collectivization and the resurgence of the market economy are the ones who maintained for as long as it was rationally possible to do so their self-employed status. When they had to take employment, they looked for jobs with the maximum possible autonomy. If necessary, they were willing to accept positions of authority in order to avoid being subjected to authority. They also often picked up new skills and networks—sometimes in urban jobs—that later proved useful for self-employment as electricians or other tradesmen, for instance. People from former burgher families may have encouraged their children to continue education, to accumulate "human capital," in order to maintain bargaining power in labor markets.

Trajectories in "parking orbits" can, then, be characterized by strong and at least partially successful aspirations to autonomy, a temporary willingness to accept positions of authority rather than be subjected to authority, middle levels of credentials, emphasis on "human capital," and indifference toward "cultural capital" (Figure 3.4).

We are now ready to begin testing our own version of the interrupted embourgeoisement theory. In Chapters 4 and 5 we will operationalize our synthesis of earlier theories, offering first an ethnographic description and then a statistical assessment of the "four destinations." In the rest of the book we will show how much family origin has to say about the destinations that people have reached by the early 1980s, and what we gain by including in our investigation the analysis of the life histories of household heads.

Authority	Autonomy	Skills	Position	Process
Position of authority for extended time	Ready to swap autonomous jobs for authority	Highly educated "cultural capital"	Cadres: field of no return	Cadrefication
May have been in position of authority for some time	Self-employed as long as possible; autonomy in work	Emphasis on human capital, technical skills	"Contradictory positions"—"parking orbit"	Embourgeoisement
Not in position of authority	Gives up self-employment early; no autonomy at work	Deskilling	Proletarians: field of no return	Proletarianization

FIGURE 3.4 *The three dimensions of the cadre/proletarian axis and the "parking orbits" around it*

4

The four destinations

An ethnography of household economies

To establish firm criteria for the statistical separation of the four destinations—cadres, proletarians, peasant-workers, and entrepreneurs—we rely mainly on ethnographic evidence from several years of fieldwork in rural Hungary. We describe the logic of entrepreneurial agricultural households and the qualities, both economic and attitudinal, that distinguish them from peasant-workers; we then perform the same exercise to separate proletarians and cadres from peasant-workers. Finally, because we believe that the most recent significant development in the rural societies of state socialist countries is the emergence or reemergence of entrepreneurship, we make a particular effort to work out the "ethnography" of entrepreneurial households: the ways by which rural families, after decades of collectivization, can establish commercial minifarms; what can be done without capital or much expertise; or with some capital and some expertise. If, tomorrow, you decided to establish a commercial minifarm in a Hungarian village, what advice could we give you? What should you produce; what production techniques should you apply; what technical and managerial knowledge should you have; how much capital will you need?

In Chapter 5 we show that we can arrive at statistically meaningful subpopulations and give a brief demographic and sociological profile of the different subpopulations headed in different directions. Then we develop a sample selection model to assess the relative explanatory power of the competing theories laid out in Chapters 2 and 3. We distinguish among the four destinations, disaggregating our dependent variable, the aggregate value of family agricultural production (FAP), into the value of family-produced goods sold in markets (FAPS) and the value of family-produced goods consumed by the producer families (FAPC).

DISTINGUISHING ENTREPRENEURS FROM PEASANT-WORKERS

We use several criteria to distinguish the four destinations and the types of household economies which correspond to them. Besides the sheer *volume* of production, we also take into account the significance of *market orientation*, the emphasis on *economizing with capital or labor*, or just on *cost saving*, and, finally, the degree and nature of *specialization* of production. (See Table 4.1.)

TABLE 4.1 *Household economies of families at different destinations*

Characteristics of household economy	*Entrepreneur*	*Peasant-worker*	*Proletarian/ cadre*
Volume of production	High	High	Low to medium
Proportion marketed	High	Medium to high	None
Priority given to:			
Economizing with capital	High	Low	Low
Economizing with labor	High to low	High	Low
Saving costs	Low	Low	High to low
Degree and nature of specialization of production	High to low, trend to fragmented production chains	Medium, trend to uninterrupted production chains	Low to high specialization, no integration

Producing for markets

The fact that agricultural producers sell some of their products on the market is not necessarily an indication that they are entrepreneurs. Peasant-workers are far from merely being subsistence producers. They also bring produce to markets and try to generate cash incomes.

Eric Wolf emphasized the importance of production for markets even in the definition of "peasants." According to Wolf, peasants are distinguished from tribal agriculturalists by their systematic exposure to markets. Peasants form partial societies, always subordinated to a nonpeasant order. They must pay rents, taxes, or tributes (Wolf, 1966, pp. 7–10); therefore they need cash, and cash they can get only by marketing their produce.

East European peasant-workers are like peasants proper in that they produce not only for subsistence but also for markets. But their motives for marketing produce are quite different: while peasants proper need cash to pay rents and taxes or buy land, peasant-workers want cash to achieve a higher standard of consumption, to depend less on state employment as their sole source of income.

Economizing with labor or capital?

Peasant-workers are first and foremost wage laborers. The main source of their livelihood is wages and salaries, and their attitudes are those of the wage-laborer. They are engaged in family agricultural production mainly to make use of spare labor time after the day's work in a state labor organization, neither hoping nor planning to become fully self-employed. Their main purpose is to supplement wages by earning extra income working a "second shift" in a family work organization. Peasant-workers despise idleness. As István Márkus (1973, 1978) pointed out so persuasively, they are driven by an extreme form of the "Protestant" work ethic. But for the early capitalist entrepreneurs hard work and asceticism were primarily directed toward capital accumulation; for the East European peasant-workers, this asceticism is in the last instance that of a wage laborer, directed toward consumption rather than accumulation. East European peasant-workers work hard and delay consumption only to save more toward strategically important consumption targets: better housing for themselves or their children, and, after that, the purchase of other consumer durables. Peasant-workers will, therefore, try to earn from family production as much as possible, with as little capital investment as possible. Spending money merely on productive investments would be irrational, would further delay the achievement of the consumption goals that motivate them in the first instance.

The peasant-worker cannot, of course, get away without capital accumulation, but it is often linked to the accumulation of consumer durables, particularly housing. The subordination of productive investment to consumption goals sometimes produces rather distorted, in some ways dysfunctional outcomes. The so-called "square house" of the Hungarian peasant-workers is a good example.

Consumption over productive investment: the Hungarian "square house"

During the 1960s and early 1970s square houses of a new type mushroomed in Hungarian villages. The square house radically transformed the traditional peasant house of the nineteenth or early twentieth century.[1] The traditional house organically combined residential and economic functions within the same building, typically preserving the front for residential purposes (one or several rooms and the kitchen), while expanding toward the yard with additions for economic activities.

The square house breaks with this tradition. It has an important symbolic function: to show that its owner is no longer a peasant. Unlike peasant farmsteads, it is emphatically residential, with three rooms (or two rooms and one bathroom) in three corners of the house, and a large kitchen in the fourth. It is only the size and location of the kitchen which indicate the existence of a family enterprise on the premises.

Architects tried for years to promote standard "urbanized" house designs for what they believed to be a new rural working class. These standard designs usually presumed that the inhabitants of the house would be wage laborers only; they linked the kitchen to dining areas and limited its size to maximize living space.

These architects believed in the "proletarianization theory"; they did not comprehend the reality of peasant-worker existence. The square house was a popular revolt against these urban designs, a compromise between the old peasant house proper and the ideal of an urban proletarian home. The new square houses provide a large kitchen, which serves the family agricultural enterprise as well. There, for instance, fodder is prepared for hogs or chickens. These roomy kitchens open up to the yard, rather than to a dining area; they link the residential and economic functions of the household.

Professional architects resented the success of these square houses, designed and built by poorly qualified rural builders, but the rejection of the otherwise better designed standard homes was a rational decision by consumers. The unimaginative and indeed quite ugly square houses fitted the real needs of a postpeasantry better; they expressed their aspirations to move beyond peasanthood, but at the same time to maintain ties with agricultural production.

These houses expressed the emphasis of the rural "new working class" on consumption values, their reluctance to spend money purely

[1] The following discussion is informed by a delightful article by Mihály Hoppál, (1983).

on productive investments. At the same time they provided new space and facilities for the productive activities of the households, linking consumption to investment to production investment. In building homes for themselves, peasant-workers to some extent expanded their fixed capital, but in doing so subordinated production to consumption, with distorting, dysfunctional consequences. Most important, the square house proved to be a rigid, inflexible structure, which, unlike the older peasant house, was unable to expand as agricultural production in the household grew. By the early 1980s some of the earlier peasant-workers were becoming entrepreneurs; they began to enlarge their houses into quite horrible hybrids, adding utility buildings toward the yard. Whereas the old row-style structure of the traditional peasant house could easily be expanded this way, the expanded square houses turned into messy, dysfunctional structures.

Since peasant-workers try so consciously to avoid purely productive investments, their household economies will often bear the marks of a "putting-out" system. This is particularly true for peasant-workers employed by the kolkhozes, which try to exploit the willingness of their members to work extra hours by turning certain tasks over to family cultivation. In a sense, kolkhoz members can take work home after hours. Those activities that they pursued during working hours under bureaucratic control they now continue under a self-exploitative system.

Some of the glass houses, for instance, in the "Árpád" kolkhoz in the city of Szentes are allocated to family production among the members of the gardening brigades. For eight hours a day the members of the brigade work in the collective glass houses; after working hours they move to their family lots and keep on doing exactly the same thing under a different control and reward system.

The economic rationale of peasant-workers' households is shaped by a "wage-laborer consciousness." Because income from family production is only of secondary importance and family security is guaranteed by employment, purely productive investments are avoided. Peasant-workers produce in the family enterprise when labor is available: it would be "sinful" to be idle. If one has the time, one must earn money to achieve consumption goals as quickly as possible. Any productive activity which produces income higher than overtime salary will be accepted as rational, particularly if it does not tie down disposable income in the form of "useless," nonconsumable constant capital.

With the appearance of entrepreneurs or burghers on the scene, accumulation of production capital is emphasized, and can be seen even in the changing house designs. With the making of the new agricultural entrepreneurial class has come a new type of rural house, the "two-storey villa", which is as distinct from the old peasant house proper as it is from the square house of the peasant-worker. The villa reunites residential and productive functions in a new, in many respects "urban" way. The new entrepreneurs spend a significant amount of money on the basement level of their houses, creating large garages and workshops which serve the capital-intensive family agricultural business located behind the house.

We are beginning to see an end to the rather unhappy marriage, in the square house, of household consumption functions and a technologically quite old-fashioned agricultural production function—preparing pig food and the family dinner in the same kitchen, often at the same time. The workshops of the two-storey villa serve a technically more advanced economy, which requires engineering or electrical engineering skills and facilities. The villa of the new entrepreneurs says that money is spent on productive functions too, but in an "urbanized," genuinely burgher way because of increased capital intensity and the general industrialization of agricultural enterprises.

The shift toward capital accumulation

To begin to take risks with productive investments, to think in terms of return on capital, are the first important steps on the road from peasant-worker to entrepreneur. The shift is gradually occurring over a long period of time.

Many families who by the early 1980s were on an entrepreneurial trajectory were once peasant-workers, who began by pursuing consumption goals: a new house, a decent dowry for their daughter, new furniture, a refrigerator, a car, or a color TV set. They dreamt of a more leisurely life at "the end of the road"; two shifts a day would not last forever. They hoped that by the time their children left home, they could settle into a comfortable, even affluent wage-laborer position. When István Márkus repeatedly emphasized that the postpeasant phenomenon could only be transitory, that such a hard life could not last forever, he told us merely what he heard from rural people during the early or mid-1970s. He took seriously—as later events show, probably too seriously—what his respondents told him. Typically, these dreams were never fulfilled. Most of the peasant-workers could not slow down, and a small, but significant minority of them, mostly against their original intentions, began to intensify production. They not only kept working long hours but also began to take risks with the small fortunes they had accumulated; they began to shift toward entrepreneurship.

The hero of the documentary film "Földi Paradicsom" [Paradise on Earth], János Kerekes, is a good illustration of an unintended shift from a consumption-oriented wage-laborer consciousness toward a capital-accumulating entrepreneurial outlook. When the Kerekes family began to build up their tomato-producing minifarm they were driven primarily by the usual consumption motives. They had teen-aged children and wanted them to have a better start in life. If they worked hard for a couple of years, they could help them with a downpayment for a house or purchase of furniture or a car. When they first began to produce tomatoes in their plastic-covered greenhouses the market was good and they were operating with minimal capital, borrowed from friends and acquaintances in order to buy their small farm and plastic greenhouses (Kerekes's initial debt was around 100,000 Ft). With little capital and a lot of work they quickly attained a respectable income.

This first success simply increased Kerekes's appetite. He began to compare himself with more established market gardeners in his city. Some could heat their greenhouses and started selling tomatoes two or three months earlier than Kerekes could. Kerekes began to calculate how much more he could earn if he purchased a heating system. Because profits were high and the return on capital investment appeared secure, he relatively easily found people who were willing to lend him money, though at an exorbitant 25–30 percent interest rate.

Kerekes now borrowed several times more than the amount with which he had started his venture. He expanded production quickly, but about that time the market began to deteriorate. High profits were attracting more and more people to tomato production and more of them were heating their greenhouses too. First-in-season tomato prices began to stagnate, while production costs, particularly fuel, soared.

If Kerekes wanted to maintain the relatively high living standard his family had suddenly achieved, let alone repay his creditors, he had to expand production to counteract the shrinking profit margin. The "only" solution was to try to borrow more and to increase the volume of production. We say "only" because he could, of course, have resisted the pressures and temptations to shift from a peasant-worker lifestyle to an entrepreneurial one; he could have accepted the life of a wage laborer. But to abandon embourgeoisement for a proletarian position may not have been so easy. He was also under some pressure from his children. It turned out that the family's initial consumption targets were flexible. The more he gave to his children, the more they wanted. Sinking under the combined pressures of greater marketplace competition, shrinking profit margins, and his family's increasing consumption expectations, Kerekes had to work harder and take greater and greater risks just to keep the boat afloat. By 1983–84 he owed more than 1 million Ft to loan sharks on the credit black market. After a decade of desperate work and struggle for survival, he would at best have barely repaid his debtors had they foreclosed on his farm. Merely to avoid bankruptcy, he had to produce about 1.4–1.5 million Ft worth of tomatoes a year (quite a gross income in a country where the average annual industrial income was just above 50,000 Ft a year!). Was it ten years of hard work for nothing? Not really. After all, he had built up an impressive, highly capital-intensive minifarm; he had become an entrepreneur.

Entrepreneurial and wage-laborer attitudes clashed even within the Kerekes family. As the family business slid toward entrepreneurship, Mrs. Kerekes became increasingly tense and unhappy. Kerekes in a way is a gambler. He is nervous and insecure, but at the same time he quite enjoys the dangers of his business; he likes taking risks. His wife is different: she can't bear the idea of their increasing debts, she feels cheated. She believes her husband irresponsibly dragged her into this mess. She would like to quit, envying those neighbors who live on their wages. Whenever Kerekes is interviewed, he is optimistic. He keeps telling us that in the end they will make it. Mrs. Kerekes on the other hand is deeply pessimistic. She repeatedly criticized her husband in front of the television camera and a couple of months after the shooting of the "Földi Paradicsom" episodes she moved out (not the only time she did so). She told the film director and interviewer that she could not take it any more, but in fact returned to her husband within a few weeks.

These tensions within the Kerekes family dramatize the anxieties linked to the transition from postpeasanthood to entrepreneurship, from economizing with labor to risk-taking with capital. In this family drama of "the making of an entrepreneur" Kerekes's mother has taken sides with her son. She may be the most entrepreneurial, the most addicted to gambling of all. She pushed her son all the way and so clashed repeatedly with her daughter-in-law.

Kerekes's mother is the daughter of a burgher-entrepreneur. Her father rented 100 holds—a huge enterprise by the standards of prewar Hungary. She was also married to a *koupetz-kulak*, a man who traded horses, cattle, and hogs in great numbers. It was probably she who never accepted the proletarian existence that collectivization offered them, and when her son in 1960 lost his 17-hold farm, she may have been quite operative in making sure he did not accept a proletarian position and that he tried to bounce back to entrepreneurship as soon as possible. János had been under contradictory pressures most of his life.

His mother pushed him to entrepreneurship, while his wife preached to him about the security, abundance of leisure, and relaxed life of their wage-laborer neighbors.

The family psychodrama of the "new petty bourgeoisie" is thus complete. The Kerekes story tells us how the temptations of market opportunities pull and the "iron law of competition" pushes some peasant-workers from consumption-centered economic behavior toward capital accumulation and entrepreneurship.

The "putting-out system": a first step toward family enterprise

Changes in the putting-out system, particularly in animal husbandry, have promoted the shift toward risk-taking with private capital. Even the large socialist enterprise may play a role in promoting the "primitive accumulation" of private capital. Above we referred to the putting-out system as the prototype of peasant-worker economic activities. Indeed, at least in its initial stages, the system, for instance in market gardening, could be understood simply as a kind of overtime, an extension of the working day beyond the legally permitted eight hours. For some time, putting out hogs or cattle to families worked this way too. The kolkhoz did so in order to rationalize the organization of labor and relieve the bureaucratic center of responsibility for organizing the labor process and exercising costly and quite ineffective control. Such putting-out contracts had no implications for capital accumulation or ownership. The stock remained the property of the kolkhoz, which also retained all risks linked to capital invested in the stock. If animals put out into the household economy died or lost value the loss was the kolkhoz's, and its only recourse was to penalize the workers for negligence.

Experience with the putting-out system in animal husbandry began to shed doubt on the rationality of such an arrangement. In the early 1980s, kolkhozes began to experiment with a new type of putting-out contract[2] in which they passed on not only the control of stock but also the risk (and gradually the ownership) to families. In the village of Szentlászló (in southwest Hungary) the cooperative, which was losing money on the cattle herd in the collective farm, began to put cattle out to individual families, who might get up to 20 or 25 cows. In its contract the kolkhoz offered a gradual purchase arrangement whereby the cows became the property of the family if they remained with them for several years.

This lease-purchase arrangement gives guarantees to the kolkhoz against possible mismanagement of the stock within the family firm. If

[2] The first was introduced by the Sovhoz of Szigetvár in 1982.

the value of the stock declines more rapidly than scheduled, then the leasing family must compensate the kolkhoz for the unanticipated decline in value. The arrangement is quite advantageous for the better farmers. If they maintain the quality of the stock, which thus keeps its value longer than scheduled, then they begin to accumulate capital and can become private owners. The introduction of this new contract is one step on the trajectory from a peasant-worker to an entrepreneurial position.

The emerging new entrepreneurs therefore begin to take risks, accumulate capital, and increase the capital intensity of their enterprises. They are in the long run also likely to earn most of their incomes from their family businesses. Some of them may gradually become full-time private farmers. But in 1987 we are still in the very early stages of this process.

How many entrepreneurs?

Only a tiny minority of rural families, probably as few as 3–4 percent of all households, as we earlier noted, make more net income from the "second economy" than from state employment. We must emphasize—particularly in considering the formulation of social and economic policy—how decisive wages and salaries are for the overwhelming majority of the population. The significance of the second economy in general and family agricultural business in particular as a source of family incomes is often exaggerated by sociologists and journalists.

The trend for these new family entrepreneurs to become full-time private farmers is in its very early stages. After 1970 the proportion of full-time private farmers continued to decline slightly. But the average age of private farmers began to decline between 1970 and 1980, whereas from 1960 to 1970 it had increased. The fact that the average private farmer was becoming younger indicates that this is not a "dying species" for the time being. As the old guard retire or die, young people replace at least some of them. But most people are slow to give up their jobs, having little "business confidence" in the regime. Perhaps the new wave of private entrepreneurship will not last very long—so people keep their jobs for worse times. Some people keep their jobs for social security reasons; income from a job makes pension prospects brighter, helps to get a loan from the Savings Banks, and has a lot of advantages in a society where for so long being in the "private sector" has been suspect, being a government employee has been the normal way of life.

Some former peasant-workers have become de facto even if not de jure full-time farmers. On our field trips during the summers of 1983 and 1984 we found examples of people taking "quasi-jobs." One of our respondents, for instance, became a night watchman. Such "quasi-jobs" appear on the personal identity card, but allow their holders to be de facto full-time entrepreneurs. Official statistics may underestimate to some extent the proportion of people who are full-time in the private sector.

The new entrepreneurial class, then, is only a class *in statu nascendi*. Only a small proportion of households are genuinely and in the full sense of the term entrepreneurs, placing primary emphasis on economizing with capital, with significant capital already accumulated, and working full-time for themselves. But the proportion of families on the embourgeoisement *trajectory*, on the road toward an entrepreneurial destination, may be quite significant. This is the pool of potential entrepreneurs, families which have not yet accumulated much capital but have begun to take risks with capital and move beyond the wage-laborer consciousness.

Peasant-workers and entrepreneurs: different types of production regimes

The diverse minifarm of the peasant-worker

As a household turns from a peasant-worker economy toward entrepreneurship, both the degree of specialization and the nature of the production regime in the family enterprise begin to change.

Peasant-worker households typically achieve a medium level of specialization; usually they are "uninterrupted production chain economies." Because the main purpose of peasant-worker production is the generation of cash revenues, and production of food consumed in the household is a secondary consideration, the postpeasantry could in principle radically reduce the range of its products. But the ideal peasant-worker household resists too much specialization and strives for some, usually well-planned diversity of production.

The production patterns of most peasant-worker families follow the prewar middle-peasant marketing and production regime. Middle peasants traditionally tried to establish a farm that was a somewhat diversified and uninterrupted production chain economy. Unlike commercial farmers, they had a cautious attitude toward the market. They produced for it but at the same time tried to defend themselves against its uncertainties. For instance, middle-peasant hog farmers during the interwar years were inclined to maintain several production chains on their farms. Rather than buying pig food, they would produce most or all that they needed. They also tried to avoid fragmented production chains; thus within hog production they usually combined feeding and breeding. Besides the few dozen pigs to be fed, they would have a couple of sows.[3] Middle peasants often built their farms on more than two uninterrupted production chains. Families might complement an uninterrupted hog production chain with a similarly uninterrupted duck or turkey production chain. Often the final products of these uninterrupted production chains were far beyond the consumption needs of the families and thus were sold in the market. These middle peasants were less concerned than peasants usually are to produce everything they needed for their own consumption. In this sense they were no longer peasants. But they were not yet farmers either, because they did not trust other producers enough to depend on them for deliveries. By producing several crops they made sure that even if the weather were bad or market conditions unfavorable for any crops, they could survive the year without bankruptcy.

But the maintenance of uninterrupted production chains was often also culturally motivated. The traditional rural conception of professional competence was difficult to reconcile with too much specialization. Breeding the pigs one planned to feed was not simply an economically rational action. The typical middle peasant also liked to believe that he was the best breeder in the village. By buying pigs on the market, he would confess to lack of sufficient competence. Distrust of others, caution, professional pride, and self-respect were important reasons for the middle-peasant preference for uninterrupted-chain economies. By emphasizing cultural factors like suspicion of strangers, caution, and the high value attached to security, all of which are *peasant* cultural characteristics, we do not question the economic rationality of such behavior. Particularly with a poorly developed insurance and banking system, an uninterrupted production chain may be an effective way to guarantee security.

When, during the late 1960s or early 1970s, rural families on the peasant-worker trajectory began to increase commodity production, the cultural and organizational pattern they found ready to hand in the villages was that of the prewar middle peasants. The farms of their parents or, if they were from a poor-peasant or rural proletarian background, the farms of their more successful, market-oriented neighbors were uninterrupted production chain economies. Some of the macroeconomic conditions of the late sixties and early seventies also encouraged peasant-workers to adopt this production regime: during those years rural services, in particular insurance and banking, were

[3] The division of labor between farmers who only feed and farmers who only breed hogs is an example of "fragmentation of the production chain."

even less developed than before the war. The socialist transformation destroyed the small service, insurance, and banking infrastructure that was slowly evolving in prewar Eastern Europe. Uninterrupted-chain production was the known and economically most rational way to move beyond traditional peasant production and to increase the proportion of marketed goods within total family production.

If it was the dominant, it was, however, far from the only production regime by which the peasant-worker household economy was organized. Where the kolkhozes began successfully to integrate family production, they often broke up these production chains within households. The kolkhoz, for instance, freed the family from the obligation to grow corn, which was grown more cheaply and effectively by the latifundium. Families could now specialize only in feeding hogs. Hog feeders were also freed from the "burdens" of breeding. Without loss of prestige, they could now purchase young pigs from the kolkhoz (they themselves may have been the "professional breeders" in the kolkhoz). Some peasant-worker households, therefore, became highly specialized, limiting their activity to a single phase of the total production process. They were becoming "fragmented production chain" household economies, more like an American commercial farmer than a prewar East European middle peasant, though purely in terms of the microeconomics of the family business.

The fragmented production chains of the new entrepreneurs

In contrast to peasant-worker households, for the new entrepreneurs the fragmented production chain is the rule or at least the emergent trend, and the uninterrupted production chain the exception.

In their degree of specialization and shift toward fragmented production chains, the new agricultural entrepreneurs did not simply reenter the embourgeoisement trajectory at the point where the middle peasants left it around 1949. By the early 1980s, some of the new entrepreneurs were running more specialized enterprises than the wealthiest peasants had before the socialist transformation of the villages. Limited access to land may currently be a major reason that entrepreneurial families have given up traditional peasant caution. Since the maximum land available is 1.5–3 acres per family, one must fragment the production chain in order to build up a proper entrepreneurial cattle or hog farm. An intensive chicken farm (the larger ones may produce 40–50,000 chickens a year), the larger dairy farm (20–25 milk cows), and the "big" hog producer (selling 100–200 hogs for meat a year) cannot produce the feed they need. These farmers will buy from the kolkhoz and concentrate on a single phase of production.

Furthermore, they have learned a good deal about agricultural techniques on the cooperative farms. They know that high-quality seeds and breeding animals can often be produced more effectively in the latifundium, under the supervision of university-trained experts. By fragmenting the production chain, they bring technical innovations into the household economy.

But this production shift has its problems. The banking and insurance infrastructure is less developed than it was even 40 or 50 years ago. The kolkhozes are often unreliable partners. Unpredictable delivery of fodder and fluctuating quality of seeds or breeding animals may push entrepreneurial households back toward uninterrupted production chain economies.

This was happening during the summer of 1984 in the kolkhoz of Szentlászló. One August day, a group of family producers from the satellite village of Ibafa came to complain to the president of the Szentlászló kolkhoz about the way in which the kolkhoz was fulfilling its obligations toward the families which had received cattle under the putting-out system. The technocratically minded kolkhoz president permitted us to observe his confrontation with his "subcontractors." The main complaint of the minifarmers was the unreliability of the kolkhoz. They cited numerous occasions when feed did not arrive in time, causing a decline in milk production. They also complained that tractors or other machinery they wanted to lease from the kolkhoz were not made available when they were needed. The president tried to defend his shop for more than an hour, explaining why it had all happened. He tried to give guarantees that it would not occur again. But as the debate progressed he lost confidence in his own story. He was aware that he could not offer the services required accurately and on time with kolkhoz workers who were not highly motivated to work overtime, particularly over weekends, for rather poor wages. At the end, he concluded: "Look, I tell you what the final solution is. Now you have the cattle from the kolkhoz. But this is not enough. Sooner or later I will lease land to you too. You can rent 40 acres, 50 acres or as much as you need to grow enough hay for your cattle. You can then also buy tractors and machinery, from the kolkhoz or from the shop as you please. Then you will be on your own, and you will be able to produce efficiently." This sounds somewhat strange from the president of a kolkhoz, but it illustrates well the pressures toward uninterrupted-chain economies for small entrepreneurs as long as the "first economy" operates ineffectively.

The trends that counteract the shift toward fragmented production chain economies suggest that degree of specialization and nature of production regime are of only limited value in distinguishing peasant-worker from entrepreneurial minifarms. A more fundamental difference between the two destinations is that those on the peasant-worker trajectory are economizing with labor, those on an entrepreneurial track are already oriented toward risk-taking and capital accumulation.

RURAL CADRE AND PROLETARIAN HOUSEHOLDS

In rural Hungary today—in rural Eastern Europe in general—the overwhelming majority of families, including many proletarian or cadre ones, produce some agricultural goods. Many cadres have their gardens or hobby farms, and most rural proletarian families keep a sizeable vegetable garden. To achieve our dual task, to distinguish with greater precision proletarian and cadre families from the rest of rural society and then to separate the proletarians from the cadres, we must have a closer look at what is grown on these hobby farms and gardens, and how it is grown.

Cadre and proletarian gardens

Cadre and proletarian gardens at first glance often look strikingly similar. Cadre families frequently keep a rather diversified backyard vegetable garden, indiscriminately producing virtually everything the family is likely to consume. The production profile and even the appearance of this cadre utility garden are almost identical to those of the proletarian vegetable patch, though the cadre is more likely to "hide" his vegetable garden behind the house or behind a strip of grass. The lawn is something peculiarly cadre in rural Hungary. Everybody grows flowers, particularly in front of the house, but only the cadre spends time and water on useless lawn, especially in the backyard.

With a stretch of the imagination one may compare Hungarian cadre and proletarian vegetable gardens to middle-class and working-class vegetable patches in the West. In Australia or in the U.K.—in the U.S. probably less so—the habit of growing your own vegetables crosses class lines. But the middle class will keep a vegetable patch emphatically separate from lawns and flowers, and the lawns will dominate the front of the houses, occupying most of the land. In working-class families the utility garden often spreads all over, telling the world that gardening is not just a pastime around here.

But one should not stretch this comparison too far. Rural cadres in Hungary are less conspicuously leisure-oriented than their Western middle-class counterparts. The more populist, and in a way more ascetic East European rural morality requires the cadre to "work." If all day in their offices cadres are just bossing people around, then at least after hours they must show that they can work too; this is the popular dictum. By proving that he is able to grow larger cucumbers or better lettuce than his neighbors, the cadre can gain some respect for his professional competence.

But in one way proletarian minifarms are easily distinguishable from cadre operations, which are more in the nature of a hobby. Even in the tiniest gardens, most proletarian families will feed and slaughter one or two pigs a year. This is most unlikely to happen in cadre households. There are hog producers of cadre origin too, but if the cadre decides to keep pigs, then he does so on a large scale and does not just keep one or two for his family's consumption. Apparently only the smell of money takes away the smell of pigs for the cadre! These larger cadre hog producers may be on their way out of cadre existence and toward embourgeoisement anyway.

This antipathy toward hogs is not restricted to the Hungarian cadre. In our case study of Wisconsin part-time farmers, we noticed that middle-class "gentlemen farmers" were also very unlikely to be hog producers. When we did our field research in Wisconsin, profit margins in hog production were among the best in Midwestern agriculture, but we found pigs only in working-class part-time farms. Somehow hogs are associated in the middle-class mind with "dirt"; middle-class farmers shy away from hog feeding or even breeding. Cattle and particularly horse breeding are much more acceptable middle-class activities.

The cadre hobby farm

If feeding and slaughtering one or two pigs is a typical proletarian activity in rural Hungary today, we can also identify a special type of hobby farm which is typically cadre. After about 1975, cadre families began to build up "hobby farms proper," highly specialized, often highly mechanized, capital-intensive minifarms. These are kept mainly as a pastime, for prestige and leisure, but with one eye on capital gains from the inflation of real estate prices. Examples of such operations are the private vineyard or orchard.

Possession of a vineyard has long been an almost universal status symbol, crossing class boundaries, in rural Hungary. Peasants, peasant-workers, and nonagricultural entrepreneurs would all like to have a vineyard. Agricultural entrepreneurs are probably the only ones among those who can afford to who are unlikely to own vineyards. But the cadre vineyard will excel itself by the quality of the vines, the capital intensity of production, and the value of the cellar and the house built upon that cellar in the vineyard.

If proletarian families also aspire to produce a variety of agricultural products and if they do so in reasonably large quantities (including slaughtering one or two pigs), how can we distinguish them from tradition-oriented peasant-worker households? The most important criterion is that for proletarian families there is no cash income from family agricultural production. One should not, of course, be too rigid about this. Everybody sells something for cash in a rural village—fruit, eggs, or even vegetables—but such sales will be rare and insignificant for the proletarian families and will constitute a more important part of family productive activities for peasant-workers. Peasant-workers are engaged in family agricultural production because they economize with labor, using time available after working hours to earn income from the second economy. This is an active strategy to counteract exploitation in their state jobs, to achieve a living standard higher than that which the position assigned them in the redistributive-bureaucratic division of labor would offer. Those who are fully proletarianized have given up the hope of engaging in such struggles; they accept that their fate has been determined by their employment status. The only purpose of proletarianized families in producing agricultural goods is to save money. They cannot significantly alter their level of income, but try merely to increase the purchasing power of their income by spending less on food. Statistically speaking, then, we anticipate that the most meaningful cutoff point between peasant-workers on the one hand and proletarian or cadre families on the other hand will not be the amount of agricultural production, but the presence or absence of significant cash revenue from such production, sometimes even when levels of overall production are quite similar.

TOWARD A TYPOLOGY OF PEASANT-WORKERS AND ENTREPRENEURS

So far we have focused our attention on "pure" or "ideal types" of peasant-worker or entrepreneurial household economies. In reality there is no single continuum from peasant-workers to entrepreneurs: both of these destinations can be divided into subtypes.

Tradition-oriented and transitory peasant-workers

Earlier we emphasized the extent to which the ideal peasant-worker household followed the pattern of the pre-1949 or prewar middle-peasant enterprise. But many peasant-workers may more closely imitate the former poor peasant ways of running a farm. Hereafter we will identify the latter type as "tradition-oriented peasant-workers" or "peasant-workers 1"; the former, peasant workers in transition to market-oriented production, we call "transitory peasant-workers" or "peasant-workers 2."

What are the distinguishing features of the "traditional peasant" subtype, those who share the old poor-peasant values and cultural and economic traditions? They are reluctant to specialize to any significant extent and maintain the diversity of a traditional peasant farmstead. Resistance to specialization is motivated by cultural and symbolic considerations. These tradition-oriented peasant-workers want their farmsteads to look like the old peasant households: they want to have one or two milk cows in the backyard, to breed and feed the hogs they will slaughter, and to maintain diverse crop or vegetable production. One of their main motives is to show how affluent, sophisticated, and skilful they are.

A certain "object fetishism" (a term coined by Bálint Magyar) characterizes these tradition-oriented peasant workers. They want to own certain objects like a cow or a horse for their symbolic importance and not primarily for their use-value. These objects are status symbols; those who own them have really "made it" and are not worse off than peasants always were in their village. The strong attachment to the peasant tradition proper is reflected by the housing choices of tradition-oriented peasant-workers, who rarely build "square houses" but prefer to buy the older peasant farmsteads.

Those who fit the peasant-worker 1 category have only loose contacts with the market. They rarely produce, intentionally and systematically, more of any single crop than they can consume. For families in the peasant-worker 2 category the cash value of the produce determines what families will produce; for the traditional-peasant subtype, family food consumption needs shape the production profile of the minifarm. Tradition-oriented peasant-workers usually also accept the market channels offered by the bureaucratically coordinated sector of the economy. If they have occasional crop surpluses, they most likely sell them through the kolkhoz. In contrast, peasant-workers in transition to market-oriented production will evaluate different marketing channels carefully and will choose the more profitable or convenient ones.

Many tradition-oriented peasant-workers are so obsessed with symbols and prestige because they are from a rural proletarian background, sons or daughters of former servants from manorial estates or the children of other nonagrarian proletarians, like rural construction workers or miners. For them to become peasants means upward social mobility. Some of the former rural proletariat made this upward move in the social hierarchy right after the land reform. Many who received land in 1945 had become peasants by 1947–48. There were, in contrast, other rural proletarians who had to wait until the "second land reform" came. Collectivization and then a tough land-ownership law of the early 1970s prohibiting ownership of second or third lots or gardens led to a major democratization, making access to land equal and also easy for everyone. Former rural proletarians used this opportunity in large numbers. The final abolition of all private monopoly, collectivization thus gave a major impetus toward "peasantization." (Since a full-time peasant lifestyle was discouraged, these former agrarian proletarians became peasant-workers of the traditional-peasant subtype.)

One of the fascinating features of the transformation of Hungarian rural structure is the almost universal upward filtering in the system of social stratification: everybody takes a step foward. The former rural proletariat entered the "peasant-worker 1" category; many of the former poor peasants or their children were by the early 1980s peasant-workers in transition to market-oriented production, running their household economies like middle peasants did in the past; and finally, quite a few of the former middle peasants or their descendants became genuine entrepreneurs and ceased altogether to be peasants.

Typology of entrepreneurs

How does one become an agricultural entrepreneur? What skills does one need, how much capital is advisable, and given both skills and capital, what is there to do with it? What can be produced, how much time will it take, and what profit margins can one hope for? How fast can a new entrepreneur grow, and what are the limits, if any, to the growth of private agricultural business in a socialist country like Hungary today? We start this description with a short theoretical exploration and then enrich it with our ethnographic field experience (Table 4.2).

Protoentrepreneurs with middle-peasant skills and mentality

Those who possessed the skills of middle peasants or had access to the farmsteads of former rich or middle peasants often started with cattle or hog farming when they began their new family enterprises in the late 1970s or early 1980s.[4] The largest hog farmers feed 100–200 pigs a year

[4] See, for a fine ethnographic description of a few part-time hog raisers and dairymen in the village of Tap in western Hungary, Sozan, 1983, pp. 123–43.

TABLE 4.2 *Types of small agricultural entrepreneurs*

	Skill required		
	Middle peasant	*Gardening*	*Industrialist*
Typical activities	Hog breeding, cattle, fodder	Market gardening, orchards	Chickens for eggs, meat, breeding; hog feeding; rabbit houses; ducks; heated greenhouse
Need for land	Farmstead; well; buildings with economic function	Garden; plumbing, electricity	Yard; plumbing, electricity
Income return on capital	25%	33–50%	33%
Proportion of fixed capital which is self-produced	Half of fixed capital could be produced by family	Only a fraction of fixed capital can be produced by family	About 25% of fixed capital can be produced by family
Expansion of production	Discontinuous	Continuous, but first has to pass a minimal threshold	Discontinuous
Labor input	Family	Family and occasional wage labor	Individual
Other inputs	Fodder from kolkhoz; services from second economy	From government commercial firms and second economy	Kolkhoz
Outputs sold to	Government wholesale firms, coops, kolkhoz; village market	Urban markets, coops, kolkhoz, or other small producers	Kolkhoz
Prices and markets	Guaranteed prices, secure markets	No guaranteed prices and insecure markets	Some prices guaranteed and insecure markets
Competition	No competition	Private producers against each other	Private producers against latifundia

and clear a net annual income of 50,000–200,000 Ft. Entrepreneurial cattle farms start with 3–4 cows (providing 35–40,000 Ft net income a year) and the largest ones by the early 1980s kept 20–25 cattle.[5]

Possession of a large and well-equipped farmstead is the precondition for establishing such a hog or cattle enterprise. The value of such a farmstead can be significant, 1 million Ft or more. Without a proper credit system it is difficult to find startup capital, and this in itself would be sufficient to explain why cattle farming is dominated by former middle peasants or their children, and why inheritance of suitable farmsteads is an important advantage.

The cattle farmers of the Szentlászló district, already mentioned, are an exception to this rule. Szentlászló is a district center of 11 rather small hill villages in somewhat isolated areas.

The landscape of these villages is shaped by beautiful farmhouses, with large stone stables for cattle, built during the last hundred years by ambitious and quite prosperous German settlers. Following World War II these Germans were deported from Hungary. The new inhabitants of their homes could never recreate the earlier prosperity. They were probably not sufficiently skilled or motivated, and agricultural policies after 1949 were also less than favorable to rebuilding prewar cattle farming. The new Hungarian settlers thus became discouraged, and began to leave the villages, many of them moving to neighboring cities like Pécs. Smaller villages like Ibafa, Kisibafa, and Korpád lost population particularly rapidly after 1960 (by 1984, only four families were left in Kisibafa, for instance). The farmsteads were left vacant and were selling for low prices.

By the second half of the 1970s these decaying villages has begun to attract a new population—unexpectedly for regional planners, who had simply extrapolated earlier population trends and anticipated a continued exodus from these settlements. Former agrarian proletarian families, even "lumpen" elements from the industrial outskirts of large cities, became suddenly interested in the property markets of the decaying villages. By the mid-1980s, many of the inhabitants of these small satellite villages of Szentlászló were such characters. Pál Schiffer, director of the documentary film "Paradise on Earth," also directed a film about the changing fortunes of these people. The following account is based on evidence from Schiffer's still largely unedited films and also on interviews I conducted with the same people.

One of the most recent immigrants to Kisibafa is Dénes Csiki, a young, bearded working-class fellow from Érd, a proletarian suburb of

[5] Such large numbers of stock were usually not owned by the individual farmers, but put out by the kolkhozes or government farms.

Budapest. The other vacant house in the village—with a beautiful stone stable which could easily hold up to 20 cows—has been rented by Laci Sánta (who comes from a family of manorial laborers from southeast Hungary) and his half-gypsy companion. Both Dénes and Laci are "pioneers." Kisibafa is an adventure, a challenge, an opportunity for them to break out, to make it. Kisibafa is their Wild West. Indeed, they display a real Wild West nostalgia. Though they hardly need horses, each bought one to ride when taking the cattle to pasture, like real "cowboys." Neither Dénes nor Laci is an entrepreneur yet. They may make it, but they might also fail, go bankrupt, disappear from the village, and probably try again somewhere else.

Both of them leaped at the opportunity when the Szentlászló kolkhoz proposed to put out its cattle to families. Each took ten cows from the kolkhoz and began upon an almost hopeless uphill struggle. When he started his cattle farm, Laci dreamed of earning up to 25,000 Ft net a month. This soon turned out to be an illusion. Both were, and to a large extent still are, utterly incompetent. When the cattle first arrived in their stables from the kolkhoz, they hardly knew anything about dairy farming. Their only piece of luck was that Laci's companion had had some experience with cows; she helped them through the first difficulties. After a year of struggling against their own ignorance, the inefficiency of the kolkhoz services, and bad luck, they were still in business by mid-1984; probably their chance of surviving and of becoming real entrepreneurs in the end may have improved somewhat.

Dénes Csiki and Laci Sánta are quite atypical entrepreneurial cattle farmers. I have told their story in order to show that prospects for family entrepreneurship are in a way wide open in Hungary today. One can take a shot at becoming an entrepreneur even in a delicate agricultural operation like cattle farming without starting capital or initial skill! Most of the dairy farmers who have enterprises as large as Csiki and Sánta are of middle-peasant background, operate their farms in the old family farmstead, and use skills they picked up from their parents or grandparents.

People like Csiki and Sánta, from poorer families, with fewer skills and fewer inherited capital assets, are more likely to try hog farming first. Not hog breeding, though—hog breeding, like dairy farming, is a prestigious activity. Newcomers to agricultural commodity production rarely dare to experiment with breeding; rather, they build hog feeding operations.

But in other respects the troubles of Csiki's and Sánta's dairy farms are not atypical. Their incompetence has not been the only constraint upon the expansion and success of their entrepreneurial venture. They are confronted with structural constraints that better-qualified family dairy farmers will also encounter everywhere in Hungary. As we showed in Table 4.2, in all those entrepreneurial forms where middle-peasant skills are useful the kolkhozes play a major integrative role. This is inevitable, because, given existing land laws, entrepreneurial dairy and hog farmers can under no circumstances grow the stock feed they need. In Hungary, as in most other state socialist societies, land ownership is limited to about 2–3 acres per family. In the 1980s this law was not being strictly administered. Some people began to buy land in the names of relatives, others to rent it semilegally. There is a fair amount of "squatting" on uncultivated land too, particularly in isolated and decaying villages like Kisibafa. The authorities pretended that they did not notice such irregularities and rarely prosecuted the violators. Thus some families may have significantly increased the amount of land under family cultivation. Since this is a grey area, we could find no reliable data on the expansion of private land possession. Some of our expert informants believed, however, that by the mid-1980s family holdings may have grown through such semilegal practices to 12–14 acres. But even taking the largest estimates, it is still improbable that this semilegally cultivated land is enough to grow feed for 20 cows or 100 pigs. Almost all the larger dairy and hog family farmers depend on the latifundia for hay and corn. The kolkhozes or state farms usually have a contract with the individual entrepreneur. Within the terms of such a contract the latifundia put out stock to the families, guarantee feed for the animals, and purchase the final product at fixed prices.

Integration of private enterprises by the latifundia is a mixed blessing. The division of labor helps to modernize the production regime of the farm and allows the development of more efficient fragmented production chains instead of the more traditional uninterrupted production chains. But at the same time the kolkhoz limits both the profitability and expansion opportunities of the family enterprise. As we saw from the controversy between the president of the Szentlászló kolkhoz and his private subcontractors (both Csiki and Sánta took part in the debate), the kolkhoz was unreliable in its deliveries, affecting daily milk production and stock quality and threatening the prospects of the new enterprises.

In the end, however, the most important limitation on the profitability and expansion of the middle-peasant type of enterprise is the legal limitations on the private ownership of land. If in the future Hungarian agricultural policy wants to encourage the expansion of entrepreneurial family dairy and hog farms, farmers must be allowed to buy or rent land without legal restrictions.

Entrepreneurs with market gardening skills

Market gardening proved to be another area in socialist Hungary where family entrepreneurship became possible for people with gardening skills and horticultural knowledge. In particular, gardening under plastic tunnels rapidly expanded after the mid-1970s.

The restrictions on private ownership of land were less of a constraint upon the expansion of such operations. Gardening under plastic tunnels, particularly heated tunnels, is a new technology which was virtually unknown in Hungary before the late 1960s and which revolutionized market gardening during the 1970s. It tremendously increased per acre productivity of paprika, peppers, tomatoes, and other produce and generated high incomes with a fast rate of return on investments.

Those with market gardening skills could start producing in a small backyard, with relatively small capital investment, could accumulate capital quickly, and expand production rapidly. One important advantage of market gardening is its independence from the latifundia. Family market gardeners do not need services, materials, or marketing assistance from the kolkhozes. Market gardeners often reach the urban markets themselves; thus government manipulation of wholesale prices affects them less than cattle or hog farmers.

We return again to the Kerekes family to show the prospects and the constraints upon expansion of family market gardening. The title of the documentary film in which the family appeared ironically expresses the contradictions in the life experiences of the emergent entrepreneurial class in Hungary today: in Hungarian, *paradicsom* has a double meaning, both "paradise" and "tomato." Is the tomato-producing family enterprise the "paradise on earth" that many jealous urbanites see it as, or is it just another hard, unpleasant way to make a living?

Quickly reviewing the history and economics of the Kerekes business: after the Kerekes family lost its family farm (impressive by Hungarian standards: 17 holds of land, 100 hogs, 3 horses) to collectivization, János drifted with his mother and wife, trying to avoid "third serfdom." In 1960 they left their village, tried different jobs here and there, and finally in 1968 arrived in the city of Szentes. They bought land far out of the city and started gardening there. Szentes is famous for its market gardens. Before arriving there the Kerekes knew little about gardening, but they decided to pick up those skills there. By the early 1970s János and his family were experimenting with unheated plastic tunnels. After some initial difficulties they were successful and by 1975 had saved some 100,000 Ft. With the money in his pocket, his "ears were itching," as János put it, so he bought a farm for 500,000 Ft and started to build up his gardening enterprise, constructing plastic-covered tunnels heated by oil furnaces (one 80-meter tunnel costs about 250,000 Ft.) He built five of these for himself, while his mother and the family of one of his married daughters added more tunnels to the enterprise. To cover these costs he had to borrow more than 1 million Ft. Since government policy prohibited the Savings Bank or any other bank at that time from giving loans for private businesses, he had to borrow from loan sharks at a 25–30 percent interest rate (about five or six times the official rate, and about four times the inflation rate). Kerekes thus suddenly became a major entrepreneur—one of the bigger ones in Szentes. With good luck, he could sell produce from each tunnel for 150,000 or even 200,000 Ft a year, so the family's gross income was well into the million.

János rarely works in the plastic tunnels any more. During peak season he acts as manager. Although his family members still do manual work, he also employs seasonal wage laborers to pick and pack tomatoes. The Kerekes business is totally oriented to the Budapest market. Late at night he leaves with his truck and drives up to the wholesale vegetable market in Bosnyák Square in Budapest. He noses around, tries to figure out how prices are going, then sells his daily harvest partially to wholesalers on Bosnyák Square, partially to retailers—old acquaintances elsewhere in the city. These are stressful hours. Prices are unpredictable; the trip can easily turn into a disaster, but it could be a big success.

According to János, the market is getting worse, in the long run. Costs, particularly heating costs, have climbed rapidly. In May 1983, Kerekes estimated that the price of tomatoes had not risen in five years but the price of fuel had increased fivefold. Profit margins are deteriorating, and he is envious of those market gardeners who began before him. They don't have excessive debt. If your capital is your own, you can still live well from market gardening, argues János. The problem is tough competition, in a rather limited consumer market, with no export possibilities for private entrepreneurs; thus the future is not very bright.

Kerekes, like Csiki and Sánta, started business with no capital and little expertise. The "itching in his ear" may have turned him into an entrepreneur, though in his case also it is still far from certain that he can ever repay his debts and financially consolidate his family business. Most market gardeners of Szentes, unlike Kerekes, knew their profession when they began to turn their minifarms into enterprises proper; most of them also had more family capital with which to begin production. But the difficulties of the Kerekes family farm are far from exceptional. All other market gardeners suffer from the lack of credit and are forced to borrow on the black market. They all suffer from the uncertainties of the market. In the early 1980s the domestic market became saturated. The inflexible and monopolistic nature of commercial organizations also hurt market gardeners. In particular, the government monopoly of foreign trade makes the international market inaccessible. If all these constraints are accepted as unchangeable, then private enterprise may have reached its limits in market gardening in Hungary. Unless capital accumulation is made easier, credit for productive investments is made available, and new commercial forms, including cooperatives with export licenses, are allowed, businesses cannot grow any further. If Hungarian economic policy hopes to rescue the Hungarian economy by encouraging small private business, it may have to take further steps toward liberalization.

Agricultural family entrepreneurs with industrial skills

The third type of agricultural enterprise in Table 4.2, that based on industrial skills, is rather a mixed bag. It includes a great variety of production profiles, mainly small-animal production in closed systems—chickens, rabbits, ducks—which require considerable industrial, technical, and engineering skills. These enterprises are based on quite advanced technology: complex heating, lighting, ventilation, and automatic feeding systems. Rural people learned these skills either in industry, when they commuted during the 1960s or early 1970s, or in the kolkhozes. Armed with such skills, they can now build their minifarms alone or with the help of friends and relatives.

The minifarms of entrepreneurs with industrial skills are usually fragmented production chain economies; more often than not, they are integrated by the latifundia or by government commercial organizations. Large chicken or egg farmers are producing meat or eggs in quantities too large for direct marketing, and because it is difficult to secure feed, they almost always operate on contracts, with prices guaranteed by the kolkhozes, commercial firms, or coops.

During the summer of 1984, I visited such an automated chicken farm in the city of Hajdunánás, in northeast Hungary. We found the farm by accident. Driving around the town, we noticed the white, modest building on the outskirts. The young co-owner manager—he was about 25 or 26 years old—showed us around hospitably. There was a service room, neatly furnished with a bed, television, an impressive automatic switchboard, and a shower room in the corner. The chicken farm is a 24-hour operation; he runs it with his father-in-law in two shifts, so they try to make it comfortable for themselves at night as well.

From the switchboard they can control air quality, temperature, and humidity in the chicken house. The feeding system is also completely automated. In the chicken house were 10,000 chickens. They buy day-old chicks, keep them for six weeks, until they weigh 2 kg, and then sell them to a government commercial firm. In one year they can repeat this exercise five times, so they are selling something like 50,000 chickens or 100,000 kgs of meat a year—quite a farm even by American standards. They also earn well: their joint net income is something like 400,000 Ft a year. Our guide used to be a skilled bricklayer. Working for a government construction company, he used to earn a third, or at the very best half of his present income. He not only now earns more but is his own boss. We chatted about the world market in chickens. He impressed me as an intelligent, well-informed businessman, who could comment on foreign trade policy and the international prospects for chicken production as knowledgeably as any farmer I interviewed in Wisconsin.

Our guide was indeed an "industrialist," with excellent training and valuable skills. He had built the farm with his father-in-law, with some help from friends in the automatic heating, ventilation, and feeding system. They spent only 700,000 Ft on the construction of the chicken house, a reasonable investment indeed if it keeps producing 400,000 Ft net income each year.

This fine chicken farm is probably as big as a private farm can become under present circumstances. According to our local informant, the sociologist Imre Kovách, there are about 15 such farms in Hajdunánás. Further growth is limited by the availability of wage labor and access to the world market. Further expansion of the business is only imaginable if the owners can gradually become managers and can employ wage laborers to do the boring and unpleasant manual tasks, which are simple (keep checking that the installations are working properly) and filthy (collecting dead birds). People like our young bricklayer in Hajdunánás, skilled, intelligent, and with entrepreneurial talent, are in a way wasting their time by performing such tasks. It would not be surprising for them to want to hire others for these operations and concentrate their efforts on management. But although private employment for seasonal work is quite widespread, permanent employment of the kind needed in an automated chicken farm is still very unusual and may border upon illegality.

Until now we have developed a typology of entrepreneurs on the basis of skills. A complementary typology could be based upon differences in the ways in which they economize with capital. All families on an embourgeoisement trajectory by definition economize with capital to some extent, but the capital intensity of entrepreneurial households can be quite different. From this perspective, one can distinguish at least two subtypes of entrepreneurial households:

1. Those which accumulate capital in order to reduce live labor input and increase production by inceasing capital intensity (capital-intensive enterprises). Such a strategy is prevalent among mini-farmers specializing in animal husbandry.
2. Those which purchase new means of production in order to be able to employ wage labor and thus expand their production (labor-intensive enterprises). Market gardening enterprises are likely to be more labor-intensive.

In this analysis I have tried to describe the ways to become an agricultural entrepreneur and the clear structural constraints upon

TABLE 4.3 *Limits on the growth of private agricultural enterprises under state socialism*

Constraints on	
Inputs	*Outputs*
From "above"	
Limits on private ownership of land	
Lack of capital and credit	Saturation of market, domestic and foreign
Inadequate services	Government monopoly of trade and processing industry
	Legal constraints on the forming of private firms, which could break such monopolies
From "below"	
Number of small producers increased by:	Consumer demand is narrowed by:
(a) in-kind payments to kolkhoz	(a) the existence of hobby farms
(b) underurbanization, which created a large rural peasant-worker population that produces for sale	(b) underurbanization, which produced a rural cadre and proletarian population with some subsistence production that do not become consumers
(c) too many people, having no alternative for self-employment elsewhere, become agricultural producers by default	

entrepreneurship. Table 4.3 summarizes these structural constraints on the growth of private agricultural enterprises under state socialism.

The stories we have told have, we hope, given readers an impression of what agricultural entrepreneurship means in a socialist country like Hungary today—admittedly rather unusual in its liberalism toward family business. Table 4.3 also indicates the limits to entrepreneurial growth—as we have already noted, perhaps 3–5 percent of all rural households qualify. But if we add those that I have called "protoentrepreneurial" middle-peasant households, then a significant proportion of rural families, probably about a fifth or sixth, may be regarded as being on an "embourgeoisement trajectory." In the broadest terms, we estimate the following distribution of the rural population among different trajectories: 40 percent proletarian or cadre, another 40 percent on a peasant-worker trajectory, and the rest on an embourgeoisement trajectory.

In the first part of Chapter 5 we will attempt to measure this distribution with greater precision.

FIGURE 1 *With [100,000 Ft] in his pocket, his "ears were itching," as János put it, so he bought a farm for 500,000 Ft and started to build up his gardening enterprise.*

FIGURE 2 *Kerekes . . . is a gambler. He is nervous and insecure, but at the same time he quite enjoys the dangers of his business: he likes taking risks.*

FIGURE 3 *[Mrs. Kerekes] can't bear the idea of their increasing debts. . . . She believes her husband irresponsibly dragged her into this mess.*

FIGURE 4 *Kerekes's mother . . . may be the most entrepreneurial, the most addicted to gambling of all. She pushed her son all the way. . . . The daughter of a burgher-entrepreneur, . . . probably she . . . never accepted the proletarian existence that collectivization offered.*

FIGURE 5 *János rarely works in the plastic tunnels any more. During peak season he acts as manager. . . . His family members still do manual work.*

FIGURE 6 *János Kerekes builds a "square house" for his daughter. The square house . . . has an important symbolic function: to show that its owner is no longer a peasant. . . . It is emphatically residential. . . . Only the size and location of the kitchen . . . indicate the existence of a family enterprise on the premises.*

FIGURE 7 *The landscape of these villages [around Szentlászló] is shaped by beautiful farmhouses, with huge stone stables for cattle, built during the last hundred years by ambitious and quite prosperous German settlers.*

FIGURE 8 *One of the most recent immigrants to Kisibafa is Dénes Csiki, a young, bearded working-class fellow from Érd, a proletarian suburb of Budapest.*

FIGURE 9 *The other vacant house in [the village of Kisibafa] . . . has been rented by Laci Sánta (who comes from a family of manorial laborers from southeast Hungary) and his half-gypsy companion.*

FIGURE 10 *In [Szentlászló] . . . the cooperative, which was losing money on the cattle herd in the collective farm, began to put cattle out to individual families, who might get up to 20 or 25 cows.*

FIGURE 11 *[Sánta and Csiki] each took ten cows from the kolkhoz and began upon an almost hopeless uphill struggle. . . . Both were . . . utterly incompetent. When the cattle first arrived in their stables, . . . they hardly knew anything about dairy farming.*

FIGURE 12 *When [Sánta] started his cattle farm [he] dreamed of earning up to 25,000 Ft net a month. This soon turned out to be an illusion.*

FIGURE 13 *Their only piece of luck was that Laci's companion had had some experience with cows. . . . After a year of struggle against their own ignorance, the inefficiency of the kolkhoz services, and bad luck, they were still in business.*

FIGURE 14 *Both Dénes and Laci are "pioneers." Kisibafa is an adventure, a challenge, an opportunity for them to break out, to make it. Kisibafa is their Wild West.*

FIGURE 15 *[Dénes and Laci] display a real Wild West nostalgia. Though they hardly need horses each bought one to ride . . . like real "cowboys." Laci Sánta on his way home from the pasture.*

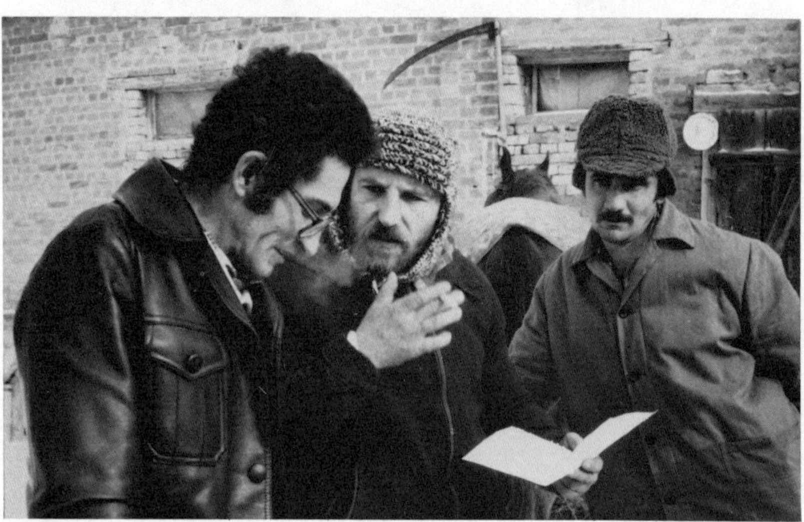

FIGURE 16 *The kolkhozes are often unreliable partners. . . . The president tried to defend his shop for more than an hour. . . . But as the debate progressed he lost confidence in his own story.*

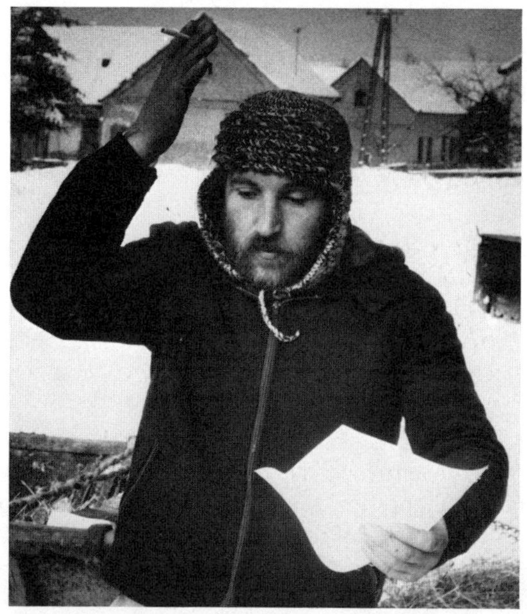

FIGURE 17 *The main complaint of the minifarmers was the unreliability of the kolkhoz. They cited numerous occasions when feed did not arrive in time, causing a decline in milk production.*

FIGURE 18 *Disobedient hogs on the winter road in Kisibafa. In one way proletarian minifarms are easily distinguishable from cadre operations. . . . Even in the tiniest gardens, most proletarian families will feed and slaughter one or two pigs a year.*

5
Measuring the four destinations

From ethnography we turn to dry numbers and quantify what we have so far described in theoretical and qualitative terms. First, we will try to put figures to the typology of destinations developed by Pál Juhász and Bálint Magyar and will compare the results with different monetary measures of family agricultural incomes that the Hungarian Central Statistics Office (CSO) has provided.

Second, we will develop a complex regression model, a "sample selection model" to assess the relative explanatory power of the alternative theories we discussed in Chapters 2 and 3; in particular we show how our models improve as we begin to distinguish more accurately among the "four destinations" we hypothesized in Chapter 4.

DISTRIBUTION OF THE RURAL POPULATION AMONG THE FOUR DESTINATIONS

In this section our task is twofold.

First, we try to quantify directly the ethnography of household economies that we presented above. We do so by relying on the work of Juhász and Magyar, who in 1985 developed a typology of household economies based upon natural measures of production. (We refer to this as the Juhász–Magyar typology, or the typology of destination.) As a first step in this descriptive work, we use this typology to estimate how many families may be at our different destinations.

Second, we use the Juhász–Magyar typology to evaluate how well nonnatural, monetary measures approximate the different destinations. Our task is to assess whether we can use these monetary measures (which are, technically speaking, preferable for sample selection models to the theoretically more meaningful typology of destinations) to distinguish among cadres, proletarians, peasant-workers, and entrepreneurs.

Natural indicators of family agricultural production

What proportion of rural families is at each destination, according to the Juhász–Magyar typology?

In Chapter 1 and Appendix A we noted that the monetary indicators we most frequently use to measure family agricultural production have methodological problems. They were constructed by the CSO in a very complex process of estimating prices and costs and distributing undeclared production. In the ethnographic description of Chapter 4 we noted another limitation: a typology of household economies that is sufficiently sensitive will have to take into consideration, besides the sheer volume of production or even of commodity production, other characteristics, most importantly the substantive indicators of production such as degree of specialization and nature of production regime.

Thus we decided to construct our typology of household economies using alternative dependent variables based on natural indicators of family production. We hope this exercise will help in two respects. First, we can put more "meat" on our analysis. With natural indicators we arrive at a typology less abstract than the picture that our models convey. It can also be directly linked to our earlier ethnographic or phenomenological descriptions of household economies and, we hope, bridges the ethnographic discourse and the highly abstract, multivariate analysis of this book. Second, the exercise acts as a control: we can assess the reliability of monetary measures by contrasting monetary estimates of the proportion of families at different destinations with estimates reached by using only natural measures.

Relying on their extensive field experience, our Hungarian colleagues, Juhász and Magyar, acted as a "jury" and assessed family agricultural production in natural measures (in kilograms, numbers of cows or chickens, etc.). They sought, first, to assess production of individual items and categorized levels of production as indicating commodity production, subsistence production, or sub-subsistence production. By aggregating those product measures at the level of the household, they assigned households to one of the three categories. Second, within these broad categories they created further subcategories, by estimating the degree of specialization and character of the production regime. Thus they could distinguish, for example, the middle-peasant type of entrepreneur from entrepreneurs with market gardening or industrial skills, and tradition-oriented peasant-workers from transitory peasant-workers.

Using this method, Juhász and Magyar produced 17 types, which in themselves were statistically acceptable. We measured the between-group and within-group variance in the distribution of family agricultural production (FAP) in this typology and arrived at a highy significant *F* value of 510.9. Still, in order to make comparisons between the Juhász–Magyar typology and our own theory of destinations easier and to assure that each type could also be linked to our ethnographic descriptions, we reduced the 17 types to seven. This shorter typology performed even better in the variance test: the comparison of between-group and within-group variance produced an *F* value of 1420.6, highly significant indeed. The distribution of the rural population into the Juhász–Magyar typology is presented in Table 5.1.

We believe that our "jury" produced a very useful and meaty typology of destinations that effectively categorizes our sample, but for technical reasons we will hereafter use monetary measures as our dependent variables when developing statistical models. How well do these monetary measures capture the four destinations? Let us now compare them with the Juhász–Magyar typology.

Disaggregated monetary measures of the value of family agricultural production

Our task is twofold: (1) we disaggregate the monetary value of family-produced agricultural goods (FAP) into the value of goods sold on the market (FAPS) and the value of goods consumed by producer families (FAPC); (2) we analyze the distribution of FAP, FAPS, and FAPC according to the typology of destinations.

We hope that the disaggregating of FAP into FAPS and FAPC will have both theoretical and methodological benefits. Theoretically, FAPS should help us to distinguish more clearly between peasant-workers and entrepreneurs, FAPC to distinguish proletarian and cadre destinations from peasant-worker and entrepreneurial destinations. Methodologically, we expect to gain measures which are "cleaner," less manipulated by the CSO. As explained in Appendix A, the agricultural statistics division of the CSO estimated the total family agricultural production to be 20 percent higher than declared in the Income Survey. The CSO income statistics division therefore increased FAP by 20 percent (but did not alter the original FAPS and FAPC estimates on the data tapes), basically allocating the "undeclared production" in 1982 equally among the smaller and greater producers. This manipulation

TABLE 5.1 *Distribution of the rural population by destination*

	N			Percent of all rural families
Proletarian/cadre 1 (proletarian and cadre families with no production)	750[a]		9.7	
Proletarian/cadre 2 (proletarian and cadre families with sub-subsistence production, but no sales)	1080		13.9	
Proletarian/cadre 3 (proletarian and cadre families with sub-subsistence production and some sales)	1418		18.3	
All proletarians and cadres		*3248*		*41.9*
Peasant-worker 1 (tradition-oriented peasant-workers)	2359		30.4	
Peasant-worker 2 (transitory peasant-workers)	991		12.8	
All peasant-workers		*3350*		*43.2*
Protoentrepreneurs (entrepreneurs with middle-peasant skills)	799		10.3	
Entrepreneurs	357		4.6	
1. With market gardening skills	260		3.3	
2. With industrial skills	97		1.3	
All entrepreneurs		*1156*		*14.9*
All rural families in sample		*7745*		*100.0*

Source: Our calculations from 1982–83 CSO Income, Social Mobility and Life History surveys.

[a] In our sample of 7754 families there are 754 households with no records of production in monetary estimates; 4 of them, however, had records of production in natural measures.

significantly influenced the distribution of FAP, with the political advantage that the data were biased toward those apologists for the regime who claim that inequalities are being reduced in Hungary, that class divisions are disappearing, and that everybody participates about equally in the "second economy." Any rationally grounded correction procedure unaffected by political considerations would have allocated most or all of the undeclared production to the biggest producers. The only reasonable assumption one can make is that bigger producers do not declare their true production figures, because taxation of family agricultural production begins at a yearly amount of 200,000 Ft.

By using FAPS and FAPC instead of FAP we at least eliminate the politically induced bias in the income distribution curve. FAPS is less exponential than the actual distribution of income from sales, since we ignore the problem of underreporting. Because our main task, however, is to allocate families into destinations, the distance of those destinations from each other is of secondary importance for our analysis, and we can live with such a bias.

In Table 5.2 we present the distribution of all three monetary measures, FAP, FAPS, and FAPC, according to the typology of destinations established in Table 5.1.

Table 5.2 helps us to assess how much distortion may have resulted from the CSO manipulation of FAP. For the total population FAP is just 20 percent more than FAPS + FAPC; but the same ratio for entrepreneurs is 6 percent, whereas for the proletarian 2 category it is 43 percent. Thus the CSO gave a big boost to the proletarianization theory by overestimating production by small producers and underestimating the incomes of big producers. From the CSO's "manufactured" FAP it appears that entrepreneurs earn only about ten times as much as very small, almost totally proletarianized households, but in reality their

TABLE 5.2 *Weighted means of FAP, FAPS, and FAPC according to the typology of destinations (monthly family income in Ft)*

	FAP	*FAPS*	*FAPC*
Proletarian/cadre 1	0	0	0
Proletarian/cadre 2	586	142	267
Proletarian/cadre 3	1070	295	446
Peasant-worker 1	1686	625	682
Peasant-worker 2	2617	1439	808
Protoentrepreneur	4991	3662	943
Entrepreueur	5683	4541	820
All	*1765*	*926*	*543*

Source: Our calculations from 1982–83 CSO Income, Social Mobility and Life History surveys. $N = 7754$.
Note: FAP = aggregate net value of family agricultural production; FAPS = value of family-produced agricultural goods, sold on markets; FAPC = value of agricultural goods, consumed by the producer families.

earnings are at least 15 times higher. Thus we anticipate more reliable results using FAPS and FAPC as our dependent variables.

Furthermore, Table 5.2 gives credence to the typology of destinations and also to our theoretical attempt to distinguish among the "four destinations." With FAPC it indeed appears possible to bisect the rural population on a line between the categories defined by Juhász and Magyar as proletarian 3 and peasant-worker 1, respectively, at a level of subsistence production valued at 5000–6000 Ft per year. FAPC climbs only slowly from the peasant-worker 1 category toward the proto-entrepreneur category and shows very little variance among the top 50 percent of family producers; it even falls back among genuine entrepreneurs.

FAPS behaves very differently, increasing exponentially all the way, and makes it possible to cut the top 50 percent of producers into two further categories. The protoentrepreneur and entrepreneur categories of the typology of destinations show strikingly different figures from tradition-bound peasant-workers and even from the more market-oriented peasant-workers (a cutoff point around 2000 Ft sale income per month per family seems to be valid). Income from sales for peasant-workers 2 is only 80 percent more than the value of family consumption (the two figures are about equal for the tradition-bound peasant-workers), but protoentrepreneurs sell almost four times as much as they consume and entrepreneurs 5.5 times as much. Thus it makes sense to distinguish households with sub-subsistence production from those that grow most of their own food. It is, similarly, statistically meaningful to distinguish those who are primarily subsistence producers from market-oriented producers.

Thus we must conclude that: (1) Natural and monetary measures complement each other effectively: using two fundamentally different methods, we arrived at the same "destinations." (2) FAPS is a better indicator of entrepreneurial orientation than FAP. In the future we will rely primarily on FAPS to distinguish entrepreneurs from the rest of the rural population or from peasant-workers. (3) FAPC seems to be a particularly sensitive measure for distinguishing proletarian and cadre households from peasant-workers and entrepreneurs.

We can now turn to building regression models to assess the relative explanatory power of the alternative theories of family agricultural production. We first create the simplest possible model using the most elementary independent variables that we can derive from the theories elaborated in Chapters 2 and 3, with FAP as the dependent variable. In the last section of Chapter 5 we fine-tune our dependent variable, moving from FAP to FAPC and FAPS. In Chapters 6 and 7 we fine-tune our main independent variables—first mobility and then life history indicators.

DEVELOPING A SAMPLE SELECTION MODEL

Four models for assessing the three theories: aggregate value of family agricultural production (FAP) as dependent variable

In working out our strategy for assessing the relative explanatory strength of the three theories of family agricultural production in socialist collectivized agriculture, we first use as our dependent variable the value of family agricultural production (FAP),[1] including both consumed and marketed goods. The value of both was estimated by the Central Statistical Office on the basis of going market prices.[2] FAP is a net figure: from the total aggregate value of sales and self-consumption, production costs were deducted (but time spent by family members on production was not considered). Our main task in this section is to explain, first, which families have incomes from FAP, and, second, what causes the variation of FAP among those with such incomes. We achieve this task by using a nested model-building strategy.

As a baseline model we use the hypotheses of the proletarianization theory (compare Table 2.1): the first model (Model A) tests the impact of demographic factors on variance in family agricultural production; the second model (Model B) measures the effect of the current occupation of the head of the household.

Demographic variables are very important for the proletarianization theory because of the assumption that successive cohorts are more and more socialized into wage-laborer status; they thus lose interest in family agricultural production and possibly also in other forms of private economic activities. The proletarianization theory postulates that under socialism, becoming a wage laborer is the normal course; private economic activities are rooted either in the past or in extraordinary family conditions. The demographic effect anticipated by the proletarianization theory is, therefore, twofold:

1. Because family producers are motivated primarily by the surviving elements of a peasant culture, households with older heads are more likely to be numbered in their ranks. As a measure of age we will use

[1] Whenever we estimate variance of FAP we use the log transformation of the income variable, following Featherman and Hauser, 1978, pp. 288–89, and Hauser, 1980, pp. 4–5.

[2] In the survey they asked for the actual quantity of production and asked the respondents to estimate the percentage of self-consumption from total production.

both natural age (AGE) and the square root of age (AGESQUARE). Despite the expected positive correlation between age and family production, it is also reasonable to assume that the very old will actually produce less, and conceivable that the likelihood of family production will peak with the middle-aged rather than with the eldest.

2. Families with a larger labor supply should produce more. We presume that the labor supply in families will be larger if the number of active wage earners is higher (ACTIVNO), the spouse of the household head is not employed but works full time in the household, or there are other unemployed adult members in the household (HOMEDUTY). We also hypothesize that school-aged or younger children "consume" the time of the adult members of the family, particularly housewives; therefore, we anticipate that the number of dependent children under 19 years of age (CHILD) will be negatively correlated with FAP. Furthermore, we assume that labor supply and family production will be greater if the number of retired people in the household is higher (RETIRNO). We also anticipate that "two-parent families" with both husband and wife (ONECOUPLE) and three-generational families (MORECOUPLE) will produce more than "single-parent" or other fragmented families.

In Model B, still remaining within the hypotheses derived from the proletarianization theory, we explore the influence of current occupation. According to the proletarianization theory, families where the head of the household does not take an industrial job but stays on the land, joins the cooperative and becomes an agricultural manual laborer will be the most active in family agricultural production. In Model B, we therefore enter a dummy for head of household working in agriculture as a manual laborer (AGRAR).

As should have been obvious from the discussion of our own "theory of four destinations" we anticipate that the variables included in Models A and B will have some explanatory power. We believe that proletarianization does occur and that some family producers are indeed people driven by tradition to produce. But although these variables are closely enough linked to family motives and capacities for part-time farming that they provide a reasonably powerful indicator of which rural families engage in agricultural production at all, we contend that they will add relatively little to our understanding of which rural producers grow more and, especially, which produce primarily for markets. We hope that these later questions will be better explained by insights from the peasant-worker and in particular the embourgeoisement theories.

The third model (Model C) tests the relative explanatory value of these last two theories. Here we presume that family status before the socialist transformation will have an independent effect on the value of family production. In accepting the embourgeoisement theory, we anticipate that people from pre-1949 entrepreneurial families will be among the larger family producers in 1982.

We try to measure two effects. First, we hypothesize that people from families who were producing for markets before the socialist transformation are more likely to turn toward commodity production and thus to produce higher FAP values today. In Model C we enter into the equation a dummy value if the family of the household head had more than 10 holds of land in 1944 (OFARM44) (perhaps the top 20 percent of family farms before the land reform of 1945; Berend and Ránki, 1972, pp. 150, 230; Donáth, 1969, p. 361). Though 10 holds was really not large enough to support a truly commercial farm, these family farms nevertheless had significant commodity production and required managerial and entrepreneurial skills. The 10-hold cutoff point is liberal, but not unreasonable. The period between 1945 and 1949 is of vital importance for the study of "embourgeoisement" in rural Eastern Europe. The radical land reform which took place right after World War II destroyed the previous rank order and began a new wave of embourgeoisement. It is important, therefore, to measure the impact of land reform: in Model C we enter a dummy value if the family held more land in 1948 than in 1944 (REFORM).

Finally, with the fourth model (Model D), we begin to test our own theory of "reentry to an interrupted embourgeoisement trajectory." We try to prove that the life history of the head of the household must be considered in explaining the variance of FAP, particularly when identifying the bigger producers and commodity producers.

In operationalizing these life history variables we rely on the analysis summarized in Figure 3.4. To measure resistance to both proletarianization and cadrefication we enter the number of years spent in a position of authority on the job (BOSYEAR). We anticipate that those who were "bosses" for too long, or who became bosses in times when entrepreneurship existed as an alternative to both proletarianization and cadrefication (for instance 1945–49 and to some extent even 1955–59) have permanently entered the ranks of the cadres and are unlikely to be "big" producers. We also hypothesize that those who never held positions of authority became proletarians and are also unlikely to produce much in a family enterprise. We anticipate, therefore, a weak, but positive correlation between BOSYEAR and FAP.

We also try to capture the significance of aspirations toward autonomy by experimenting with two measures: number of years the head of household spent in cooperatives (COPYEARS) and the number of years he/she worked as self-employed (SELFYEARS). The first measure particularly is rather problematic. Isn't it a way of smuggling back in the impact of agricultural employment? After all, it is damaging both to the peasant-worker and embourgeoisement hypotheses, particularly our own hypothesis of "reentry to an interrupted embourgeoisement trajectory," if years spent in agricultural employment are sufficient to explain family production. But we believe that the measure of years spent in cooperatives versus those in government-owned enterprises is potentially useful. Although cooperatives in Eastern Europe are not truly cooperatives—they are strongly controlled by the central government—they offer more opportunities for self-management than the government sector proper. In cooperatives, managers are at least de jure elected by the members, the wage system is usually more flexible, and there is at least the illusion that coop "members" take part in making decisions about the management of their firms. Consequently it makes some sense to assume that those who value autonomy will prefer jobs in a cooperative to positions in state-owned and centrally managed enterprises. Furthermore, our COPYEARS variable does not simply measure agricultural employment, because current employment has been controlled for already in Model A. A few people who are currently not kolkhoz members spent years as employees of industrial and service-sector cooperatives.

The SELFYEARS variable is less problematic, although, as we have mentioned, too long a time self-employed, too stubborn an insistence on maintaining independence after the full-scale collectivization drive of 1960 may be seen as "irrational," measuring stubbornness rather than rational commitment to autonomy. Thus we anticipate a rather weak, significant, and positive correlation between SELFYEARS and FAP.

Measurement of the effect of skills is also quite complicated. As we indicated in Figure 3.4, both "too much" and "too little" education may work against embourgeoisement. Those who received "too much" education, particularly nontechnical education, and especially those who obtained credentials after promotion to legitimate a position of authority became cadres and thus were lost to embourgeoisement. At the other end of the scale, too little education indicates people who gave up, accepted subordinate positions in society, and did not really aspire to move up in the first place.

In Model D we enter two educational history variables in the equation: one is a dummy for those who attended evening schools at a high-school or university level (EVENING), the other is a dummy for those who had no more than five years of education (FIFTHYEAR). According to our theory of "parking orbits," both of these variables should have a negative impact on FAP.

Our strategy of analysis in building our four nested models is summarized in Figure 5.1.

Our main contention is that by moving to Models C and D we will significantly improve our understanding of the variance of FAP. Any improvement which results from including Model C indicates that the "interrupted embourgeoisement theory" is indeed useful in explaining socialist part-time farming; further improvement in Model D shows that our extensions and modifications of this theory may be justified. At this stage we aim to show only that variables describing family background and life histories do affect the phenomenon we are investigating. How they exercise this effect is a question that will be explored later.

The 1982 CSO Income Survey, which gave us our dependent variable (FAP), and the 1983 Mobility and Life History Survey, which generated our independent variables, were carried out using the same national random sample. Respondents were interviewed on two different occasions, using the same sets of identifiers, so that we were able to merge the two data sets. From a total of 8172 rural households, we found life history and other relevant information for 7754 heads of households: this merged data set is the basis of our present analysis.

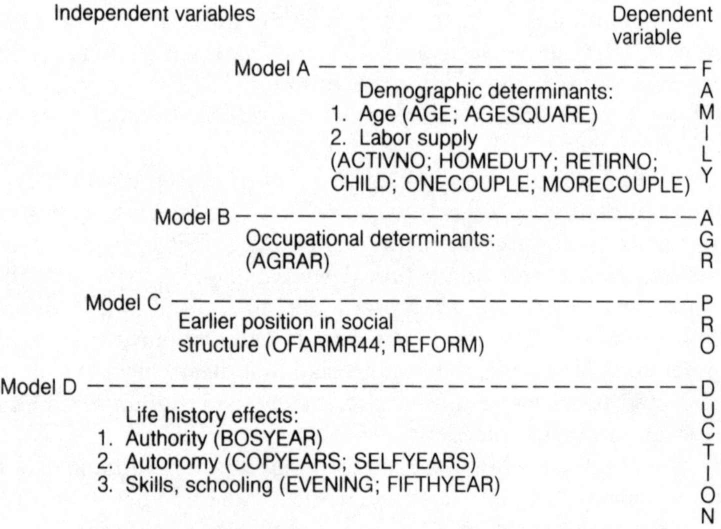

FIGURE 5.1 *The four nested models and their statistical measures*

In our statistical analysis we seek answers to two different questions:

1. *Who is producing at all*? Which variables are of particular importance in predicting the families that, from the total rural sample of 7754, will be among the 7000 families who declared at least some production?
2. *Who among the 7000 producers is likely to produce more?*

To answer both these questions we developed a maximum-likelihood, simultaneous, two-equation sample selection model, in which the first equation produced probit estimates of participation in FAP or, in later stages of our analysis, in intensive commodity production, and the second equation estimated the log values of different measures of family incomes by carrying simultaneously into these log-value estimates the statistical effects of the variables operating at the first selection stage.[3]

In this section of Chapter 5 we discuss how the parameters of individual variables in the sample selection models change as we move from Model A to Model D (Tables 5.3 to 5.6) and we also generally assess the fit of our models (Table 5.7).

Briefly restating, in light of the specific properties of the statistical instrument used, what we expect to achieve in Tables 5.3 to 5.6: This first empirical test of our theory is conducted under the least advantageous conditions for that theory. We use only the aggregate net value of family agricultural production (FAP), without distinguishing consumption from commodity production, although in Models C and D we do specify the new variables that anticipate an entrepreneurial orientation. We also allow the theories we criticize to have the first bite, as it were—to explain as much as they can—and then we try to show that even under such conditions the hypotheses derived from the "interrupted embourgeoisement" theory improve our understanding. We suggest that our theory passes this test—that it is worthwhile to continue our explorations—if (1) the fit of the model significantly improves as we move from Model A to Model D; (2) comparatively speaking, the demographic and occupational variables do better in the probit equations, the social mobility and life history variables in the regression equations; and (3) as we move from Model A to Model D the role of demographic and occupational variables in the second equation steadily diminishes whereas the role of the social mobility and particularly the life history variables steadily increases.

[3] We are grateful for methodological advice we received from Robert Mare and David Grusky in our search for the appropriate model of analysis.

TABLE 5.3 *Nonstandardized (NS) and standardized (ST) parameters of the sample selection model for Model A (N = 7754/7000)*

	Probit			*Regression*		
	NS	*ST*	*t values*	*NS*	*ST*	*t values*
AGE	.103	1.624	12.6	.068	1.075	12.1
AGESQUARE	−0.0008	−1.358	−10.2	−0.0005	−0.969	−11.5
ACTIVNO	.137	.147	4.0	.122	.131	8.4
HOMEDUTY	.438	.077	2.1	.154	.027	2.5
RETIRNO	.205	.144	4.5	.056	.039	2.8
CHILD	.079	.083	3.1	.010	.011	0.8
ONECOUPLE	.540	.244	9.9	.475	.215	14.6
MORECOUPLE	.395	.096	2.7	.451	.109	7.4
Constant					4.828	26.8
σ	.850		118.1			
ρ	−0.019					

Source: Our calculations from 1982–83 CSO Income, Social Mobility and Life History surveys.

TABLE 5.4 *Nonstandardized (NS) and standardized (ST) parameters of the sample selection model for Model B (N = 7754/7000)*

	Probit			*Regression*		
	NS	*ST*	*t values*	*NS*	*ST*	*t values*
AGE	.107	1.746	12.7	.071	1.154	15.5
AGESQUARE	−0.0009	−1.102	−11.1	−0.0006	−1.102	−15.0
ACTIVNO	.236	.160	5.7	.157	.137	10.1
HOMEDUTY	.305	.081	4.5	.121	.029	4.5
RETIRNO	.339	.161	6.4	.122	.056	5.7
CHILD	.073	.076	2.8	.010	.006	0.8
ONECOUPLE	.418	.258	6.3	.427	.223	13.6
MORECOUPLE	.190	.108	1.1	.402	.120	6.3
AGRAR	.661	.296	10.8	.455	.206	20.2
Constant					4.654	37.3
σ	.824		118.3			
ρ	−0.017					

Source: Our calculations from 1982–83 CSO Income, Social Mobility and Life History surveys.

We believe that Tables 5.3 and 5.4 prove that our theory passes the test.

Tables 5.3 and 5.4, for models A and B, demonstrate the strength of the proletarianization theory. In particular, if our task is simply to explain which rural families will produce agricultural goods in their household economies, then the hypotheses derived from this theory take us a long way indeed.

In the first equation for Model A (Table 5.3), natural age and age squared are by far the most important variables, followed at some distance by ONECOUPLE, ACTIVNO, and RETIRNO. If we set out, then, to explain the selection of producers from among the total rural population by using only demographic variables, we can conclude that the rural families more likely to be involved in production are those (1) where the head of household is middle-aged; (2) which are "two-parent," nuclear families; (3) which have a higher number of economically active adults; and (4) which have more retired people whose labor can be mobilized for family production.

In the second equation for Model A (Table 5.3), both age variables lose much strength, as does the RETIRNO variable (which becomes only marginally significant), whereas ONECOUPLE and ACTIVNO hold their strength well.[4] MORECOUPLE, which showed only a weak association and was only marginally significant in the first equation, now becomes undoubtedly significant. Even this simplest model shows, then, that proletarianization theorists face some difficulties, if they want not only to explain the fact of family production, but also to hypothesize about the reasons for greater production. The relative weakening of the AGE, AGESQUARE, and RETIRNO variables, if compared with the stability of ONECOUPLE and ACTIVNO, suggests that among those who produce families younger than middle-aged may play a greater role than the proletarianization theory would suggest. Surprisingly, also, the retired people, who presumably are the most tradition-bound, closest to the peasant past, are not so important for greater production.

Model B in Table 5.4 demonstrates two things:

1. One of the strengths of the proletarianization theory is indeed the hypothesis that agricultural manual laborers are likely to be agricultural family producers. As AGRAR enters the first equation, it

[4] When, in interpreting the models here and later, we use the terms "lose" or "gain" strength, we always do so *relatively speaking*. Parameters of the two equations cannot be compared—what we compare is the *ranking* of parameters of different variables, or the distance between the parameters of different variables in the probit and regression equations.

becomes the third most important variable after AGE and AGE-SQUARE.

2. Somewhat surprisingly, AGRAR does little better in the second equation than AGE. It loses a lot of its strength and is pushed to fourth place by ONECOUPLE. As in Model A, ACTIVNO performs relatively better in the second equation of Model B.

Thus Model B, like Model A, gives qualified support to the proletarianization theory. The theory works well when the task is to predict who will produce, but it begins to run into difficulties when one begins to explore who is producing more among producers. In searching for an answer to the second question, the two most important variables in the proletarianization theory—age and current agricultural employment—lose strength. Those variables which gain strength cannot easily be conceptualized by proletarianization theorists. How can they explain that people below middle age—therefore, people who are less tradition-bound—are better represented among the bigger producers than among producers in general? The same appears to be true for those who hold nonagricultural occupations.

There are some unanticipated results in Model A and Model B too. HOMEDUTY and CHILD in both models and both equations are weak and either marginally significant or nonsignificant. Thus the number of dependent children does not seem to be related to family agricultural production; if it is, then its effect is more likely to be positive than negative, as we first hypothesized. The CHILD variable may behave like this because it has two effects on family production, canceling each other out. We had hypothesized that the number of dependent children might reduce the labor time of adult members that is available for family production—children are "consumers" of adult time—and thus be negatively related to FAP. But, in fact, greater numbers of dependent children may increase the need for family production. CHILD limits resources, but increases need. This proposition is supported by data in Table 5.3, where CHILD shows a weak, positive, and significant association in the first equation, but loses more strength than any other variable in the second equation and becomes nonsignificant. Thus people with dependent children are more likely to produce ("need" wins the day). But among those who do produce the presence of dependent children is irrelevant (the "need effect" is countered by the "resource effect").

The poor performance of the HOMEDUTY variable is more disturbing and more difficult to interpret. HOMEDUTY performs somewhat better in Model B, where it becomes clearly significant, though weak. Earlier

(Szelényi et al., 1983), we had noted the somewhat unexpected behavior of women working at home toward agricultural production. In analyzing data from the 1972 Rural Survey of the Institute of Sociology of the Hungarian Academy of Sciences, we commented that families where the wife did not work outside the home were less likely to be among the larger producers than families where wives were employed in the kolkhozes. We speculated that this may be linked to motivation. Women at home may have more time, but the fact that a married woman sought outside employment is probably an indication of aspirations to autonomy and higher motivation to increase family income. So again two trends may cut across and cancel each other: women at home may have more time but less motivation, employed women have less time but greater motivation. This hypothesis is at least not contradicted by our data. In Model A and Model B, HOMEDUTY is an even weaker variable in the second equation than in the first one. Where motivation matters more—in becoming a bigger producer—wives at home make less of a contribution.

What happens if we begin to move beyond the proletarianization theory, shift to Model C, and add social mobility variables to the selection model?

TABLE 5.5 *Nonstandardized (NS) and standardized (ST) parameters of the sample selection model for Model C (N = 7754/7000)*

	Probit			*Regression*		
	NS	*ST*	*t values*	*NS*	*ST*	*t values*
AGE	.102	1.615	12.0	.067	1.051	14.6
AGESQUARE	−0.0009	−1.460	−10.5	−0.0006	−1.037	−14.4
ACTIVNO	.160	.172	4.3	.131	.141	9.1
HOMEDUTY	.179	.064	2.4	.092	.033	3.1
RETIRNO	.277	.194	5.6	.103	.072	5.3
CHILD	.079	.083	3.1	.014	.014	1.1
ONECOUPLE	.535	.242	8.9	.467	.211	16.2
MORECOUPLE	.468	.114	3.0	.497	.121	8.6
AGRAR	.603	.269	9.8	.425	.189	18.9
OFARM44	.470	.179	6.3	.332	.126	12.6
REFORM	.366	.147	6.0	.182	.073	7.4
Constant					4.749	38.2
σ	.816		118.3			
ρ	−0.004	(restricted)				

Source: Our calculations from 1982–83 CSO Income, Social Mobility and Life History surveys.

As anticipated, in Table 5.5 Model C shows that both family background variables are positively and significantly associated with FAP. OFARM44 and REFORM perform well though not spectacularly in both the first and second equations, anticipated doing better in the second, which focuses upon explaining why some people produce more. In the first equation, OFARM44 ranks sixth, after the two age variables, AGRAR and ONECOUPLE, and close behind RETIRNO. In the second equation, it remains sixth in ranking: RETIRNO is now behind OFARM44, whereas ACTIVNO overtakes OFARM44 in the regression equation. But, it is important to note, in the second equation OFARM44 comes closer to AGE, AGESQUARE, and AGRAR; relatively speaking, it gains strength in comparison with the two strategic proletarianization theory variables, age and agricultural manual occupation of the head of the household. REFORM is slightly weaker than OFARM44 in the probit equation and loses more strength in the second equation.

Model C thus gives weak but unambiguous support to the claims of the peasant-worker and embourgeoisement theories—especially of the latter, because the mobility variables were specified according to the embourgeoisement theory. Family background is a variable that sociologists must consider in order to comprehend the survival of family agricultural production in socialist collectivized economies, particularly if they want to explain why some people produce more than others.

Turning to Model D, let us see how our extension and modification of the embourgeoisement theory fares.

In Model D (Table 5.6), the relative strength of the demographic variables declines as we move from selection to the regression estimate of earnings (although the most important demographic variable, age, remains the strongest among all variables). The relative contribution of the SELFYEARS and COPYEARS variables to the explanatory power of the model increases in the second equation, thus strongly supporting our emphasis on the importance of life history variables for the explanation of entrepreneurship.

The contribution of BOSYEAR to the model is modest, but the change in its effect by moving from the first to the second equation is fascinating. In the selection equation, BOSYEAR is negative and statistically significant; in the substantive equation, however it is positive and nonsignificant. Somewhat hypothetically, we may interpret this change as follows: Perhaps long years in a position of authority move individuals firmly into the ranks of the cadres, negatively affecting production (equation 1). However, among those relatively few families that are large producers, experience in exercising authority may be an asset. Bosses or former bosses do not generally produce anything, but if they do, they

TABLE 5.6 *Nonstandardized (NS) and standardized (ST) parameters of the sample selection model for Model D (N = 7754/7000)*

	Probit			Regression		
	NS	*ST*	*t values*	*NS*	*ST*	*t values*
AGE	.096	1.512	10.9	.052	.878	11.1
AGESQUARE	−0.0008	−1.372	−9.5	−0.0005	−0.905	−11.6
ACTIVNO	.169	.182	4.4	.118	.142	9.3
HOMEDUTY	.181	.065	2.3	.077	.031	3.0
RETIRNO	.286	.201	5.7	.102	.080	5.8
CHILD	.084	.088	3.2	.018	.021	1.61
ONECOUPLE	.515	.233	8.3	.323	.159	11.5
MORECOUPLE	.395	.096	2.5	.321	.089	6.4
AGRAR	.461	.205	6.9	.309	.115	10.2
OFARM44	.415	.158	5.3	.211	.091	8.9
REFORM	.356	.143	5.7	.119	.054	5.4
BOSYEAR	−0.009	−0.045	−2.1	.003	.015	1.4
COPYEARS	.023	.180	5.2	.018	.162	15.1
SELFYEARS	.011	.074	2.4	.012	.087	8.4
EVENING	−0.424	−0.132	−6.9	−0.077	−0.025	−2.2
FIFTHYEAR	−0.285	−0.102	−4.4	−0.132	−0.052	−5.0
Constant					7.270	447.4
σ	.797		113.9			
ρ	−0.112					

Source: Our calculations from 1982–83 CSO Income, Social Mobility and Life History surveys.

[a] The nonstandardized parameters in this model were estimated from standardized parameters using two formulae developed by Robert Mare of the University of Wisconsin–Madison. These formulae were:

$$\text{Nonstandardized probit parameters} = \frac{\text{Standardized probit parameters}}{\text{Standard deviation of independent variable}}$$

$$\text{Nonstandardized regression parameters} = \frac{\text{Standard deviation of dependent variable}}{\text{Standard deviation of independent variables}} \times \text{Standardized regression parameters}$$

For the probit equation, the standard deviation is calculated for the whole sample (in this case $N = 7754$); for the regression equation, it is calculated for the subsample into which selection occurred (in Table 5.6 $N = 7000$).

are likely to be quite big producers. These findings illustrate clearly the problems of and prospects for analyzing life history variables. Aware of the limitations of such interpretations we will nevertheless proceed, in the hope that with better specifications of our dependent and independent variables the hypothesized positive relationship between BOSYEAR and entrepreneurship will at some point also become statistically significant.

The contradictory consequences of the number of years spent in a position of authority support some of our earlier speculations that the BOSYEAR variable could indicate either moving into cadre ranks or resistance to the pressure to become proletarianized. Positions of authority may function as "parking orbits" that facilitate a return to an entrepreneurial course. In order to make BOSYEAR or other possible indicators of authority work for our theory, then, we must fine-tune them. The consequences of holding a position of authority may vary depending not only on how long one was in such a position—the figure directly measured by BOSYEAR—but also on how and at what historical point one reached it.

The historical time at which one enters a position of authority is, we believe, very important. We ran a few cross-tabulations and calculated ordinary least squares (OLS) estimates in order to assess this effect. According to these data, the fact that somebody entered a position of authority in 1945–49 or in 1955–59 has significantly negative effects on the value of their family's production today. For those who became bosses between 1950 and 1954 or 1960 and 1964 the opposite is true: these years had a significant and positive effect on family agricultural production. This is a most fascinating contrast. During the years 1945–49 and the few years from 1956 to 1960 in Hungary, possibilities for entrepreneurship were reasonably good; one could have been a private farmer, with hope for the future of market-oriented family farming. Presumably people who during those years sought positions of authority in the redistributive, bureaucratic rank hierarchy were ready and eager to become cadres and did not have entrepreneurial motivations. To have become a boss in 1949, 1960, or a few years after that, when the pressures to give up entrepreneurship and join the cooperatives were at their height, is quite another story. For those who were on embourgeoisement trajectories between 1945 and 1949 or 1957 and 1959, the alternatives in 1949 and 1960 were either to become a boss or to be bossed around. To accept a position as president of a newly formed kolkhoz in 1960 was a sign of the will to resist proletarianization and to seek a "parking orbit" where one might be able to survive difficult times.

Up to this point we have compared the parameters of individual variables within each model, seeking to demonstrate that mobility and life history variables individually produce parameters which are significant and sometimes significantly greater than the parameters of variables derived from the proletarianization theory. Our next task is to compare the models themselves with each other. Does including these variables improve the overall fit of our model and thus justify including them? Does the complex theory indeed more fully describe the phenomenon we are investigating than earlier theories do? For an answer we turn to Table 5.7, which shows that moving from Model B to Model C and then to Model D significantly improve the overall fit of our model.

TABLE 5.7 *Goodness of fit for sample selection models A to D*

	*−2*loglikelihood*	*Degrees of freedom*
Model A	22,070	7735
Model B	21,468	7733
Model C	21,266	7729
Model D	20,796	7719
Model B vs Model A	602	2
Model C vs Model B	202	4
Model D vs Model C	470	10

This analysis was conducted merely to show that in explaining FAP and, more theoretically speaking, reemergent family entrepreneurship, one must consider both family background and life history. Later we will specify in more detail our main independent variables as we did in our brief comments on time spent in positions of authority. This first exploratory analysis was intended to assess the viability of the whole project—whether it was worthwhile to pursue this strategy of research—and we found the results reassuring. Our main conclusions are:

1. The hypotheses derived from the proletarianization theory offer some insight into the extent of family agricultural production, but their explanatory power is quite limited. To understand this phenomenon we must include variables drawn from outside that theory.
2. There are two sets of such variables. The peasant-worker and interrupted embourgeoisement theories correctly emphasize that

family background helps to explain family production and, in particular, the reemergence of entrepreneurship. If one specifies family background variables according to the interrupted embourgeoisement theory, that is, if one assumes that people from middle- and rich-peasant backgrounds are more likely to be family producers, and on a larger scale, then the explanatory power of our model is improved.

3. Our extension of the interrupted embourgeoisement theory to include the idea of "four destinations" and "reentry to an embourgeoisement trajectory" and our emphasis on life history are also supported by the evidence presented earlier. Two main points follow:
   (a) We regard the distinction between the "total rural population" and the "producing population"—7000 families from our total sample of 7754—as the first approximation of different destinations: it reflects the difference between the proletarian and cadre families on the one hand and peasant-worker and entrepreneurial families on the other. Even with this first approximation we can show that social mobility and, particularly, life history variables are important in explaining which families arrive at peasant-worker and entrepreneurial destinations. We are optimistic that with further refinements in the measurement of destinations we will be able to make our point even more persuasively.
   (b) Our contention about the significance of life history and indirectly, our belief in an "activist view" of class structure are as fully supported by the above evidence as one can expect from an exploratory analysis. Adding life history measures to the sample selection models improved their predictive powers, and these measures seem to be as important—if not more important than—indicators of positions in the present social structure or the impact of family.

Fine-tuning the dependent variable

In the previous section, the aggregate value of family agricultural production (FAP) was our dependent variable. This very crude measure hardly enabled us to do more than show the inadequacy of the proletarianization theory, the need to consider family background in the study of family agricultural production, and, beyond that, the importance of investigating the effects of life history.

Our task in the remainder of Chapter 5 is to fine-tune our dependent variable, to disaggregate FAP, separating more clearly the four "destinations" on the "class map" of state socialist rural societies. FAP did not allow us to test in any systematic way whether these destinations could be statistically distinguished. In the first place, it did not allow us to distinguish between the value of produce consumed by the family (FAPC) and produce sold in the market (FAPS); thus we could not separate peasant-worker and entrepreneurial destinations proper from each other. Secondly, the distinction we could make with FAP between producers and nonproducers was very crude; even our distinction of proletarians and cadres versus peasant-workers and entrepreneurs was not sufficient (the cutoff point in FAP was no production at all versus any amount of production). Proletarian or cadre families can easily grow some agricultural products. "Hobby farming" is a great fashion among rural cadres; a small vineyard or a small garden with a couple of fruit trees are very much the thing to have. These hobby farms should in no way be seen as indicating absence of cadre status; in fact, quite the reverse. Likewise, thoroughly proletarianized families may have a vegetable garden, mainly to save money from supermarket bills for other purposes. Thus some kinds of small household agricultural production may go hand-in-hand with either proletarian or cadre status. Using FAP as defined above, we could not distinguish proletarian and cadre households from peasant-worker and entrepreneurial families with sufficient precision.

In this section we rerun our sample selection models with our disaggregated and fine-tuned dependent variables. With FAPC and FAPS we hope to prove that the closer we come to the entrepreneurial destination, the better our specifications of the mobility and life history variables work.

First, we run Models B and D with FAPC as dependent variable.[5] We also use a new cutoff point to define the population for which we calculate the regression equation. Zero production is an inaccurate measure of proletarian and cadre status: because most rural proletarians and cadres did produce some agricultural goods, they should be distinguished from peasant-workers not by the total absence of production but by their inability to come anywhere near subsistence production. Our peasant-workers and even our entrepreneurs produce a substantial part of the food they consume, whereas for proletarians and cadres family production is of lesser significance. Searching for a cutoff point to divide the population somewhere between the

[5] We will call them Models B/FAPC and D/FAPC. See their parameters in Tables 5.8 and 5.9, later.

proletarian/cadre 3 and peasant-worker 1 positions in the typology of destinations (see Table 5.1) we found this to be 5000 Ft or more production for self-consumption per year (Table 5.2). We thus select from the total sample of 7754 those 4389 families who could not be regarded in any meaningful sense of the term as proletarian and cadre, but who are either peasant-worker or entrepreneur. If our earlier theoretical elaborations are on target, Model B should effectively explain who are selected, but should have little or nothing to say about how much they produce for their own consumption. We expect little improvement by moving from Model B to Model D: Model D should work rather poorly with FAPC as dependent variable.

Second, we begin to use FAPS as our dependent variable, defining two cutoff points. The first, very liberal point was defined to allow all peasant-workers who by the most relaxed criteria could be regarded as "market-oriented" to join the entrepreneurs and protoentrepreneurs. This point on FAPS is 5000 Ft yearly production for sale; it selects 3703 families from the 7754. We present both Model B and Model D with this first cutoff point;[6] for our theory to hold water, Model D should perform better. Finally, we also experiment with a more rigorous cutoff point in FAPS at 24,000 Ft yearly production for sale. This way we narrow our target population approximately down to those who are defined in the typology of destinations as "entrepreneurs" and "protoentrepreneurs," 1254 families. In Table 5.12 we present Model D with this second cutoff point in FAPS (Model D/FAPS2). Our comparisons of Model D/FAPS1 and Model D/FAPS2 (Tables 5.11 and 5.12) show the limitations of our current mobility and life history variables and the need to fine-tune them further to comprehend who the biggest producers really are.

How well do Models B and D explain the division between proletarian/cadre and peasant-worker/entrepreneurial destinations?

First, we compare the performance of Models B/FAP and B/FAPC (Tables 5.4 and 5.8); we will do the same for Models D/FAP and D/FAPC (Tables 5.6 and 5.9). Second, we analyze what happens with FAPC as the dependent variable when we move from Model B to Model D; thus we compare Models B/FAPC and D/FAPC (Tables 5.8 and 5.9).

[6] We call these models Model B/FAPS1 and Model D/FAPS1. See their parameters in Tables 5.10 and 5.11.

TABLE 5.8 *Nonstandardized (NS) and standardized (ST) parameters of the sample selection model for Model B with FAPC as dependent variable (Model B/FAPC; N = 7754/4389)*

	Probit			*Regression*		
	NS	*ST*	*t values*	*NS*	*ST*	*t values*
AGE	.123	1.937	17.6	.017	.266	6.2
AGESQUARE	−0.001	−1.860	−16.7	−0.0001	−0.244	−5.7
ACTIVNO	.331	.355	12.6	.076	.082	10.0
HOMEDUTY	.442	.201	10.0	.058	.026	4.4
RETIRNO	.383	.269	10.9	.068	.048	6.5
CHILD	.058	.060	3.0	.020	.021	3.1
ONECOUPLE	.623	.281	12.9	.091	.040	5.0
MORECOUPLE	.509	.123	4.8	.107	.026	3.4
AGRAR	.573	.255	15.3	.063	.028	5.6
Constant					9.14	1621.3
σ	.337		93.6			
ρ	−0.1 (restricted)					
−2*loglikelihood	= 11,830					
DF	= 7,733					

Source: Our calculations from 1982–83 CSO Income, Social Mobility and Life History surveys.

Comparing Model B/FAP with Model B/FAPC and Model D/FAP with Model D/FAPC

The disaggregation of FAP into FAPC positively affects Model B, particularly in the first equation (compare Tables 5.4 and 5.8). The parameters of Model B appear very comfortable with FAPC as a dependent variable; their level of significance for the probit scores is dramatically higher than it was in Model B/FAP or for that matter in any other model we have produced or will produce in this book. In Model B/FAPC the standardized probit parameters are also systematically higher than those in Model B/FAP, the only exception to this being our AGRAR variable, which was the third strongest variable in Model B/FAP in the probit equation but falls back to sixth place in Model B/FAPC. But the demographic variables all do very well; even the otherwise unimpressive HOMEDUTY and CHILD are solidly significant.

In the regression equation, Model B/FAPC does not fare so well when compared with Model B/FAP. All variables, including CHILD, remain significant, but the t values decline in comparison with both the

probit equation of the same model and the regression equation of Model B/FAP. The normalized parameters are drastically reduced, and AGRAR further loses some of its relative strength; usually one of the most powerful variables, it now features as one of the weakest.

This, of course, all makes sense. Because FAPC measures the value of agricultural goods produced for consumption by the family, the demographic variables should indeed play a prominent role in explaining who is involved in such activities. Our decision to stick with the HOMEDUTY and CHILD variables, despite their poor earlier performance, has also been justified. A wife at home and number of dependent children (thus more mouths to feed) are indeed important in explaining why rural families get involved in subsistence production. HOMEDUTY

TABLE 5.9 *Nonstandardized (NS) and standardized (ST) parameters of the sample selection model for Model D with FAPC as dependent variable (Model D/FAPC; N = 7754/4389)*

	Probit			*Regression*		
	NS	*ST*	*t values*	*NS*	*ST*	*t values*
AGE	.113	1.780	15.5	.016	.249	5.8
AGESQUARE	−0.001	−1.780	−15.1	−0.001	−.241	−5.5
ACTIVNO	.247	.265	10.1	.065	.069	9.3
HOMEDUTY	.269	.096	5.4	.043	.016	3.1
RETIRNO	.307	.216	9.3	.059	.041	6.1
CHILD	.068	.071	3.5	.019	.021	3.1
ONECOUPLE	.782	.354	17.1	.110	.049	6.4
MORECOUPLE	.841	.205	8.4	.150	.036	5.3
AGRAR	.297	.132	7.1	.033	.015	2.7
OFARM44	.289	.110	6.2	.041	.016	3.0
REFORM	.233	.094	5.8	.025	.010	2.0
BOSYEAR	−0.004	−0.019	−1.2	−0.004	−0.002	−0.4
COPYEARS	.022	.186	9.9	.003	.022	4.3
SELFYEARS	.012	.140	7.0	.002	.028	4.1
EVENING	−0.536	−0.167	−9.8	−0.023	−0.007	−1.0
FIFTHYEAR	−0.209	−0.075	−4.4	−0.059	−0.021	−3.7
Constant				8.46		112.5
					9.13	1606.1
σ	.333		93.6			
ρ	−0.1	(restricted)				
−2*loglikelihood	= 11,394					
DF	= 7,719					

Source: Our calculations from 1982–83 CSO Income, Social Mobility and Life History surveys.

and CHILD are even important in explaining which subsistence producers will produce more. But otherwise, in identifying the bigger subsistence producers in the regression equation, this sample selection model performs understandably poorly. As we saw in the earlier statistical description (see Table 5.2), there is little variation in the value of subsistence production, particularly above the 5000 Ft per year cutoff point. Given this lack of variation, the mere fact that the model fits the data is quite an achievement.

The comparison of Model D/FAP with Model D/FAPC (Tables 5.6 and 5.9) shows that the mobility and life history variables are much less at ease with FAPC as dependent variable than are the demographic characteristics of the families. Mobility and life history variables perform reasonably in the first equation of Model D/FAPC, about as well as they did in Model D/FAP. In the probit equation of Table 5.9 only BOSYEAR is nonsignificant and the other life history variables in both tables do about as well as the weaker demographic variables. But when we move to the regression equation, the situation changes dramatically. In moving from the first to the second equation of Model D/FAP only BOSYEAR lost its significance; some of the life history variables gained strength and cut into the explanatory power of some demographic variables. Now the opposite seems to be happening in Model D/FAPC: in the regression equation, two out of the seven mobility and life history variables are nonsignificant at a *t* value of 2.0 or higher (whereas all eight demographic variables remain highly significant, and though AGRAR loses some of its relative strength, it also stays solidly significant). The changing importance of HOMEDUTY and CHILD in explaining income variance speaks to the reversal of power relationships between demography on the one hand and mobility and life history on the other. In the regression equation of Model D/FAP, both HOMEDUTY and CHILD were weaker variables than most of the mobility and life history variables. In the second equation of Model D/FAPC, HOMEDUTY and CHILD perform better than four out of the seven mobility and life history variables. Whatever we were able to explain about the variance of FAP by introducing indicators of mobility and life history, we explain for FAPC by the indicators of wives at home and number of dependent children.

Comparing Model B/FAPC with Model D/FAPC

Despite the uneasiness of the mobility and life history variables with FAPC as a dependent variable, our model gains in explanatory power by addition of these types of indicators. Purely statistically speaking, Model D/FAPC produces a significantly better fit than Model

B/FAPC: in moving from Model B/FAPC to Model D/FAPC, −2*loglikelihood was reduced by 436 points and the degrees of freedom were cut by 14. Thus those who oppose the proletarianization theory could use these models to show its limitations; even the explanation of subsistence production needs insights from the interrupted embourgeoisement theory.

Right now, though, we don't want to be too hard on the proletarianization theory. It is, after all, a powerful tool (Tables 5.8 and 5.9) if our task is to explain which rural families will produce food for their own consumption. These are mainly older and larger families, with larger numbers of retired people and dependent children, where the husband is an agricultural manual laborer and the wife does not work outside the home; it matters relatively little what background they come from, what sort of life trajectories they have pursued. It is also not unreasonable to hypothesize that as real incomes begin to increase, as the pressure to supplement wages by reducing grocery bills eases, most of these families may give up subsistence production altogether and will slide into a purely proletarian or cadre existence. As we have seen in Chapter 1, this happened, even in Hungary, the paradise of socialist part-time farming, and even during the crucially important decade of the 1970s. Some families who were only subsistence producers during the 1960s gave it up, swapped their houseplots for cash from the kolkhoz, and limited their family agricultural production to proletarian or cadre hobby gardens. In 1982, compared with 1972, fewer families were producing their own food, and they cultivated a shrinking proportion of the arable land.

Thus, reinforced by the results of comparing Models B/FAPC and D/FAPC, we accept the proletarianization theory in two respects: (1) it is a valid explanation of the dominant trends in rural Hungary between 1949 and the late 1960s (and possibly the dominant trend in other East European societies ever since); (2) even after the late 1960s or early 1970s it captures one tendency in rural society, the continued decay of subsistence-oriented production.

But we claim that our theory of reentry to the interrupted embourgeoisement trajectory is necessary to explain a different phenomenon, commodity production on family minifarms. This phenomenon is relatively new, limited to a much smaller proportion of rural families, and unlike subsistence production is not in retreat but is expanding quite dynamically. Here we turn to analysis of the performance of sample selection models when family income from the sale of agricultural goods (FAPS) is used as the dependent variable.

How well do Models B and D explain commodity production, the division between the peasant-worker and entrepreneurial destinations?

In this concluding section of Chapter 5 we first contrast Models B/FAPS1 and D/FAPS1 (Tables 5.10 and 5.11) to prove that including mobility and life history variables dramatically improves the fit of the model; second, we contrast Model D/FAP with Model D/FAPS1 (Tables 5.6 and 5.11) to show that, indeed, income from the sale of agricultural goods is the proper dependent variable for the interrupted embourgeoisement theory; third, we show some of the difficulties we face, when we try to close in on our target population, the "real entrepreneurs," by moving from Model D/FAPS1 to Model D/FAPS2 (Tables 5.11 and 5.12). This last contrast helps us to identify the research tasks for Chapters 6 and 7.

Comparing Model B/FAPS1 with Model D/FAPS1

A first glance at Model B/FAPS1 (Table 5.10) shows that the proletarianization theory is in deep trouble in explaining the variance of

TABLE 5.10 *Nonstandardized (NS) and standardized (ST) parameters of the sample selection model for Model B with FAPS as dependent variable (Model B/FAPS1; cutoff point 5000 Ft; N = 7754/3703)*

	Probit			*Regression*		
	NS	*ST*	*t values*	*NS*	*ST*	*t values*
AGE	.081	1.277	12.1	.024	.375	3.7
AGESQUARE	−0.001	−1.250	−11.6	−0.0002	−0.389	−3.8
ACTIVNO	.112	.120	5.0	.097	.104	5.3
HOMEDUTY	.097	.035	2.1	.037	−0.013	−1.0
RETIRNO	.106	.075	3.5	−0.028	−0.019	−1.1
CHILD	−0.015	−0.015	−0.8	.011	.012	0.7
ONECOUPLE	.501	.227	11.5	.196	.089	4.8
MORECOUPLE	.568	.138	6.3	.066	.016	0.9
AGRAR	.739	.329	20.9	.233	.104	8.4
Constant				8.96		51.2
					9.84	714.3
σ	.776		85.6			
ρ	−0.2 (restricted)					
−2*loglikelihood	= 18,465					
DF	= 7,733					

Source: Our calculations from 1982–83 CSO Income, Social Mobility and Life History surveys.

TABLE 5.11 *Nonstandardized (NS) and standardized (ST) parameters of the sample selection model for Model D with FAPS as dependent variable (Model D/FAPS1; cutoff point 5000 Ft; N = 7754/3703)*

	Probit			*Regression*		
	NS	*ST*	*t values*	*NS*	*ST*	*t values*
AGE	.069	1.084	9.7	.020	.324	3.2
AGESQUARE	−0.001	−1.216	−10.5	−0.0002	−0.434	−4.2
ACTIVNO	.107	.115	4.7	.095	.102	5.3
HOMEDUTY	.105	.038	2.2	−0.033	−0.012	−0.9
RETIRNO	.143	.100	4.6	−0.010	−0.007	−0.4
CHILD	−0.008	−0.008	−0.4	.010	.011	0.6
ONECOUPLE	.464	.209	10.2	.203	.092	5.0
MORECOUPLE	.507	.123	5.5	.083	.020	1.1
AGRAR	.408	.182	10.2	.164	.073	5.5
OFARM44	.283	.108	6.4	.069	.026	2.1
REFORM	.221	.089	5.7	.014	.006	0.5
BOSYEAR	.001	.007	0.4	.009	.047	3.5
COPYEARS	.033	.278	15.8	.009	.077	6.2
SELFYEARS	.019	.230	11.9	.010	.120	7.6
EVENING	−0.119	−0.037	−2.2	.108	.034	2.2
FIFTHYEAR	−0.194	−0.069	−4.2	−0.021	−0.007	−0.5
Constant				9.01		51.2
					9.79	−4.1
σ	.764		85.9			
ρ	−0.2 (restricted)					
−2*loglikelihood	= 17,648					
DF	= 7,719					

Source: Our calculations from 1982–83 CSO Income, Social Mobility and Life History surveys.

incomes from market-oriented production. In predicting who is likely to produce for sale, our demographic variables perform reasonably well; only one out of the eight variables is nonsignificant, though the standardized parameters are not very impressive (compare Model B/FAPC, Table 5.8). But in the regression equation, where we attempt to identify the bigger commodity producers, the model begins to disintegrate. In the second equation of Model B/FAPS1, four out of the eight demographic variables are nonsignificant.

As we move to Model D with FAPS1 as the dependent variable (Table 5.11), the model gains impressively in explanatory power. The goodness of fit statistics show this: whereas in Model D/FAPC versus Model B/FAPC the difference of −2*loglikelihood was only 436, in Model D/FAPS1 versus Model B/FAPS1 (Tables 5.11 and 5.10) it is 817 (in both cases the difference in degrees of freedom is the same, 14).

In the probit scores the gains are not yet obvious. In the first equation of Model D/FAPS1 (Table 5.11), the variables from Model B perform well; only one out of the nine is nonsignificant, whereas one out of the seven mobility and life history variables is also nonsignificant. But in the regression equation of Model D/FAPS1 the balance of power alters radically: four out of the nine variables from Model B are nonsignificant, whereas five out of the seven mobility and life history indicators remain significant. Two of them, COPYEARS and SELFYEARS, become, in fact, the most significant in the whole equation after the age variables.

Thus the comparison of Model B/FAPS1 with Model D/FAPS1 demonstrates with absolute clarity that, when using income from the sale of agricultural production as a dependent variable, we in general gain a lot by informing our analysis with hypotheses taken from the interrupted embourgeoisement theory. Our gains are the greatest, however, when our task is not simply to predict who will produce goods for sale, but who will produce the larger amounts.

Comparing Model D/FAP with Model D/FAPS1

This comparison (Tables 5.6 and 5.11) also shows that disaggregating FAP into FAPS was beneficial for the embourgeoisement hypotheses. The variables in the first equation in the two models perform similarly: in Model D/FAP all variables are significant, but in Model D/FAPS1 only one of the mobility and life history variables and one of the variables from Model B is nonsignificant. But in Model D/FAPS1, COPYEARS and SELFYEARS, and to some extent even OFARM44, do a relatively better job than they did in Model D/FAP. In Model D/FAP, for instance, COPYEARS was in seventh place; in Model D/FAPS1 it is now in third place. The improvement in the relative strength of SELFYEARS is now even more impressive; it moved from fourteenth place in Table 5.6 to fourth place in Table 5.11 (in the first equation).

The benefits of disaggregating FAP into FAPS for the embourgeoisement theory are even more obvious in the regression equation. In Model D/FAP the demographic variables lost some ground to the mobility and life history indicators, but most of them remained significant. In Model D/FAPS1, other than the age measures only ACTIVNO and ONECOUPLE retain their power. In comparing Models D/FAP and D/FAPS1 we should, of course, remember that our task in

Model D/FAPS1 is much more difficult statistically: we must explain selection into and variance of income within a much smaller and more homogeneous group of 3703 households. The difficulty of this endeavor makes even more remarkable the goodness of fit of Model D/FAPS1 and in particular the contribution to it of the mobility and life history variables.

Closing in on the target population: Model D/FAPS1 versus Model D/FAPS2

Our last task in Chapter 5 is to show how well our mobility and life history measures perform when we attempt to identify the population headed for the entrepreneurial destination proper and income variance among the biggest commodity producers.

By introducing a second cutoff point for FAPS at 24,000 Ft yearly net income from the sale of agricultural goods and narrowing our target population down to 1254 families, we set ourselves a difficult statistical problem, further increasing the homogeneity of our target population and reducing the variance of our dependent variable within this population. It will be increasingly difficult to find a model to fit the data.

We cannot indeed claim that Model D/FAPS2 is particularly successful. Comparing Model D/FAPS1 with Model D/FAPS2, we merely hold our position while being confronted with an increasingly difficult task (Table 5.12). For Model D/FAPS2, in the probit equation the number of nonsignificant variables increased to five out of the 16 (there were two in Model D/FAPS1); in the regression equation the number of nonsignificant variables remained six (the same as in Table 5.11). By and large, the relative contribution of the variables from Model B and the mobility and life history indicators is unaltered. But, rather disturbingly for us, it appears from Table 5.12 that we are unable to identify clearly the larger commodity producers. With the mobility and life history variables as specified for our first empirical test of the interrupted embourgeoisement theory we could significantly advance our identification of rural families who will be involved in commodity production—who are likely to be headed toward an entrepreneurial destination—but we face difficulties in explaining the variance of entrepreneurial incomes.

Some of the results from Model D/FAPS2 are encouraging for the interrupted embourgeoisement theory. In the regression equation of Table 5.12 particularly, BOSYEAR, COPYEARS, and SELFYEARS perform well. These three variables together give their best performance to this point in our analysis, thus supporting our claim that life history is of central importance in explaining entrepreneurial behavior.

TABLE 5.12 *Nonstandardized (NS) and standardized (ST) parameters of the sample selection model for Model D with FAPS as dependent variable (Model D/FAPS2; cutoff point 24,000 Ft; N = 7754/1254)*

	Probit			*Regression*		
	NS[a]	*ST*	*t values*	*NS*	*ST*	*t values*
AGE	.063	.995	6.3	.017	.443	2.8
AGESQUARE	−0.001	−1.243	−7.5	−0.0002	−0.591	−3.5
ACTIVNO	.161	.173	6.1	.038	.079	3.3
HOMEDUTY	.050	.018	0.9	−0.009	−0.007	−0.4
RETIRNO	.056	.039	1.5	−0.002	−0.003	−0.1
CHILD	−0.012	−0.013	−0.5	−0.000	−0.000	−0.0
ONECOUPLE	.513	.232	7.9	.125	.096	3.1
MORECOUPLE	.440	.107	3.9	.079	.044	1.7
AGRAR	.429	.191	9.3	.093	.093	5.4
OFARM44	.241	.092	4.8	.056	.051	3.3
REFORM	.127	.051	2.7	.040	.034	2.1
BOSYEAR	.010	.046	2.4	.006	.059	3.4
COPYEARS	.027	.219	11.5	.002	.048	3.0
SELFYEARS	.041	.272	10.6	.009	.143	6.1
EVENING	.045	.014	0.7	.012	.007	0.4
FIFTHYEAR	−0.089	−0.032	−1.5	−0.017	−0.011	−0.6
Constant					10.07	353.1
σ	.553		47.1			
ρ	.6 (restricted)					
−2*loglikelihood[b]	= 7,550					
DF	= 7,719					

Source: Our calculations from 1982–83 CSO Income, Social Mobility and Life History surveys.

[a] The nonstandardized parameters in this model were estimated from the standardized parameters with the formulae developed by Robert Mare of the University of Wisconsin, Madison. For details see the note to Table 5.6.

[b] The loglikelihood statistics for Model B with FAPS as dependent variable at the second cutoff point in FAPS are:
−2*loglikelihood = 7,964
DF = 7,733.

Thus we refuse to be discouraged with the somewhat disappointing performance of Model D/FAPS2. After all, so far we have relied upon the crudest possible specification of both the mobility and life history measures. Next we will try to fine-tune them, in the hope that we can make them work more effectively, particularly in Model D/FAPS2.

6

Historical continuity in embourgeoisement

The effect of family background

The purpose of this chapter is to fine-tune our family background variables. Are people on an embourgeoisement trajectory indeed from a different social background than families heading toward other destinations? In Chapter 5 we disaggregated our dependent variable in order to distinguish with greater precision among entrepreneurial, peasant-worker, and proletarian household economies. In Chapter 6 we fine-tune our family background variables, in order to explain which family background leads to each destination. We achieve this task in two steps.

First, we present some general hypotheses about differences in the social origins of entrepreneurs, peasant-workers, and proletarians. These hypotheses are derived from theoretical propositions and based on ethnographic evidence.

Second, we return to our regression models and retest them with the fine-tuned mobility variables.

THE SOCIAL ORIGINS OF ENTREPRENEURS, PEASANT-WORKERS, AND PROLETARIANS

The most general and therefore somewhat simplistic hypotheses suggested by the theoretical elaborations of Chapters 2 and 3 are summarized in Table 6.1. In what follows we will further specify these general hypotheses, relying on ethnographic evidence and working out more detailed mobility hypotheses for as many types as possible from the typology of destinations.

TABLE 6.1 *Social origins and destinations*

Destination	Social origin
Entrepreneur	Middle- and rich-peasant background
Peasant-worker	Poor- and small-peasant background
Proletarian	Mainly former rural landless laborers
Cadre	No clear hypotheses; possibly from rather varied social background

Social origin of the new entrepreneurs

Protoentrepreneurs: former middle peasants

The general hypothesis about the middle- and rich-peasant origins of entrepreneurship is particularly true for the protoentrepreneurs. The skills and relatively large initial capital investment required for dairy farming or hog breeding are such that people without access to a middle- or rich-peasant farmstead and childhood training may find it difficult to enter these branches of production. These structural constraints are not, of course, absolute—there are the Csikis and Sántas who try to overcome them—but they are quite serious.

Entrepreneurs with market gardening skills: former poor and small peasants

Market gardening is very different. Even before the war it was a channel of upward social mobility, understandably, since the land and capital requirements of gardening are less pressing than those of entrepreneurial animal husbandry, for instance. Between the two world wars, ambitious individuals from poor-peasant families (with 1–3 holds of land) or even from the families of seasonal agricultural laborers began to buy or lease small plots of land; some became successful gardeners. This happened especially in the sandy soil between the Danube and Tisza rivers, an area not particularly suitable for wheat or corn production and somewhat neglected before 1900, when wheat was the most important crop. The value of the area for agricultural use improved around the turn of the century, as wine-growing spread to sandy soils and as rapidly growing Budapest created a major market for produce from this small nearby region. Some of the earliest and the most recent work of István Márkus (1979) and the very early work of Ferenc Erdei (for instance, his first book, *Futóhomok* ["Drifting Sand"], 1937) were stimulated by the experiences of such pioneer poor peasants, who were trying to exploit the new opportunities in cities like Nagykőrös and their environs (Márkus, 1979, pp. 65–78).

A dual change occurred during the 1950s in the social character of market gardening:[1]

1. During the interwar years, poor peasants played the pioneering role in market gardening; from the 1950s on, people from a small-peasant background (with 5–10-hold farms) began to take up gardening.
2. This second wave of upward mobility into gardening was not a phenomenon restricted to ambitious or talented individuals, but was genuine collective mobility. During the interwar years a small number of poor peasants improved the lot of their families by market gardening, but the bulk of the poor peasantry was left in desperate poverty. After 1950, a very significant proportion of the former small peasants who stayed in the villages and on the land took up market gardening. Collectively they filled the vacuum which was created by declining competition for urban vegetable markets from kulaks or capitalist big estates.

The new "industrial" entrepreneurs: former small peasants and their children

The "industrialist" category of agricultural entrepreneurs is probably of quite mixed social origin. Vital for entrepreneurship in this group are industrial skills like electrical engineering, tool making, or truck driving, and people from the most diverse backgrounds have picked up such skills. We would anticipate that small peasants are well represented, for two reasons:

1. People from small-peasant backgrounds were apparently more likely than any others to become skilled industrial workers. Katalin Hanák, for instance, found people whose parents were small peasants to be strongly overrepresented among skilled industrial workers (Hanák, 1982, p. 251). Former small peasants were more ambitious than people from poorer families; they did not accept a life as unskilled or semiskilled laborers and learned industrial skills. At the same time, because they had sizeable land holdings, they were more likely to stay in the villages than former agrarian proletarians or poor peasants. Thus it is reasonable to assume that

[1] These ideas were elaborated by Pál Juhász during the summer of 1985 in a tape-recorded interview in Madison, Wisconsin.

they were particularly attracted to those industrial skills that could be utilized in the villages.

2. It can be argued that as opportunities for agricultural entrepreneurship open up again, smaller peasants are more likely to move back to agriculture and to try to utilize their newly acquired industrial skills there. Those middle or rich peasants (or their children) who became electricians or builders may be more likely to succeed in the "industrial second economy." They can use their family networks to generate enough consumer demand for their industrial services that they do not have to return to agricultural production proper. From a small-peasant background, people may return to agriculture where competition is less stiff, because they have not succeeded in the industrial second economy (Juhász, personal communication).

Thus we would not be surprised if the hypothesis about the middle-peasant origin of entrepreneurship would be primarily true for proto-entrepreneurs. At the entrepreneurial destination proper, both in its industrialist and market gardening version, we might well find a larger proportion of people from small- and even from poor-peasant background. When it comes to entrepreneurship proper, family inheritance may play a somewhat more modest role and the life history of the individual may matter relatively more.

Former middle peasants and the rural cadre after the 1960 collectivization

Temporary power in the collectives

Until now we have assumed that former middle and rich peasants automatically preferred embourgeoisement and resisted at all costs absorption into the ranks of the proletariat or the cadre. This hypothesis requires qualification. Many former middle peasants who by the early 1980s were on an embourgeoisement trajectory were at one stage tempted by the possibilities of the cadre, and quite a few former middle peasants and their descendants did indeed become cadres. If children of small peasants are overrepresented among rural skilled workers, the descendants of former middle peasants are overrepresented among the rural cadre (Hanák, 1982, p. 251).

During the 1960 collectivization drive, the middle and some of the rich peasants no longer opposed the formation of the kolkhozes. Some middle peasants, like János Kerekes, rejected collectivization and escaped the "third serfdom" at whatever cost, but others—probably the majority of the middle peasants—felt that they had learned the "lesson of history." They had fought against collectivization during the Stalinist period, in the early 1950s, but the bloody defeat of the 1956 uprising taught them how merciless the regime could be, how hopeless was stubborn resistance. The whole of the Hungarian peasantry enjoyed the brief pause in collectivization efforts after 1956—the regime was prudent enough to leave a breathing space to the peasants before resuming the organization of the kolkhozes—but few peasants had any illusions. They suspected that they had received only a brief suspension of the death sentence passed on private farming and not a reversal of the sentence itself.

By late 1959 and early 1960 the villages were once again flooded by "men in leather jackets."[2] These kolkhoz organizers were party apparatchiks, teachers, plainclothes policemen, military officers, and a few industrial workers who in hope of promotion to an office job joined the drive. Upon their arrival the peasants may have been angry, but they were not surprised. Most of them, often led by former middle peasants, "signed on" with some irony and without much resistance.

This, of course, does not mean that the collectivization of agriculture in 1960 was "voluntary" in any meaningful sense of the term (cf. Bell, 1984, pp. 135–36). All of us who spent time in the villages as professional or amateur ethnographers collected stories about the abuses of power: the peasant who was ordered to stand in his heavy winter coat beside the overheated stove in the town hall and was asked every hour if he was ready to sign; the teacher–kolkhoz organizer who soon became known for his strange habit of pushing his pencil—the symbol of his profession—up a man's nose, toward his brain, while he lectured him about the social and economic advantages of the collective farms. Bell also writes about "psychological pressures" applied in the village of Kislapos:

> Agitators visited families for hours on end, not leaving until an application form was filled out. Whenever a new family signed up, the fact was announced over the loudspeakers spread out over the village. Once or twice outings were organized for villagers to visit nearby successful collective and state farms. Many villagers, remembering the beating of a decade earlier and unsure of the purpose of these bus trips, went with great trepidation; . . . for Lapos's inhabitants this increased the feeling of inevitability of the collectivization
>
> [1984, p. 136].

[2] A leather jacket around that time was a symbol of cadre status, a "uniform" of the members of the secret police but also of other party officials.

So collectivization was, of course, not voluntary, but the choreography of coercion was different from that elsewhere, particularly from the 1930s in Russia. In Hungary in 1960, both the peasants and the kolkhoz organizers knew from the outset that the villagers would give in without murder or torture. The "symbolic coercion" sketched above was only to remind both the rulers and the ruled that the act which occurred was an act of power. The peasants were not fools; they gave in, but with style, preserving their self-respect, registering their dissent from collectivization and putting the record straight for future historians of the epoch.

The regime had also learned the "historic lesson" of the 1950s and of Stalinism. The 1960 Hungarian collectivization drive was designed by a group of politicians who listened closely to the advice of Ferenc Erdei. Erdei not only knew peasants better than anybody else, but unlike the typical Bolshevik politician loved them, and tried to devise the least painful collectivization strategy. In 1960 Erdei acted as president of the so-called National Front. This was a largely ceremonial post, but since he had a close personal relationship with the first secretary of the Hungarian Communist Party, János Kádár, he actually had a major impact on agrarian policy until his death in 1971.

One of the most important lessons the post-1956 Hungarian regime had learned from past experiences in Hungary and elsewhere in Eastern Europe was that there was no point in alienating the middle or even the rich peasants. These were, after all, the people who had run larger farms and who might be able to cope with the task of managing the relatively small cooperatives, some of them only 1500 or 2500 acres, which were formed around that time. In 1960, in sharp contrast with the early 1950s, kolkhoz organizers often began with the most prestigious middle or rich peasants. They would persuade him to join or even to become president of the new cooperative and thus more easily build support in the village.[3]

Offsetting the many like Kerekes, then, there were other middle peasants who joined the kolkhozes immediately; in many kolkhozes they collectively occupied most of the managerial positions. They were elected as presidents, they became brigade foremen, supply department managers, wagon and tractor drivers, and even party secretaries. In many Hugarian kolkhozes by the mid-1960s a solid "middle class"

[3] The same is reported by Bell 1984, pp. 132–33, 238, 240. According to Orbán the greater role of middle peasants may not have been intended by the regime; at least certain elements of the party were concerned that "class enemies" were playing such a role in the newly formed kolkhozes. Orbán, 1972, pp. 238–39, particularly fn. 368 on p. 238.

formed from the former middle peasants occupied all positions of authority and autonomy. In a sense they reproduced within the kolkhozes the power and prestige hierarchy of the villages before collectivization.

Changing the guard: the rise of the technical intelligentsia in the cadre

The rule of the villages and kolkhozes by middle-peasant cadres did not last very long. Pál Juhász (1983a) has described the struggle between university-trained agricultural professionals and cadre management personnel from middle-peasant background for control of the agricultural cooperatives during the late 1960s and early 1970s. The ultimate replacement of most of the older generation of kolkhoz leaders by young, university-trained agricultural engineers[4] is an important episode in what we have elsewhere called the "struggle of intellectuals for class power" during the 1968 reform epoch in Hungary (Konrád and Szelényi, 1979), but it is also important in explaining the reemergence of rural entrepreneurship—the decision of the former middle peasants to reenter the embourgeoisement trajectory.[5]

The middle peasants were well prepared for the second collectivization drive, but were taken completely off guard by the challenge to their newly acquired "cadre power" within the kolkhozes by the young agricultural professionals in the late 1960s. Around 1968–69 a new generation of freshly trained agricultural engineers appeared in Hungarian agriculture. They were not only armed with scientific agricultural knowledge but were also filled with the ambitions of the East European reform intelligentsia of the 1960s. This was the time when the ethos of the "scientific-technical revolution" exerted such a strong influence. Radovan Richta's *Civilization at the Crossroads* (1969)—then a best-seller among Hungarian intellectuals—is a powerful statement of the views of this generation of socialist intellectuals. The new agricultural engineers who were graduated by the late 1960s were also influenced by Richta's version of socialist scientism. They did not think much of the earlier kolkhoz management: former peasants were not ready to manage modern agricultural enterprises. They underestimated the value of the work and knowledge of former middle peasants and expected to receive significantly larger salaries, better housing, and greater social prestige than the existing kolkhoz leadership.

If the incoming new agricultural engineers were arrogant, the former

[4] See also Hann, 1983, pp. 82–90.

[5] The following account of the rise of agricultural engineers to power is based on Juhász 1983a and on interviews conducted with Juhász.

middle peasants, now in managerial positions, often responded foolishly to the challenge. In their eyes, the young agricultural engineers were ignorant and bookish; viewing them as apprentices, management gave them ridiculously low salaries and talked to them like children. The former middle peasants stubbornly resisted the technical innovations that the new college graduates wanted to bring in. They ridiculed them for wanting to apply American techniques and to increase the sowing density of corn; they resisted use of the silo system and artificial manure for pastures.

A full-fledged "class struggle" broke out; the agricultural engineers soon gained the upper hand by producing powerful new ideologies of agricultural organization and implementing reform of the kolkhoz system. Their main ideological weapon was the superiority of "industrial methods" in agriculture. The industrialization of agriculture required reorganization of the kolkhozes, in particular of the labor process. During the early 1970s amalgamation of the cooperatives proceeded apace. In 1960 each village had usually had several cooperatives, sometimes as many as four or five, but by the early 1970s the policy became one cooperative for each village, which sometimes meant one cooperative for one central village and its several satellite villages. As a result the size of the cooperatives increased from as little as 1200 acres to 12,000 or sometimes even 36,000 acres (Donáth, 1977, pp. 243–50). The amalgamation of the cooperatives typically occurred together with a major new investment drive. Huge hog or cattle complexes housing several thousand pigs or cows were built, huge heated greenhouses were erected. The amalgamation and massive capitalization of cooperatives resulted indeed in an impressive increase in crop yields per acre, but also in a major decline in the ratio of productivity gained to capital invested. Thus these new coops represent a doubtful achievement in a country where labor is cheap, land abundant, but capital scarce (the amount of land left uncultivated increased during the same period; Donáth, 1982–83; 1977, pp. 259–60). But the sociological purpose of the amalgamation and industrialization drive was achieved. In these new large kolkhozes, cathedrals for pigs and cows, full of fancy technology, the former middle peasants were lost, and the shift of power into the hands of the new technocrats was inevitable.

The new agricultural engineers also pushed for new methods of work organization; they wanted to bring "Taylorism" into the kolkhozes, breaking up production chains. So, for instance, in the cattle stable they separated those who prepared the feed from those who did the feeding and those who milked cows. Each brigade now had its own foreman, who was directly responsible to the agricultural engineers in charge of animal husbandry. Thus the skills of the old "cattle farmer" were downgraded or disappeared altogether. The former middle peasants lost their function: in managerial positions they were replaced by agricultural engineers and on the production line they became semi-skilled workers—like feeders or feed makers. The result was a massive "proletarianization" of all who did not have university degrees. After such a reorganization of the labor process, managerial positions were open only to those with university credentials, possessors of "cultural capital." Taylorist work organization within the cooperatives and amalgamation of the kolkhozes together represented a major step toward bringing agriculture under the control of university-trained experts.

The class struggle between the new agricultural intelligentsia and the former middle-peasant kolkhoz cadre occurred in two stages. At first, around 1968, the young engineers were still using "democratic methods," and for a while it appeared that a "coalition government" of university-trained intellectuals and former middle-peasant cadres might be possible within the kolkhozes. Between 1968 and 1971 the kolkhoz elite was split into two groups. The university-trained young people were agricultural engineers, mechanical engineers, or veterinarians and controlled primarily animal husbandry; the old guard of former middle peasants were still presidents, party secretaries of cooperatives, and brigade leaders (who then still had a fair amount of power). These middle-peasant cadres controlled crop production.

But this division of labor and power did not last very long. By 1971 the young agricultural intelligentsia had infiltrated agricultural policy making at different levels of the government. In 1971, county agricultural departments regained control over the kolkhozes, and the county agricultural apparatus was to a significant degree composed of young, university-trained agricultural intellectuals.[6] This enormously strengthened the position of agricultural engineers who worked in the kolkhozes, and over the next few years control of the latifundia moved completely to this new technocratic elite.

Middle peasants back on the road toward entrepreneurship

The trajectory to cadre status was thus now closed to former middle peasants. They lost many key positions to young technocrats; the positions they kept were reduced in influence, and positions in middle management like brigade leader or foreman lost their prestige and even

[6] The county government played a key role in the collectivization drive, but later lost some of its powers, which were, however, regained during the early 1970s.

autonomy in the new Taylorist labor organization.[7] The unintended consequence of this lost "class struggle" was the resurgence of family entrepreneurship among former middle peasants.[8] Some of them moved into the marketplace and started to build up their family enterprises as the channels of upward mobility within the rank stratification system were closed.

The overrepresentation of former middle peasants among entrepreneurs was not inevitable; history could have worked differently. Middle peasants were tempted by cadrefication: some of them actually entered cadre ranks, and most of them reentered the embourgeoisement trajectory only when the young agricultural engineers took away their managerial positions in the kolkhozes.

Whatever happened to the kulak families?

During the 1960s and early 1970s a new antikulak ideology emerged, particularly among the former agrarian proletarians: "It is again the kulaks who rule us!" was a complaint often heard (Orbán, 1972, p. 239). Particularly prone to articulate such views were people from poor rural families who had been politically radicalized during the 1950s and became apparatchiks in the local government system, within the party or the kolkhozes, but who later, as the regime consolidated itself, began to slide downward in the rank hierarchy of the villages.

"The kulaks rule us again" was probably never very true. The people who in fact ruled most of the villages by the late 1960s, as we just saw, were mainly from a middle-peasant background, from families with 10–25 holds of land.[9] Kolkhoz managers of middle-peasant background may have behaved like "kulaks" (see also Bell, 1984, p. 170). They may have learned from rich peasants how to behave when in a position of authority, how to give orders and get work from their subordinates, but relatively few leaders were actually kulak by origin.

Many of the rich-peasant and rural commercial and industrial entrepreneur families (the so-called "industrial kulaks") were broken and pauperized by the early 1950s. In Dunapataj, a village then with

[7] The party secretary, a powerful figure in most kolkhozes during the early 1960s had come to play a largely ceremonial role by the late 1970s.

[8] In 1982, 9.9 percent of all heads of households came from a family which was middle peasant in 1944. But 14.6 percent of protoentrepreneurs were from such a background (by contrast, only 3.7 percent of the proletarian-cadre 1 group were former middle peasants).

[9] When, during the Stalinist years, the so-called "kulak lists" were created, typically only people above 20 or 25 holds were classified as "kulaks," though the definition varied over time and across regions.

4000 inhabitants, the 90 so-called kulak families owned altogether 35 cows by 1951.[10] They were all breaking apart under the government's pressure, and many, particularly the children, left for distant cities, where they settled permanently and became urban proletariat or professionals.[11] Those kulaks who stayed in the villages may have been able to reestablish a middle-peasant existence. Some did move, together with middle peasants, to skilled jobs and even managerial positions in the kolkhozes when they were legally allowed to join the cooperatives (Donáth, 1977, p. 138). Later in the 1970s, some even became involved in the new agricultural entrepreneurship, but on both the cadrefication and embourgeoisement trajectories they were disadvantaged in comparison with middle peasants. As aspirants to cadre status their social background worked against them (Hanák, 1982, p. 254). When they tried to build new family enterprises they were often handicapped by the disintegration of their families during the antikulak campaigns; now they could not count on the extended family support which was vitally important in the early stages of reestablishing family entrepreneurship.

Rural outmigration affected different strata differently. Former kulaks resemble former agricultural proletarians and poor peasants: they were the most likely to migrate to the city. Former small and middle peasants and their descendants were the most likely to stay in villages.

At closer scrutiny, then, it is very likely that the new "kulak rule" will prove to be a myth, created by the frustrated former rural proletariat and rural poor, who missed out upon another opportunity for collective mobility. Most kulaks left the villages permanently; the few who remained fitted into the center of the former middle peasantry and moved along with them, slightly disadvantaged, toward embourgeoisement or in a few cases into kolkhoz managerial positions, toward cadre status.

[10] We are grateful to Bálint Magyar for this information.

[11] Donáth (1977, p. 138) also claims that "By the 1950s the majority of the former peasant-employers had left agriculture. They found jobs particularly in mining and in the construction industries." See also Hanák, 1982, p. 253. But in many villages the former kulak families did not disappear altogether. Bálint Magyar in Dunapataj could still find, during the early 1980s, one or more descendants of 80 out of the 90 original kulak families (though in smaller villages a much higher proportion of the families probably disappeared altogether). Most of those 80 families were quite fragmented and had "lost" several of their members to cities.

Social origins of the peasant-workers

The most problematic hypothesis in Table 6.1 is that addressing the social origins of peasant-workers. Becaue they are a kind of middle stratum between cadre and proletariat, wage laborer and entrepreneur, they may come from all kinds of social backgrounds. By breaking up the peasant-worker destination into transitory or market-oriented peasant-workers on the one hand and tradition-bound peasant-workers on the other, we will be able to offer better mobility hypotheses.

Transitory peasant-workers: former small peasants and their descendants

People from small-peasant origin are likely to constitute the backbone of the peasant-worker destination and to be well represented among market-oriented peasant-workers. Small peasants were bound to the villages through land ownership, and relatively few migrated to the city. Cadre ranks were not particularly open to them, for they lacked the political acceptability of the poor peasants and seasonal workers and the expertise or social prestige that brought middle peasants and, rarely, kulaks into managerial jobs. Some small peasants became proletarianized, but as a class, Márkus (1980) has persuasively argued, small peasants were highly ambitious, so that they were likely to try their luck with family agricultural production whenever opportunities arrived. They did not own proper farmsteads, and possessed little cultural capital; compared with former middle peasants they were at a disadvantage in developing market-oriented family enterprises. Thus we will anticipate that the more fortunate people from a small-peasant background share the "peasant-worker 2" destination with the less successful descendants of middle peasants.

Tradition-bound peasant-workers: former poor peasants and their children

The former poor peasants and their children had a quite different experience. Because their holdings were negligible, they were not tied to the villages, and many left for the cities. They were also well positioned for the rural cadre. Below them in the social hierarchy of the prewar Hungarian village were the manorial laborers, somewhat of a "lumpen" group, rarely with ambition or qualifications for bureaucratic positions. The poor peasantry was therefore the "lowest class" available for the cadre and many were indeed promoted into minor positions of power: the apparatus of the police (including the secret police), the army, and the party and state bureaucracy. Some made it, others could not adjust to the new opportunity and became proletarians. Thus we anticipate that by the mid-1980s former poor peasants or their descendants will be more sparsely represented among peasant-workers than former small peasants and their children, but they will still be ahead of the descendants of manorial laborers and, primarily in the tradition-bound peasant-worker category, of the descendants of middle peasants also.

The most proletarianized: former manorial laborers

Most of our informants believed that former manorial laborers and their children left in great numbers for the cities. According to Pál Juhász and Bálint Magyar (personal communication) this may often have been a sort of "circular migration": some may have returned temporarily to rural proletarian positions, only to try again later in another city. Those who did stay in the villages are believed to be the most fully proletarianized stratum of rural society today. The most ambitious among them may be fulfilling their century-old dream: they may have become "peasants," have built up peasant-worker household economies, mainly of the traditional peasant type. The more ambitious may have joined the ranks of the former poor peasants in the lower spheres of postpeasant existence. Thus although former manorial laborers are the most likely to be on a unilinear trajectory toward full proletarianization, some may have joined the "embourgeoisement queue." In this queue quite a few former middle peasants became real entrepreneurs; former small peasants adopted the ways of middle peasants and became market-oriented peasant-workers or even protoentrepreneurs; former poor peasants began to run their household economies as they had observed their small-peasant neighbors to do; and at the very end of the queue, some manorial laborers began to complement their wages and salaries with subsistence-oriented family minifarms, which may be similar to those of prewar poor peasants.

Social origins of the rural cadre

In our analysis so far we have offered a few, quite weak hypotheses about the social origins of the rural cadre. Recruitment into rural cadre positions may have been reasonably open over the last three decades. With the exception of the "lumpen" former manorial laborers, people from most other origins could have been recruited into a cadre position reasonably easily. Hanák's (1982, p. 251) findings seem by and large to support this claim: she found that people from most social origins were represented as expected in cadre ranks, except those from manorial laborer families (underrepresented 1 : 3), the very few from professional families (overrepresented 1: 6), and those of middle-peasant origins (overrepresented 1 : 1.6).

But the weakness of our mobility hypotheses about the cadre

destination does not worry us particularly. For our purposes, the cadre is a somewhat residual category. We define destinations in terms of the character of the household economy, not of occupation and authority, and most of the time we must collapse the cadre and proletarian destinations. In this book we are less interested in differentiating cadre from proletarian than in exploring the alternatives to that axis of social stratification.

We are now ready to reformulate the general hypotheses we presented in Table 6.1 and to base upon our discussion a more detailed but still equally hypothetical "mobility table" (Table 6.2).

RETESTING THE SAMPLE SELECTION MODEL

We will proceed in two steps. First, we report our experiments with alternative variables—which were selected for inclusion in the sample selection model, which were considered but finally eliminated, and why. Second, we present the sample selection models with the fine-tuned mobility variables (Model D′) with FAPC, FAPS1, and FAPS2 as dependent variables (Tables 6.3, 6.4, and 6.5). We compare these tables with those containing Model D and the same dependent variables, that is, Tables 5.9, 5.11, and 5.12, in order to show the improvement achieved by our fine-tuning.

TABLE 6.2 *A hypothetical "mobility table": 1944 family status and mid-1980s destination*

Destination: type of household economy in mid-1980s	*Social status of the family in 1944*				
		Peasant			
	Kulaks	*Middle*	*Small*	*Poor*	*Manorial laborers*
Entrepreneurs					
Market-gardener type		+	++	+	
Industrialist			+	+	
Protoentrepreneurs	++	+++			
Peasant-worker 2		++	+++		
Peasant-worker 1				+++	+
Rural proletarian			+	+	++
Cadre	+	+		++	
Left for the city	+++		+	++	+++

Note: Increasing number of + indicates the increasing probability, within each category of origin, of arriving at a given destination.

Selecting the new mobility variables

In Chapter 5 we used two very crude mobility measures: OFARM44 and REFORM.

As the reader may recall, OFARM44 was created to measure middle- or rich-peasant origins. In creating this variable, we combined measures of landholding by the parents of the current head of the household and of his own landholding. If the current respondent was already a head of household in 1944, then we used his own landholding, but if he was a child, we registered the size of the parental landholding, giving a value of 1 to our dummy OFARM44 for those who, one way or another, owned ten or more hold of land in 1944. Thus OFARM44 was a curious mixture of a social mobility and a life history variable.

The purpose of the REFORM variable was to measure the embourgeoisement effects of the 1945 land reform. REFORM is a dummy in which all those families that increased their landholding between 1944 and 1948 received a value of 1, irrespective of how much land they added or how much they had held before land reform.

In fine-tuning these variables using the ethnographic and theoretical analysis just completed, we worked on measures of both prewar family social position and the effect of the 1945 land reforms.

1. We created variables which described more precisely prewar social position, not only middle-peasant but other origins that we found in our ethnographic discussion to be closely related to the current level of family agricultural production.

Here we were involved in three operations. First, we decided to make our earlier OFARM44 variable more clearly a measure of "social background." Thus we created a new variable which simply described the landholding of the parents of the current head of household, PFARM44; it was designed as a dummy which took the value 1 when the father of our respondent in 1944 owned 10 or more holds of land. Cross-tabulations of both OFARM44 and PFARM44 with different monetary measures of incomes from family agricultural production persuaded us that PFARM44 would not only be a theoretically "cleaner" variable, but it would indeed be correlated to current entrepreneurship as powerfully, or almost as powerfully, as OFARM44 was. Second, we decided to create a variable which would explain proletarianization/cadrefication—that is, one which would have a strong negative correlation with current family production and particularly with FAPS. We experimented with several measures and finally settled upon a variable we labeled NONAGR38. This variable is a dummy which takes the value 1 if the father of the current head of household had a nonagricultural occupation in 1938. Third, we searched—not very successfully—for a variable that could explain the social background of people who became peasant-workers. From cross-tabulations of different social background indicators with income measures, we concluded that children of manorial laborers who remained in the villages were probably more "peasantized" than proletarianized; thus we created a dummy labeled MANORIAL which took the value 1 for those whose fathers were manorial laborers in 1938. As we will see, this was a questionably successful move, but since MANORIAL, in particular when combined with our new measure of the effects of land reform, does offer certain theoretical insights, we have left it in our sample selection models, despite its statistical weaknesses.

2. We tried to comprehend the effects of the 1945 land reform rather better. Our main aim was to create variables which would distinguish clearly between people who were put on a "peasant" trajectory by the land reform and those who moved toward entrepreneurship. Thus we created two new variables, REFORME (a measure of land reform encouraging entrepreneurship), and REFORMPW (a measure of land reform with a "peasantizing" effect). REFORME was a dummy which took the value 1 for families that owned land in 1944 but had increased the size of their landholding by 1949—thus showing an entrepreneurial attitude. REFORMPW was a dummy which took the value 1 for families who owned no land in 1944 but had become landowners by 1949. REFORME worked beautifully; it proved to be one of the most powerful measures of entrepreneurship we found, but because the *N* behind value 1 in this variable was too small we decided not to include it in the sample selection model. REFORMPW performed reasonably well in cross-tabulations with income measures, typically better than the old REFORM variable; we decided to substitute REFORMPW for REFORM.

Thus our final choice of variables for Model D′ is: PFARM44, REFORMPW, MANORIAL, and NONAGR38.

The performance of the new mobility variables in the sample selection models

The fine-tuning of our mobility variables was basically successful. As long as FAPC was used as the dependent variable, in conformity with our hypothesis, the fine-tuning did not really affect the goodness of fit of the model: the −2*loglikelihood value was 11,394 for Model D/FAPC and went down to 11,312 for Model D′/FAPC, which is a significant though not too impressive improvement in fit. When FAPS1 is used as a dependent variable, then, unfortunately, the fit deteriorates: −2*log-likelihood was 17,648 for Model D/FAPS1 but increased to 17,670 for Model D′/FAPS1. This is the only step in our analysis where we violated the principles of nested model building. In order to have theoretically "cleaner" variables we replaced two variabes from Model D when we developed Model D′ (OFARM44 became PFARM44; REFORM became REFORMPW). Although the deterioration of the model with the more precise but empirically weaker variables concerns us, we think the exercise was necessary. Furthermore, at the second cutoff point on FAPS the fit of the fine-tuned model—despite our violation of nested model building—improves slightly but significantly: the loglikelihood value decreases from 7550 for Model D/FAPS2 to 7506 for Model D′/FAPS2, a quite encouraging result.

We now turn to analysis of the individual models.

Model D′/FAPC

From a comparison of Tables 5.9 and 6.3 it is clear that fine-tuning the mobility variables left the relative strength of the nonmobility variables basically unchanged. The new mobility variables, with the exception of NONAGR38, which is quite robust, perform modestly. PFARM44 is much weaker than OFARM44 was. In Model D/FAPC, OFARM44 was strongly significant and positive in the probit equation and, although it lost some of its power, remained positive and significant in the substantive equation. PFARM44, however, is not significant in the first equation, and becomes only marginally significant in the second. We like this result: PFARM44 performs more in line with our theory than OFARM44 did. After all, a middle- and rich-peasant background should not play an important role in explaining who the subsistence producers are; PFARM44 should keep its strength for the task of explaining commodity production.

NONAGR38 also performs according to our expectations. It is negative and highly significant in both equations, confirming that those whose parents held nonagricultural jobs in 1938 are the least likely to produce even their own food.

It is somewhat more difficult to interpret how REFORMPW and MANORIAL behave in the two equations. REFORMPW works in Model D′/FAPC like the old REFORM variable did in Model D/FAPC; they are both significant in the probit equation and lose their significance in the regression equation. For REFORMPW, which is now supposed to measure peasant-worker background, this is reasonable. But MANORIAL, which in two-way cross-tabulations with income indicators appeared to be almost identical with REFORMPW, and probably even a better measure of

TABLE 6.3 *Nonstandardized (NS) and standardized (ST) parameters of the sample selection model for Model D′ with FAPC as dependent variable (Model D′/FAPC; N = 7754/4389)*

	Probit			*Regression*		
	NS[a]	*ST*	*t values*	*NS*	*ST*	*t values*
AGE	.103	1.630	14.0	.006	.226	5.2
AGESQUARE	−0.001	−1.647	−13.8	−0.0001	−0.219	−4.9
ACTIVNO	.250	.269	10.3	.023	.070	9.4
HOMEDUTY	.272	.098	5.5	.014	.016	3.1
RETIRNO	.308	.216	9.3	.020	.041	6.1
CHILD	.065	.071	3.5	.007	.020	3.0
ONECOUPLE	.790	.357	17.2	.042	.049	6.3
MORECOUPLE	.844	.205	8.4	.045	.037	5.3
AGRAR	.303	.135	6.6	.011	.014	2.5
PFARM44	.057	.019	1.1	.013	.013	2.5
REFORMPW	.172	.063	3.9	.003	.003	0.5
MANORIAL	−0.052	−0.017	−1.0	.002	.002	0.3
NONAGR38	−0.395	−0.177	−10.1	−0.020	−0.023	−3.7
BOSYEAR	−0.004	−0.021	− 1.3	−0.0002	−0.002	−0.4
COPYEARS	.023	.183	9.8	.001	.022	4.2
SELFYEARS	.022	.144	7.2	.001	.025	3.7
EVENING	−0.498	−0.155	−9.0	−0.008	−0.006	−0.9
FIFTHYEAR	−0.212	−0.076	−4.5	−0.022	−0.021	−3.8
Constant					9.13	1601.9
σ	.322		93.6			
ρ	−0.1 (restricted)					
−2*loglikelihood	= 11,312					
DF	= 7,715					

Source: Our calculations from 1982–83 CSO Income, Social Mobility and Life History surveys.

[a] The nonstandardized parameters in this model were estimated from the standardized parameters with the formulae developed by Robert Mare of the University of Wisconsin–Madison. For details see the note to Table 5.6.

the social background associated with the peasant-worker destination, is now unable to produce a significant parameter and is even negative in the probit equation. How is this possible?

In light of the performance of REFORMPW and MANORIAL in Models D′/FAPC, D′/FAPS1 and D′/FAPS2, we can formulate our social mobility hypothesis for the descendants of manorial laborers as follows: in these models, MANORIAL systematically takes negative parameter values (with FAPS2 they are significantly negative) when it enters the model with REFORMPW, because REFORMPW "controls" for the effects of land reform on manorial laborers. Former manorial laborers and their descendants are indeed more prone to proletarianization than people from most other prewar origins, *except* when they were recipients of land grants during the 1945 land reform. Manorial laborers who were land-grant recipients became peasant-workers, though they are still less likely to be entrepreneurs by the 1980s than other land-grant recipients—for instance, other agricultural proletarians and their children.[12]

Model D′/FAPS1

Comparing Tables 5.11 and 6.4, we note, as mentioned earlier, that fine-tuning the mobility variables produced a worse fit. The bad news is that for both demographic measures and mobility variables the value of

[12] We conducted experiments with restrictions imposed on our models; they supported this hypothesis. In Chapters 5 and 6 we had to impose certain restrictions on our models to make them fit the data. These restrictions became necessary since there was an unacceptably high correlation in all these models between the errors of the unexplained variance of the two equations, measured by ρ. Such high ρ values occur when very different laws govern the functioning of the two equations. Not surprisingly the need for restrictions is greater when we begin to close in on our "target population," the real entrepreneurs. These entrepreneurs are selected according to different criteria from peasant-worker producers and their behavior is governed differently than is the behavior of most other family agricultural producers. We still succeeded in fitting these models by restricting the value of ρ between -0.1 and $+0.6$ in the various models. The restrictions imposed on the value of ρ do mainly two things: (1) they affect the goodness of fit statistics; and (2) they regulate the distance between the parameters in the two equations. -2*loglikelihood values reach their lowest point at a certain restricted ρ value, and changing these values in any direction will reduce the goodness of fit of the model. In figuring out the value at which to retrict ρ we were guided by these goodness of fit statistics. Typically the restriction of ρ values has little effect on the relative explanatory power of the individual variables within each equation; it effects mainly how close or distant, numerically, the parameters are in the two equations. But on some occasions the relative explanatory power of the individual variables is also affected—REFORMPW and MANORIAL are cases in point. For instance, we experimented with increasing the restricted value of ρ in Model D′/FAPS1. In Table 6.4 ρ was restricted to $+0.2$, but we ran the same model with ρ values ranging from $+0.3$ to $+0.9$. As we increased the restriction from $+0.2$ to $+0.9$, MANORIAL and REFORMPW began to behave in complementary fashion; REFORMPW became increasingly positive, whereas MANORIAL became increasingly negative, and at one point even significant. We take this as indirect evidence that the relationship between the two variables is indeed what we hypothesized: the more we allow REFORMPW to act as a variable explaining orientation toward commodity production, the more MANORIAL becomes a variable of proletarianization. Or, to put it differently: if the behavior of manorial workers who were land-grant recipients is captured by REFORMPW, then MANORIAL will explain only the behavior of nonrecipient former manorial laborers—indeed a story of proletarianization.

TABLE 6.4 *Nonstandardized (NS) and standardized (ST) parameters of the sample selection model for Model D′ with FAPS as dependent variable (Model D′/FAPS1; cut off point 5000 Ft; (N = 7754/3703)*

	Probit			*Regression*		
	NS[a]	*ST*	*t values*	*NS*	*ST*	*t values*
AGE	.053	.839	7.4	.016	.276	2.6
AGESQUARE	−0.001	−0.940	−8.2	−0.0002	−0.360	−3.4
ACTIVNO	.119	.128	5.2	.081	.109	5.7
HOMEDUTY	.097	.035	2.1	−0.027	−0.013	1.0
RETIRNO	.140	.098	4.5	−0.007	−0.006	−0.4
CHILD	−0.001	−0.001	−0.04	.014	.017	1.0
ONECOUPLE	.367	.166	8.1	.111	.058	3.2
MORECOUPLE	.416	.101	4.5	.006	.002	0.1
AGRAR	.429	.191	10.7	.134	.080	6.0
PFARM44	.268	.090	5.4	.090	.042	3.5
REFORMPW	.169	.062	3.9	.023	.011	0.9
MANORIAL	−0.046	−0.015	−0.9	−0.055	−0.023	−1.8
NONAGR38	−0.346	−0.155	−9.0	−0.076	−0.037	−2.3
BOSYEAR	−0.001	−0.006	−0.4	.006	.035	2.5
COPYEARS	.036	.290	16.0	.007	.075	6.0
SELFYEARS	.022	.143	8.3	.008	.072	5.6
EVENING	−0.096	−0.030	−1.8	.105	.036	2.4
FIFTHYEAR	−0.232	−0.083	−5.0	−0.031	−0.013	−0.9
Constant					9.80	705.2
σ	.766		85.9			
ρ	−0.2 (restricted)					
−2*loglikelihood	= 17,670					
DF	= 7,715					

Source: Our calculations from 1982–83 CSO Income, Social Mobility and Life History surveys.

[a] The nonstandardized parameters in this model were estimated from the standardized parameters with the formulae developed by Robert Mare of the University of Wisconsin–Madison. For details see the note to Table 5.6.

the parameters was generally reduced in the probit equation. The good news is threefold:

1. In the fine-tuned model (D′/FAPS1) the new mobility variables perform better in the regression equation than the equivalent variables did in Model D/FAPS1. In the probit equation, the fine-tuned PFARM44 and REFORMPW have lower parameters and lesser *t*

values than OFARM44 and REFORM had in Model D/FAPS1. But as we move to the substantive equation, PFARM44 and REFORMPW improve their performance over OFARM44 and REFORM in the old model. This is what we would hope for PFARM44, which as a measure of embourgeoisement, should better explain who produces more commodities and does not really have to predict who produces at all.

2. The inclusion of NONAGR38 is a smashing success. This new variable is highly significant in both equations, and particularly in the probit equation it contributes greatly to the explanatory power of the whole model, ranking as the sixth most powerful variable. In the substantive equation, as anticipated from our theory, it plays a less important but still significant role. MANORIAL's parameters are negative and nonsignificant in both equations, though the variable approaches significance in the regression equation. By itself this could not be interpreted, but if we consider MANORIAL and REFORMPW together as hypothesized earlier, it is clear why MANORIAL cannot in itself contribute much to the explanation of commodity production.
3. In the probit equation, the life history variables pick up some of the explanatory power that the social mobility variables lose. This is reassuring, because we justified replacing OFARM44 with PFARM44 on the ground that OFARM44 was a mixture of social mobility and life history measures. With PFARM44, we have more closely addressed our measurement to the social mobility problem.

Model D′/FAPS1 produced a worse fit than Model D/FAPS1, but the battery of mobility variables did gain from our fine-tuning operation. In the substantive equation of Model D/FAPS1, only one of the two mobility variables had a significant association with increasing commodity production; in Model D′/FAPS1, two out of the four mobility variables have a significant association, and a third variable produces an almost significant value. Particularly in the substantive equation, the three stronger mobility measures accumulate an impressive aggregate parameter value. Thus the fine-tuning was beneficial for the model in general, and it strongly supported the embourgeoisement theory from which the new mobility variables were created or fine-tuned.

Model D′/FAPS2

Our fine-tuning operation was more successful at the second cutoff point in FAPS. Model D/FAPS2 was until now our least successful model, but Model D′/FAPS2 produces a significantly better fit. (The loglikelihood was reduced from 7550 to 7506, whereas the degrees of freedom were reduced by only 4.) Furthermore, the mobility-variable battery of Model D′/FAPS2 performs much better than before in the substantive equation of the model. Thus we are making substantial progress in our search for an answer to one of our key questions: what explains successful entrepreneurship and which entrepreneurs will produce more (Table 6.5)?

The slight loss in strength of PFARM44 in comparison with OFARM44 in both equations (compare Tables 5.12 and 6.5) is more than compensated for by the impressive performance of NONAGR38 and by the

TABLE 6.5 *Nonstandardized (NS) and standardized (ST) parameters of the sample selection model for Model D′ with FAPS as dependent variable (Model D′/FAPS2; cutoff point 24,000 Ft; (N = 7754/1254)*

	Probit			*Regression*		
	NS	*ST*	*t values*	*NS*	*ST*	*t values*
AGE	.054	.852	5.3	.025	.391	2.4
AGESQUARE	−0.006	−1.110	−6.6	−0.0003	−0.537	−3.2
ACTIVNO	.165	.177	6.2	.075	.081	3.3
HOMEDUTY	.049	.017	0.9	−0.020	−0.007	−0.5
RETIRNO	.051	.036	1.4	−0.008	−0.005	−0.2
CHILD	−0.012	−0.013	−0.5	.003	.003	0.1
ONECOUPLE	.515	.232	7.9	.206	.093	3.0
MORECOUPLE	.454	.110	4.0	.179	.043	1.7
AGRAR	.421	.187	9.1	.213	.095	5.5
PFARM44	.209	.070	3.8	.124	.041	2.9
REFORMPW	.094	.034	1.8	.118	.043	2.5
MANORIAL	−0.058	−0.019	−0.9	−0.114	−0.037	−2.1
NONAGR38	−0.307	−0.138	−5.8	−0.134	−0.059	−2.5
BOSYEAR	.009	.044	2.7	.012	.056	3.5
COPYEARS	.026	.214	11.2	.006	.046	2.9
SELFYEARS	.021	.258	9.9	.011	.130	5.4
EVENING	.062	.019	0.9	.023	.007	0.4
FIFTHYEAR	−0.086	−0.030	−1.4	−0.033	−0.118	−0.6
Constant					10.06	394.4
σ	.551		47.1			
ρ	.6 (restricted)					
−2*loglikelihood	= 7,506					
DF	= 7,715					

Source: Our calculations from 1982–83 CSO Income, Social Mobility and Life History surveys.

improvement, in the regression equation, in the strength of REFORMPW (Model D′/FAPS2) over REFORM (Model D/FAPS2). REFORMPW has a positive and solidly significant parameter, whereas REFORM lost more power at this stage. That positive, significant association with increased commodity production among entrepreneurs was not anticipated. We had tried to fine-tune REFORMPW in order to measure social background for the peasant-worker destination; now it appears to explain entrepreneurship, and rather better than the old "embourgeoisement" variable, REFORM! But if we explore REFORMPW in conjunction with MANORIAL, in light of their hypothesized relationship, then at least half of the mystery can be solved. MANORIAL in the regression equation of Model D′/FAPS2 remains negative, as in most equations and models in Chapter 6, but it does become significant. How to interpret this? Perhaps those landless families that received land during the 1945 land reform have become very big entrepreneurs by 1982, though manorial laborers in general, particularly if they were not land-grant recipients, are less likely to be big commodity producers.

Finally, after this variable-by-variable analysis, we can comment on how the whole mobility-variable battery performs in comparison with other groups of variables as we close in on the big commodity producers. From this perspective, fine-tuning appears to be a success. In Model D/FAPS2, one out of the two mobility variables in the substantive equation of Table 5.12 was only marginally significant; in Model D′/FAPS2 all four variables in the mobility variable battery are significant (one only marginally) in the same equation. At the same time, the demographic variables derived from the proletarianization theory keep losing their explanatory power. In the regression equation of Model D/FAPS2, four out of the eight demographic variables were nonsignificant; in the same equation of Model D′/FAPS2 the proportion of significant to nonsignificant demographic variables remains the same, but the t values generally decline for most such variables.

It is interesting to compare in this way Tables 6.3, 6.4, and 6.5. We divide our variables into two groups: the first nine are derived from the proletarianization theory (demography and current agrarian occupation), the second nine from our interpretation of the interrupted embourgeoisement theory (mobility and life history). Moving from Table 6.3 to Tables 6.4 and 6.5 in the regression equation, the number of nonsignificant variables from the first group keeps increasing, from zero in Model D′/FAPC to four in Models D′/FAPS1 and D′/FAPS2. For the second group of variables, the reverse occurs: the number of nonsignificant variables keeps declining, from four in Model D′/FAPC, to three in Model D′/FAPS1 and two in Model D′/FAPS2.

We are still not very good at identifying the more successful entrepreneurs among commodity producers. But the variables which we created and fine-tuned on the basis of our interrupted embourgeoisement theory perform more effectively than the variables created from the proletarianization theory.

We hope that with the fine-tuning of the life history variables we will be able to make further progress along these lines in Chapter 7. It is not unreasonable to argue that life history analysis is particularly important in explaining which producers become genuine entrepreneurs. What makes entrepreneurs exceptionally successful may depend a great deal on relatively idiosyncratic factors having more to do with personality and individual life experience than with family inheritance, and particularly with demographic factors. If this is true, then we may have to accept that the task of explaining entrepreneurial success may be to some extent beyond sociology as such. But if the task can be approached at all with sociological methods, then success should lie within the analysis of individual life histories.

7

Beyond family inheritance

The importance of life history for the reemergence of embourgeoisement

It is time to fine-tune our life history variables. We begin with people from the "right background," born into families already moving toward entrepreneurship before or shortly after World War II. We try to identify more precisely those sequences of jobs after 1949 (or, for those who began their working lives later, since the first job) which served as "parking orbits." We anticipate that reentry to an embourgeoisement trajectory will prove, historically speaking, to be possible from such parking orbits. We also try to identify those occupational choices which proved to be "fatal" for embourgeoisement, which put people irreversibly on proletarian or cadre trajectories. We then analyze the careers of people from the "wrong background," from small-, poor-peasant, or rural proletarian, nonentrepreneurial families. As we saw in Chapter 6, some of these people became entrepreneurs during the 1970s. We seek to identify those educational and occupational choices which kept people from such backgrounds in the proletariat, headed them toward proletarian status, or moved them toward the cadre. And we also look for those schooling patterns and job sequences which helped people from the "wrong background" to enter the embourgeoisement trajectory and to become protoentrepreneurs or entrepreneurs by the late 1970s, or early 1980s.

This chapter follows the pattern of the two that precede it: we begin with a theoretical, speculative section, supported with ethnographic evidence, then conclude by entering a new set of refined and expanded life history variables into the equations of our sample selection models.[1]

[1] In this chapter we also rely on tape-recorded interviews conducted with Pál Juhász and Bálint Magyar and on our own field experiences in rural Hungary.

TOWARD A TYPOLOGY OF LIFE HISTORIES

We begin with former rich and middle peasants. We work out hypothetical life trajectories since World War II and try to identify parking orbits (Figures 7.1, 7.2). Next, we go to the bottom of the social hierarchy and move upward. We explore the typical life histories of former manorial laborers (Figure 7.3), poor peasants, and small peasants (Figure 7.4), and we look for the lucky conjunctions of their stars that gave them autonomy from the rank hierarchy of social stratification by 1982. Within each social group we conduct a cohort-by-cohort analysis. We assume that the *historical timing* of occupational and educational choices may be crucial. One had to do different things in the 1950s, in the Stalinist era (1945–56), during the 1960s, in the prereform era, and after the 1968 reforms to be able successfully to resist the pressures toward proletarianization and cadrefication, which were undoubtedly greatest during the Stalinist years. To begin one's career during the late 1940s or early 1950s handicapped prospects for future entrepreneurship, but with a little luck and the right strategy the handicap could be overcome. Analogously, those who were lucky enough to begin adult life in the 1960s or particularly the 1970s generally had a better chance to move gradually toward greater autonomy from the bureaucratic rank order, but through bad luck or wrong decisions they could lose this relative advantage and end up at a proletarian or cadre destination. A cohort-by-cohort analysis may enable us to identify how one could compensate for the "bad luck" of being born at the "wrong" time.

Kulaks: from pauperization to professionalization

The oldest cohort of wealthier peasants: effects of the antikulak policies of the 1950s

The top 5 to 10 percent of the rural population, rich peasants with landholdings above 20 or 25 holds[2] and the owners of the larger shops, large machines (tractors, combines), and small factories were in 1949 labeled by the authorities as agricultural or industrial kulaks. The years which followed were most traumatic for them. They were severely persecuted until 1953 and discriminated against for several years thereafter. Most kulaks were pauperized and proletarianized during the 1950s. Of those who left for the cities, some became déclassé, others

[2] According to Berend and Ránki (1972, p. 230) they represented about 6 percent of all farms in 1949.

later climbed back to skilled working-class or lower managerial positions. Those who remained in the villages began once again to consolidate their positions in the early 1960s. They gradually re-established themselves in the rural social hierarchy, at a somewhat lower location but still in reasonably affluent and prestigious positions as small entrepreneurs or small cadres.

Their children, particularly those who started adult life between 1949 and 1953 (to a lesser extent those became adults before 1960) faced very hard times for a while. Those who began their careers after 1949 usually left the villages and rarely returned. If they took their first jobs during the Stalinist epoch, they became elite workers; if they began under Kadar, they became professionals, mostly in engineering, a few in agriculture. Figure 7.1 summarizes their life trajectories.

During the early 1950s almost all adult "industrial kulaks," owners of large shops, mills, tractors or combines, or small industrial firms, and the large animal traders (particularly horse and cattle—the *koupetz*) left for the city. Among the agriculturalists it was mainly the largest who followed them, mostly those who were not only put on "kulak" lists by the authorities but were also regarded by the villagers as kulaks and exploiters. These were the rich peasants, owning more than 50 holds, sometimes even several hundred holds. They were peasant-entrepreneurs who did little or no manual work but were full-time managers and supervisors, and who made themselves unpopular among the villagers by their harsh manners, greed, or iron-fisted labor discipline. The official "kulak" lists were much longer. As zealous village cadres wanted to prove to their county or urban superiors how alert they were, they began to expand the kulak lists to include many of the smaller peasant-burghers who were rather organically integrated into the village community (Orbán, 1972, pp. 74–78; Bell, 1984, p. 113). Peasants with 20–50-hold farms, small agricultural entrepreneurs who employed wage labor only occasionally, at peak season, who often worked side-by-side with their laborers, who married women from small- or middle-peasant families, and who had relatives and friends in the villages were put on the kulak lists too.

These were people who had often started their lives as small or middle peasants and became reasonably wealthy only because they had better luck or were more able farmer-entrepreneurs than the rural average. They were often popular elected officials of the village government and played an important political role after 1945. Many of them were the organizers and leaders of the Small Peasant Party (*Kisgazda Párt*), the liberal bourgeois party which won the overwhelming majority

	Life events			
	1949–53	1953–60	1960–70	After 1970
Those who started adult life before 1949	Industrial kulaks move to cities	Some become successful middle peasants	Coop leaders	Most involved in family agricultural production, mainly as small entrepreneurs
	Agricultural kulaks pauperized; many move to cities	Others are déclassé to lower layers of middle peasants	Lower kolkhoz management, wagon drivers, etc.	
Those who started adult life in 1949–54	All move to cities, become workers, learn skills	Most stay in city		Form consolidated middle layer, workers' aristocracy in industry or kolkhozes. Highly paid, no family agricultural production, "proletarianized"
		A few return, become middle layer in villages		
	Those who started adult life in 1954–60	Boys go to technical schools, girls to grammar schools		Most become engineers or technicians in cities
				Few who return to village become skilled, well-paid workers' aristocracy, "proletarianized"
		Those who started adult life after 1960		Typically get college training, mainly engineering, some in agriculture; cadrefied or professionalized

FIGURE 7.1 *Life history trajectories of kulaks or those whose parents were kulaks in 1944*

of votes during the first postwar elections in most villages (Bell, 1984, pp. 110–11).

These "lesser kulaks" were often put on the kulak lists for political motives: labeling them as kulaks was part of the struggle for political power in the villages. Unlike "real kulaks" they often enjoyed a significant popular support that was vitally important to their chance for future survival. Kinship networks, for instance, were critical; these "lesser kulaks" might be able to hide their crops and some of their belongings from the "requisitioners" in the houses of relatives and even friendly neighbors. They had psychological and the minimal material support to fend off starvation and to be able to start again after 1953.

But even these lesser, luckier, more popular rich peasants slid downward in the social hierarchy of the villages. Most importantly, they lost most of their land. By 1953 there were virtually no families with more than 20 holds of land. Even though the 1945 land reform distributed only the land of those who farmed over 200 holds (Berend and Ránki, 1972, p. 228), supplementary legislation and, even more typically, purely administrative measures gradually took land away from larger peasants.

An effective method of virtually eliminating rich peasants was the repeated reallocation of land which occurred in conjunction with the organization of state farms and the first agricultural cooperatives between 1948 and 1953 (Orbán, 1972, pp. 103–6; Bell, 1984, p. 118). As the new latifundia were created, local authorities reallocated land, giving valuable, centrally located land to the new state farms or the kolkhozes and marginal land to rich peasants, land not only remote but often poor or unsuitable farmland. The exercise of "reallocation" was sometimes repeated, as long as the former rich peasants continued to give in and accept that their land was lost.

After 1953 the antikulak measures were eased; in 1954 some of those on the kulak lists were "rehabilitated,"[3] and after 1956 the kulak lists were abolished altogether. There was even some talk about giving land back to rich peasants. In 1957 committes were set up to return land to owners from whom it had been illegally expropriated, but these committees merely legitimated the status quo. People who dared to apply to get their land back were told why they could not have it, but as far as we know, no significant amount of land was ever given back to private owners (Orbán, 1972, p. 165). In other words, the minority of agricultural kulaks who remained in the villages were reduced at best to a middle- or small-peasant existence.

[3] In Dunapataj, for example, according to Bálint Magyar, 27 families were removed from the list of 90.

A few of them took advantage of the brief prosperity of private farming between 1957 and 1959. Together with the most successful middle peasants, they attempted to pick up farming again where they had left off in 1949 and to move toward entrepreneurship. The rest of the former kulaks—possibly the majority—settled for a normal, more cautious and withdrawn middle-peasant existence. They had no interest in sticking their heads up above the crowd again. From here onward, the life history of most former kulaks is basically indistinguishable from that of the middle peasants.

The few more adventurous kulaks, together with the most successful middle peasants, were in 1960 elected presidents or other high-ranking officials of the newly formed kolkhozes. This usually did not happen during the first few hectic months of collectivization, but a few months or a year later, when the first kolkhoz amalgamations took place and some of the most incompetent early political appointees to kolkhoz leadership were replaced by people with more grassroots support and local prestige.

But the majority of former kulaks did not turn into cadres. Like most middle peasants, they joined the kolkhozes, and quite a few of them became lower managerial personnel or took other reasonably prestigious or autonomous positions; for example, they became wagon drivers.[4]

As entrepreneurial opportunities reopened both categories of former kulaks turned toward the second economy. But relatively few of them became large entrepreneurs. Most of those who were wealthy peasants themselves before the war were growing too old. The younger ones, having bitter experience of changing political fortunes, played it safe and kept a relatively low profile.[5] They joined the ranks of the smaller entrepreneurs or the market-oriented peasant-workers.

The next cohorts of people from a rich-peasant background had a drastically different life history.

Beginning adult life under Stalinism: "rotten egg from the wrong basket"

Those who became adults during the Stalinist epoch had a horrible start in life. Almost without exception they went to the cities. Their

[4] Wagon drivers were quite powerful and had a great deal of prestige. They controlled a strategically important, scarce resource, means of transportation. They were courted by most people in the kolkhoz. They could also set their own schedules and could not be tightly controlled by the central bureaucracy, so from time to time they could get transport for their own family plots. Mainly the former horse owners became wagon drivers; they knew how to handle horses, so they were often allowed to drive their own horses, which they had surrendered to the kolkhoz when they were forced to join.

[5] The youngest of those who were already active in 1944 were around 55 in 1975.

parents' farms were pauperized and could not even support the old folks, and there was no other place for them in the villages. The children of the wealthier peasants were treated as "rotten eggs from the wrong basket."[6] Life was impossible for them in the villages; they had to try their luck in cities. Paradoxically, many of them ended up in major new industrial constructions among the "socialist pioneers," for instance in the new city of Sztálinváros, the "socialist city" of the 1950s, built about a hundred kilometers south of Budapest. Sztálinváros was designed to become the "city of iron," the center of steel industry in Hungary, a country without iron ore or coal of sufficient quality. Despite the absurdity of the whole conception, Sztálinváros somehow created a sort of enthusiasm.

It was a frontier, a Wild West for the early 1950s. Construction jobs in Sztálinváros attracted not only the ideologically most dedicated, but also, or even more so, the outcasts, adventurers, criminals. The sons of kulaks fitted into this environment. They could hide there. Labor was short and screening of workers more relaxed. Their kulak origins were not easily discovered or were ignored. They could get reasonable jobs and learn skills. Many soon became respected foremen or skilled workers, and only a minority of them slid into the lumpenproletariat. Between 1953 and 1960 some returned to their native villages, though many remained urban skilled workers, gradually even becoming an urban workers' aristocracy. The rural return migrants had relatively little difficulty in finding work. Their newly acquired skills were sought after by many rural industrial firms within the state or the kolkhoz sector, and in rural commercial institutions. Many former kulak return migrants became skilled workers or even foremen in the industrial producers' cooperatives, and during the late 1960s some were active in setting up the industrial secondary activities of the kolkhozes. Kálmán Rupp has written a delightful book, *Entrepreneurs in Red* (1983), about kolkhoz industrial operations, set up mainly by urban outmigrants. But kulak return migrants also played a role.

Thus sons and daughters of former kulaks who started their adult lives between 1949 and 1956 were proletarianized, though by the late 1970s or early 1980s, at around 45 or 50 years of age, they had ended up in the highest strata of the rural proletariat. In today's villages they are among the most highly skilled, well-paid workers; they often fill middle

[6] Jonathan Unger in his wonderful book, *The Chen Village* (1983), analyzes the quasiracist implications of this Maoist concept of the "blood line"—the idea that children from the "wrong families" should be collectively punished for the "crimes" of their parents. Stalinism had no such explicit ideology, but Stalinist practices were identical to or worse than Maoist ones.

managerial positions, with a fair amount of authority and autonomy. But they are proletarianized; they have become wage laborers. They are unlikely to be among our new agricultural entrepreneurs and may not be particularly strongly represented among the industrial or commercial entrepreneurs either.

Beginning adult life after 1956: entry into the new professional elite

The next two cohorts of kulak descendants were much more fortunate than their parents or older siblings. Those who completed primary school by 1956 could get into reasonable urban schools. Between 1953 and 1960 boys went to *technikums*, where they were trained as highly qualified technicians or lower-level engineers.[7] Girls attended grammar schools, or *gimnaziums*, academically-oriented high schools, with good chances of university admittance. After graduation most stayed in the city, the men to become engineers or technicians, the women often doctors or other highly trained professionals. Those who returned to the villages were highly trained workers in rare and sought-after occupations, like electricians, blacksmiths, or toolmakers. They became the cream of the rural workers' aristocracy, often quite critical of the middle-peasant rural leadership of the 1960s. They were the potential and often de facto allies of the agricultural intelligentsia in their struggle against the middle-peasant rural cadre. The two groups fought together for the industrialization of agriculture and the scientific-technical revolution of industry, complemented by Taylorist methods of labor organization.

The next cohort of kulak descendants fared even better. Those who started postprimary education after 1960 went through their training and started their careers highly motivated and facing no prejudice. Most of the sons and daughters of former kulaks in this cohort went to college, mainly in engineering though there were some agricultural engineers. Whereas the earlier cohort of kulak children had become political allies of the new agricultural intelligentsia, this later cohort, together with some descendants of former middle-peasant families, formed the very core of the new professional elite. Thus the kulak families within 30 or 40 years had made a full circle: in 1945 they began as the rural elite; they became pauperized and proletarianized during the 1950s, and were pushed to the very bottom of the social hierarchy. But by the 1980s their children or grandchildren had become a new professional elite.

Two case studies from Dunapataj, both described by Bálint Magyar, illustrate the progress of former kulaks toward professionalization.

[7] This is still secondary training, for students between 14 and 18 years old.

Gyula Váradi started adult life around 1953. His family lost about 100 holds during the Stalinist years and he himself was drafted into the army before 1956. Here he learned how to drive trucks, and when he returned around 1960 to Dunapataj the newly formed Petöfi kolkhoz hired him as manager of their truck operation. Over the years he proved to be an able manager. He learned more industrial skills and began to organize profitable industrial and transportation sidelines for the kolkhoz (this time for the larger Uj Elet Kolkhoz). By the turn of the 1970s he was a respected and influential man. The agricultural intelligentsia, which around that time launched its attack against the middle-peasant cadre in Dunapataj, found an important ally in him.

Gyula Nagy is the grandson of another former kulak, whose family also owned over 100 holds. He is some 10–15 years younger than Gyula Váradi. Nagy, whose father settled into a slightly déclassé middle-peasant existence and became a middle manager in one of the Dunapataj cooperatives, was trained in college as an agricultural engineer. First he became the agricultural engineer of the large prison farm at Allampuszta, just outside Dunapataj, where some 4000 convicts worked. Gyula Nagy fought his first war with the "peasants" here. He complained bitterly about the peasant convicts who did not value his technical knowledge and expressed his preference for working with working-class convicts who accepted his authority and followed his instructions. After having been trained against the stubborn peasants, he got a job as the agrarian engineer responsible for animal husbandry in the Uj Elet Kolkhoz, joining the ranks of the agricultural intelligentsia, already solidly in power there.

A former poor-peasant cadre, Mrs Rejtő, who was town clerk during the 1950s in Dunapataj, told Zsolt Csalogh: "These kulaks outsmarted us once again—they got degrees and now they are privileged again, though in a different way than they were." There is an element of truth in this. Kulak families did indeed "bounce back," but, interestingly enough for our theory—they were almost always lost to the cause of embourgeoisement. They may have become an elite again, but they are not an entrepreneurial elite. They are more likely to belong to the professional–cadre elite or to the highly privileged workers' aristocracy than to excel themselves in the reemerging market-based system of social stratification. Under great pressure during the Stalinist years they were unable to find parking orbits and frequently became "over-qualified" for reentry to the embourgeoisement trajectory.

With the former vanguard of embourgeoisement thus déclassé or firmly in professional or cadre ranks, pursuit of that destination falls to the social group next in line, the former middle peasants and their children.

Middle peasants: in search of parking orbits

With the kulaks removed from their way, middle peasants and their children had the best prospects of becoming the new vanguard of entrepreneurship. They had family entrepreneurial traditions and were also more likely to stay in the villages during the crucial 1950s and early 1960s, when both wealthier and poorer people left for the cities and were proletarianized. The middle and small peasants stayed, partly because they owned land and partly because their families expected them to stay.

Thus most of them survived the early dangers of proletarianization, only to be tempted by cadre status during the early 1960s. As we have seen in Chapter 6, for most former middle peasants the temptation proved to be passing; most of them had lost their managerial jobs to the new agricultural intelligentsia by the early 1970s and were ready to reenter embourgeoisement exactly at the time that opportunities began to open up. The younger cohorts were also repeatedly tempted by the possibilities of the cadre, and some of the children of former middle peasants who started adult life after 1960 did become professionals, but many followed their parents toward entrepreneurship (Figure 7.2).

Parking orbits in the 1950s: self-employment or commuting to urban, industrial jobs

For the middle peasants the most successful strategy for staying in a parking orbit during the 1950s was to remain in the village. The younger generation had to commute to urban workplaces, but they too maintained rural residence and learned skills that in the future would be useful in farming.

Staying in the villages made a lot of sense for middle peasants, who did reasonably well in these years. In some ways they were socially upwardly mobile. Their former major competitors, the large estate owners and the rich peasants, were removed and they found themselves suddenly at the top of the social hierarchy. But the exploitative requisition system and antiagricultural, antipeasant policies of the Stalinist administration made them also net losers. Their standard of living declined after 1949, but they were at least partially compensated for this by the increase in their social status. The local party and government, in search of grassroots support, often promoted many

	Life events		
	1949–60	1960–70	After 1970
Those who started adult life before 1949	With kulaks removed, they become the new peasant elite, council members, etc. →	Become new kolkhoz leaders →	After intelligentsia win, become entrepreneurs
	Others are alienated, stay on land, but oppose regime's antipeasant policies →	Some escape "third serfdom," go to cities →	Some who left return
		Others become kolkhoz workers →	They start entrepreneurship early, but remain small
Those who started adult life in 1949–60	Almost all become industrial workers, but keep commuting and by late 1960s return to work in villages →	Some become rural artisans (bricklayers, electricians) →	Become industrial entrepreneurs
		Others join kolkhoz as tractor drivers, skilled workers →	Become agricultural entrepreneurs
	Those who started adult life in 1960s →	Minority learn agricultural skills, become mechanics experts in animal husbandry →	Become workers' aristocracy in kolkhoz
		Marjority learn industrial skills, become skilled workers. Some become agricultural engineers →	If return to village, become industrial entrepreneurs, join new technocracy
		Those who started adult life in 1970s	Many become agricultural engineers, women clerical workers, but since technocratic elite is closed, they try entrepreneurship

FIGURE 7.2 *Life history trajectories of middle peasants or those whose parents were middle peasants in 1944*

middle peasants to ceremonial political roles, put them into offices which were previously dominated by richer peasants.

Such positions could, of course, compensate only a minority of the middle peasants for what they had suffered from the requisition system. The majority were left out and did not forget what the regime had done to their slightly wealthier neighbors. This majority was not enthusiastic about the Communist regime. They were anti-Communists before 1945, were staunch Small Peasant Party supporters from 1945 to 1949 and were ready to give their support again to this party if the opportunity arose. In 1956, middle peasants were active in setting up the anti-Communist National Councils and reestablishing the Small Peasant Party organizations. But this majority, despite their opposition to Stalinism, did not find it rational to leave the villages even during the 1950s. They still had the land, and although they gradually began to prepare themselves for the inevitable collectivization, they were not yet ready to surrender their land, especially not voluntarily.

After 1960: changing attitudes toward education

Before 1960, middle peasants tried to keep their children in the villages; unlike the kulaks, they did not encourage them to get tertiary or even secondary education, hoping that their children would inherit their land. Their attitudes toward education changed quite radically after 1960, and for a decade or so enrolment of peasant children in academically-oriented programs increased. But this may be changing again as new entrepreneurial opportunities begin to open up in the early 1980s. During the 1960s and most of the 1970s, state socialism succeeded in making credentialing the single most important value; its meritocratic principles found their way even into the value system of rural society. Following collectivization, all of rural society, even the former middle peasants, began to accept that the only way to be upwardly mobile was to get an education, to receive credentials, to become an intellectual.[8]

This credentialing and meritocratic ethos of state socialism was shattered by the mid- or late 1970s. As the second economy began to open up, a second system of social hierarchy emerged in which market achievement and not rank or educational credentials was the source of wealth and prestige. As a result, members of those rural strata which are reentering embourgeoisement are losing to some extent their interest in

[8] The obsession with intellectual credentials, the practices of limiting access to decent incomes and positions of authority and prestige to those with university training, is one of the indicators of what we called earlier the rise of a "new dominant class of intellectuals"; Konrád and Szelényi, 1979.

education. Able young people from such entrepreneurial families, who just a decade ago would have fought to gain admittance into university programs, now seek vocational training and often join their fathers or fathers-in-law in the family enterprise.[9] Such apathy toward education, in particular toward university training, worries, even distresses many intellectuals.[10]

During the 1960s, appointment to bureaucratic office was the mechanism that pulled the older cohort of middle peasants from the parking orbits of embourgeoisement into the cadre. During the late 1960s and early 1970s, credentialing performed the same function for their adult children. Middle peasants who joined the kolkhoz management around 1960 and stayed for too long, significantly beyond 1970, are probably permanently lost for entrepreneurship. It is the same for their skilled sons and daughters: as the latifundia industrialized and kolkhoz management was taken over by the agricultural intelligentsia, these skilled descendants of middle peasants began to earn high wages, and by the early 1980s they were in the upper third of the rank hierarchy. Some members of this cohort were thus "credentialed out" from their parking orbits and may have little to do with agricultural or even with industrial entrepreneurship.

Those middle-peasant sons who were trained as agricultural engineers during the 1960s are a good example. Working with the sons of kulaks from the same cohort, they masterminded the intellectual coup d'état in the villages, in a sense unseating their own fathers or the friends of their fathers, and they are solidly in power today. Others from the same cohort learned very useful industrial skills, the most important of which was heavy-tractor driving. The heavy-tractor drivers during the mid-1970s played the most strategic role in the industrialization of the kolkhozes and were rewarded with high incomes. They are members of the workers' aristocracy, with a comfortable standard of living, and most of them are unwilling to push themselves into a second shift after the well-paid official working hours.

Credentialing, on the other hand, may not divert the youngest cohort of middle-peasant sons from embourgeoisement. Some of the most recent agricultural engineering graduates have begun to build their own

[9] The young chicken farmer in Hajdunánás is such an example.

[10] "What a loss of talent!" a well-established actress complained recently to us. "Just a few years ago all these young people would have become doctors, lawyers, actors, and writers and now they run farms, open shops, they become businessmen." The intellectuals may be concerned not only about the "loss of talent," but also about the challenge this alternative structure of reward and source of prestige may pose to the income privileges of university-trained people.

family enterprises, and some are joining their fathers' enterprises. Their ascendancy to prestige, income, and power has been blocked by the earlier cohort of agricultural engineers: most cadre-expert positions in the kolkhozes are occupied by men who are still in their thirties or, at most, in their early forties. Blocked mobility within the rank hierarchy pushes the youngest cohort of highly trained middle-peasant sons toward the market-based hierarchy, toward private business.

With Figures 7.1 and 7.2 we tried to explain why the kulaks lost their entrepreneurial dominance to the former middle peasants and their children. But about four-fifths of the big producers are of neither kulak nor middle-peasant background; most of them come from lower classes. How has this come about? To what extent can we explain the ascent from former proletarian or semiproletarian, poor-peasant backgrounds to entrepreneurship? To this question we now turn.

The "lower classes": how some former proletarians became entrepreneurs under socialism

Having investigated the top of the social hierarchy, let us now turn to the bottom and explore what happened between 1950 and 1980 to the lower 50 percent of presocialist rural society: the former manorial laborers, agrarian proletarians, poorest peasants, and their descendants (Figures 7.3 and 7.4).

Manorial laborers and their descendants

Among those with a manorial-laborer background the shift from proletarian status toward the embourgeoisement trajectory was difficult and rare; only a few lucky ones had achieved peasant-worker status by the late 1970s. Mostly manorial laborers and their children remained proletarian, typically at the bottom of the occupational hierarchy in both cities and villages. Ascent to cadre status was probably even more limited for them. There were, of course, individual former manorial laborers who became cadres, but this class is underrepresented in every single category of the cadre (Hanák, 1982, p. 251). Nonetheless, former manorial laborers live better than their parents or they themselves did before the war or before collectivization.

Life in the settlements: a symbol of relative immobility

Poverty, even hunger, were widespread in manorial laborer settlements until the mid-1960s. Though living standards increased thereafter, in the mid-1980s a large number of former manorial laborers and descendants were still living in these settlements, which were built,

	Life events			
	1945–49	1949–60	1960–70	After 1970
Those who were manorial laborers in 1944 →	Few get land, become peasants →	Most can't continue, form kolkhozes →	Successful ones become kolkhoz leaders →	Run peasant-worker households
			Most take low-prestige kolkhoz jobs →	Proletarians have gardens at most
	Most don't get land or lose it at once →	Become laborers on state farms →	Remain state farm laborer or work in construction industry, fully proletarian	
		move to cities		
	Those who started adult life in 1949–59 →	Become laborers on state farms →	If they stay in manorial settlements, become seasonal workers for new entrepreneurs	
		Move to cities, become unskilled workers, live in workers' shelters all their lives and hate greedy peasants		
		Those who started adult life in 1960s →	Most become unskilled workers, proletarianized	
			Some learn skills, e.g., become tractor drivers →	Become peasant-workers
			Those who started adult life in 1970s	Less likely to get into schools for skilled workers, worse off than previous cohort

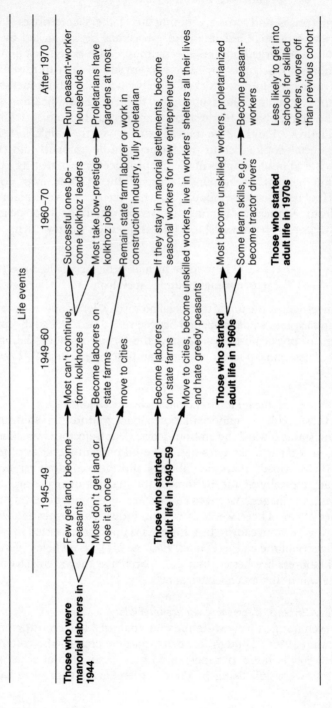

FIGURE 7.3 *Life history trajectories of former manorial laborers and their children*

mostly during the nineteenth century, by the large landlords to house their yearly contract laborers. Today they represent, after the rapidly disappearing gypsy colonies, the worst housing in Hungary. In a typical manorial settlement (*cselédtelep*), small flats were built in rows, each row containing half a dozen, a dozen, or more such units.[11] The manorial settlements—their population varies from half a dozen to several dozen families—were usually built far away from the villages, and even today they may be without electricity and running water. Some have been abolished, others upgraded, but most just survive basically unaltered (at best, they are connected to electricity and the road is paved). The population of the manorial settlements stays nearly constant. As the older generation dies out there are always children and grandchildren to occupy the old units; there are always enough "circular migrants" who had temporarily left for the villages or cities and are ready to return to keep such settlements alive.

The persistence of these manorial settlements symbolizes the limited prospects for mobility of the former manorial-laborer population. Life in these settlements has improved; people have more food than before and are well clothed, but their prospects for changing their own or their children's position in either social hierarchy, the rank hierarchy or the market, are limited.

Upward mobility trajectories

Within this general immobility we could identify at least two life history trajectories which offered some upward mobility, some movement from a proletarian existence toward embourgeoisement. On the first such trajectory are those former manorial laborers who received land in the 1945 land reform and between 1945 and 1949 proved that they knew what to do with it. In the land reform, which was in the hands of the village peasants, manorial laborers were somewhat discriminated against. The peasants regarded manorial laborers as "lumpen" elements who did not deserve land grants and who would not know what to do with land anyway. Manorial laborers, therefore, were frequently left out; if they did not show up in time or had not yet returned from prisoner-of-war camps in Russia, they found themselves without land. Of the 250,000 manorial-laborer families, only about 100,000 received land (Orbán, 1972, p. 42; Donáth, 1977, p. 22).

In a classic self-fulfilling prophecy, some manorial laborers proved the "undeserving poor" stereotype. Without the peasants' agricultural and technical knowledge, they mismanaged their farms and, although it

[11] Each flat contains a kitchen in front and a room at the back, with a very small garden in front of the unit.

was against the law, some even sold them. Others, however, broke loose from the stereotype, survived the first years, and by 1949 had established themselves as fairly respectable small peasants. The population of the manorial settlements was traditionally quite stratified. Those who successfully became peasants during the late 1940s presumably came from the top of the social hierarchy of such settlements (Pál Juhász, personal communication). They were mainly self-selected unofficial, popular leaders or "foremen" (*bandagazda*), who negotiated collective contracts with the officials of the latifundia and guaranteed discipline within their communities. They achieved their positions either by being the sons of former leaders or by showing enough skill or charisma in leadership.

Despite the skepticism of the village peasants, then, by 1949 some former manorial laborers, foremen more than rank and file, had become peasants. Indeed, this relatively successful group was important, particularly in 1948–49, in forming the few genuinely voluntary kolkhozes. Though they had proved their agricultural skills, collectivization still made more sense to them than to the village peasants. They were used to collective work organizations, had more of a sense for large-scale production, and could see the advantages of bringing back to production the abandoned but still standing agricultural buildings of the former latifundia. (Most of these buildings were quickly destroyed following land reform: peasants needed construction materials, and they also wanted to make sure that no one would recreate the latifundia system.) These cooperatives of former manorial laborers received a good share of government subsidies, too. The regime wanted them for window dressing, to show the rest of the rural population that the kolkhoz system would work. When, in 1956, the kolkhoz system fell apart, the few surviving kolkhozes were those formed by the former manorial laborers.[12] The most successful former manorial laborers, therefore, were reasonably well placed in 1960 for managerial posts within the rapidly expanding kolkhoz system, and a few did join kolkhoz management. By the late 1960s and early 1970s these successful ones were running peasant-worker household economies.

But they constituted only a minority of former manorial laborers or their descendants, who mostly lost their land, became laborers on the state farms and kept doing pretty much the same thing that they had done before land reform, working for the state instead of a private landlord. Most members of the early manorial-laborer kolkhozes did not make it to kolkhoz managerial positions after 1960; instead, they

[12] Only about 10 percent of the land remained within the kolkhoz system; see Orbán, 1972, p. 162.

were slotted into the bottom of the kolkhoz hierarchy, assigned to the least prestigious, physically most taxing, and dirtiest jobs in animal husbandry, under the managerial supervision of former middle or small peasants.

The losers: those who became adults between 1949 and 1960

The younger cohort of manorial-laborer descendants, those who entered the work force between 1949 and 1960, may be the most unfortunate of all. Left out of the land reform, they did not have the opportunity to achieve peasant status that their fathers or older brothers had. The rural job market during those years was very depressed. Some joined the state farms, typically staying in the manorial settlements, and even today at 45–55 years old they are still living there, perhaps earning a bit extra as seasonal workers for those peasants who have become the new entrepreneurs. Those from this cohort who moved to the cities in the 1950s did not fare much better. They were shovelled off to workers' shelters and many still live there after 25 or 30 years, in poverty and disorganized family conditions, pushed toward alcoholism and crime. They never had a chance to form a proper family or to own a house or rent an apartment.

The lucky cohort: those who became adults during the 1960s

The next cohort was in many respects the luckiest. During these years after collectivization, there was a lot of emphasis on training skilled workers for the kolkhozes. It was relatively easy to enter schools in which skilled agricultural workers, even tractor drivers, were trained. The sudden expansion in the training of skilled agricultural workers, particularly when the wealthier families in the villages had doubts about the future of agriculture, could not foresee the revitalization of family entrepreneurship, and were therefore encouraging their children to try their fortunes outside agriculture, opened up educational opportunities to young boys and girls from the manorial settlements. Many of them even in this epoch did not use the opportunity and either went to the state farms as laborers or ended up in the workers' shelters in the cities, but some received a solid training, and today, at the age of 35 or 40, they are respected members of the kolkhozes and running prosperous peasant-worker family economies. It appears, however, that this chance of mobility into a peasant-worker or peasant-burgher existence was, once again, a window only temporarily open onto the future. As agriculture became consolidated, the educational opportunities leading to the more prestigious agricultural occupations were monopolized once more by families from higher levels of the stratification system. For the youngest cohort of people from a manorial-laborer background, proletarianization seems to be almost the only trajectory available.

In other words, we reiterate the hypothesis presented in Table 6.2: former manorial laborers or their descendants are the most likely source of the present rural proletariat, although we can also identify at least two cohorts for which movement toward embourgeoisement was possible. Those who received land in 1945 may by the mid-1970s have moved beyond peasant status proper toward a peasant-worker existence, and those who finished primary schooling during the 1960s also had a chance to become peasant-workers or even entrepreneurs by the mid-1980s, mainly by first becoming skilled workers in the kolkhoz system.

The "Catholic work ethic" and entrepreneurial ambitions

The relative immobility of the former manorial-laborer population is a good indication that "hard work" in itself was not enough to "make it." These cohorts of former manorial laborers were hard-working, probably as much so as any other stratum of rural society. Mostly Roman Catholics, they were driven by a sort of "Catholic asceticism," which teaches self-exploitative hard work as much as the "Protestant ethos" does. When the Habsburgs, a Roman Catholic dynasty, reconquered the country from the Turks in the seventeenth century and the Catholic aristocracy returned, their serfs, the ancestors of the twentieth-century manorial-laborers, were forcibly reconverted to Catholicism, whereas the free peasants were able to maintain their Calvinism and the free, German, urban burghers their Lutheranism.

The real difference between the manorial laborers' "Catholic asceticism" and the free peasants' "Protestant ethos" was not an emphasis on hard work, but more a certain tolerance. The population of the manorial settlements has been exceptionally tolerant, almost as much so as the seminomadic gypsy communities. Unlike village peasants, manorial-laborer communities did not excommunicate marginal or deviant individuals. All of their brothers and sisters, sons and daughters could expect to find safe refuge in the settlements, regardless of the norms they may have broken. Decades after the disintegration of the old manorial system, these settlements still maintain the old tolerance, offering refuge to those who did not make it, to the "lumpens" who return after failed attempts at mobility in the cities. This is one of the forces that have kept the people of the manorial settlements at the bottom of rural society.

One last comment about the mobility chances of former manorial laborers: Curiously, the most recent cohort of women from such a family background may have reasonably good prospects of mobility through marriage. Most of the agricultural villages suffer from a shortage of young women, and the young men from middle- or small-peasant background who move toward entrepreneurship are beginning to find it difficult to marry women from their own social background. Girls from such social origins have learned urban skills and have left or are trying to leave for the cities. As Pál Juhász (personal communication) has pointed out, girls from the manorial settlements offer an alternative choice of spouse. They are ready to stay, they don't have skills convertible to city life. For them, work in an entrepreneurially oriented household economy is a major step forward, so they become "ideal" wives, hard-working and satisfied with the upward mobility they have achieved by marrying the new entrepreneurs.

Poor peasants and their descendants: strategies for resisting proletarianization

As Figure 7.4 indicates, the upward mobility prospects for former poor peasants and their descendants have been much better than those for manorial laborers. This is really the stratum István Márkus has been theorizing about (see Márkus, 1980). In many respects he is right: people from this stratum used the opportunities which opened up after 1945 in the most imaginative manner. They entered diverse trajectories: many moved toward a postpeasant existence and became prosperous peasant-workers, others pursued the cadre trajectory, and a few even became agricultural entrepreneurs.

The oldest cohort of former poor peasants: three ways to choose

Those who were poor peasants in 1945 had three trajectories to choose from. Some who received land in 1945 had become small peasants by 1949, and by exploiting the opportunity created by the decline of the kulaks moved toward market gardening. These market gardeners of poor-peasant origin usually did not get managerial positions in 1960 in the kolkhozes, but they got good jobs in the market gardening divisions, and by the mid-1970s some were ready to become entrepreneurs. They had risen two strata in the social hierarchy in one lifetime, jumping ahead of most former small peasants and even some of former middle peasants.

The second trajectory open in 1945–56 led toward cadre status. Poor peasants were regarded by the new regime as particularly suitable for cadre jobs. They had lowly origins, but unlike the "lumpen" manorial laborers were highly motivated, better educated, and more ambitious. Indeed, many members of the rural apparatus between 1945 and 1956 were former poor peasants, who had joined the Communist Party (whereas small and middle peasants were in the Small Peasant Party).

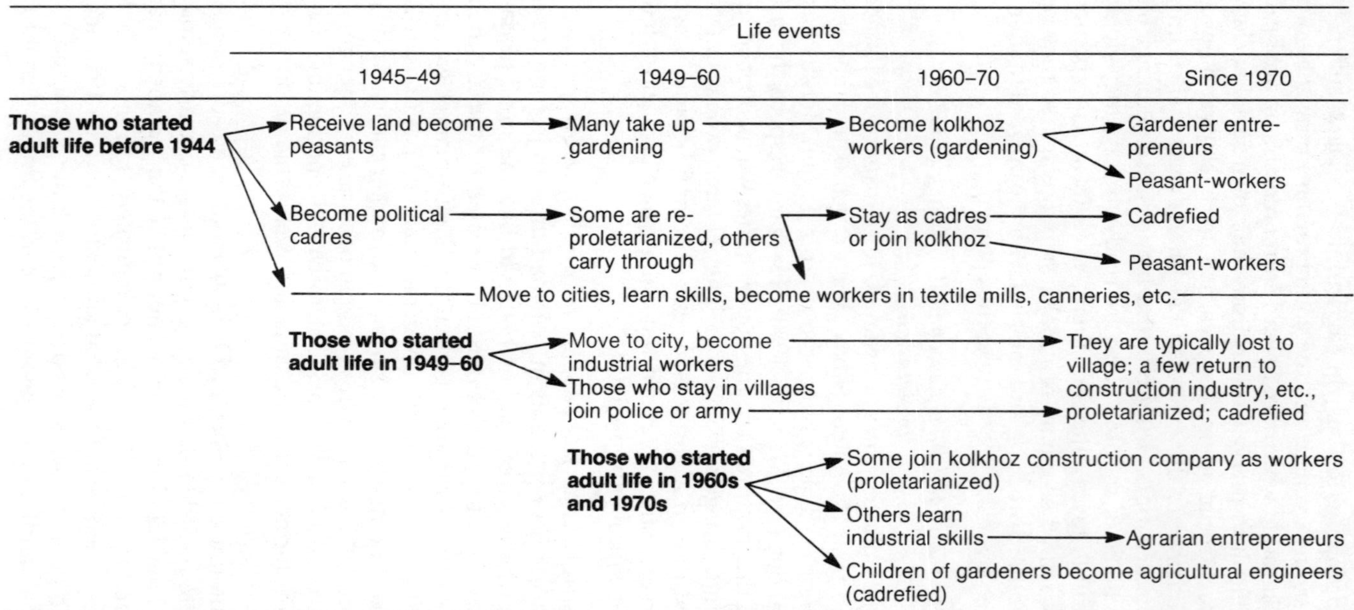

FIGURE 7.4 *Life history trajectories of former semiproletarians, poor peasants, and their children*

They were the natural candidates for positions such as party secretary; many joined the police force, including the political police and the AVO (The Hungarian version of the KGB), and they were also prominently represented among the apparatus of requisition. A few of them could not grow into their new tasks or became disappointed and dropped out. Some of them found themselves in a sort of "lumpen" existence by 1956 and may even have been in the mobs involved in the few more violent actions against Communist cadres.

The 1956 insurrection was an important turning point for most of the former poor peasants who had joined the cadre. In that traumatic year, many left their cadre jobs, returned to agriculture, and tried to identify themselves with a small- or middle-peasant existence. In 1960 many of them joined the kolkhozes, slotted into the middle of the kolkhoz social hierarchy, and by the mid-1970s they were among the more affluent, market-oriented peasant-workers. Those who did stay with the Party even after 1956 tended to move back to their native villages. Before 1956, most cadres were sent to strange villages: the regime wanted to ensure that "parachutist cadres" did not have strong ties with the local people and would loyally execute the instructions of the central party or government organs. This arrangement did not work out very well in 1956. The "parachutists" were indeed regarded as strangers and could count very little on the mercy of people subordinated to them. Having learned this lesson, many cadres who remained loyal to the regime after 1956 asked to be transferred to the villages of their birth, and there they made sure that they built up and maintained reasonable relations with the villagers. So the poor-peasant cadre remained after 1956 an important source of village and county administration, and those who did stick to such jobs between 1956 and 1960 were likely to become irreversibly cadrefied.

The third trajectory open to poor peasants between 1945 and 1956 was industry. Many, particularly women, became industrial workers, especially in the textile industry but also in the canneries. People who entered this third trajectory typically ended up in cities as skilled workers, but rarely in the highly paid, much-in-demand skills. They became proletarianized, and thus were lost for embourgeoisement.

Those who became adults during the 1960s: the embourgeoisement trajectory opens

The embourgeoisement trajectory remained open for at least one more cohort of the descendants of poor peasants. Those who finished their primary education during the early 1960s, particularly the sons and daughters of former poor peasants who had become gardeners and were heading toward entrepreneurship, were well educated, and many became skilled workers in areas very useful in agriculture—blacksmiths or electricians, for instance. Many of the new agricultural entrepreneurs with an industrial background are probably from this group. Some of the children of market gardeners went to college; they became professionals or joined the cadre and were among the young intellectuals who took power in the kolkhozes in the mid-1970s.

After this ethnographic account, we turn again to statistical analysis, in an effort to develop life history variables that will capture some of the proposed hypotheses. We enter these new variables into our sample selection model and investigate their effect on the fit of the different versions of this model.

RETESTING THE SAMPLE SELECTION MODEL

First, we will briefly describe how we fine-tuned our life history variables and created new ones using our ethnographic information. Second, we present and briefly interpret all sample selection models, using the fine-tuned life history variables (Models D″/FAPC, D″/FAPS1, and D″/FAPS2). Third, we develop the "best model" we can come up with to explain both subsistence production and commodity production. We do so by eliminating from earlier models the nonsignificant variables (we make an exception for a few nonsignificant or marginally significant variables in the "best models," if we can thereby gain theoretical insights). The resulting "best models" are not best in the sense that they fit the data better than the more comprehensive models. As we will see, leaving out nonsignificant variables usually negatively affects the goodness-of-fit statistics: these new models are "best" only in the sense that nonsignificant or theoretically noninterpretable variables are excluded. We present two such "best models," one with FAPC, the other with FAPS1 as dependent variables. In order to make our "best models" as comprehensive as possible we also include all significant interaction terms (or terms which offer theoretical insights, even if they are nonsignificant or only marginally significant).

Fine-tuning old and creating new life history variables

Our old life history variables, particularly COPYEARS and SELFYEARS (number of years in cooperatives or self-employed, respectively) served us well in the models of Chapters 5 and 6, and even BOSYEAR (number of years in a position of authority) did a good job in explaining entrepreneurial orientation. But all these variables were crude measures which could be refined in two ways: (1) why just *numbers* of years in certain types of jobs rather than a *ratio* of years spent in certain jobs to all years worked? (2) As we indicated in our ethnographic account, the *historical timing* of certain job events may be of vital importance. The ethnographic section of Chapter 7 is full of specific hypotheses about the links between current entrepreneurship and, for instance, the time at which an individual gave up self-employment, returned to the village, or took or left a position of authority.

We fine-tuned our variables for years spent in a position of authority, in cooperatives, and in self-employment in both ways. The creation of variables expressing the ratio of all time in the workforce in a specific type of work proved disappointing. We cross-tabulated these newly created variables with our measures of income and found the results unimpressive and often difficult to interpret. Fine-tuning of the BOSYEAR, COPYEARS, and SELFYEARS variables according to historical timing of life events proved, in contrast, to be successful, and the resulting cross-tabulations supported most of our more sophisticated hypotheses. Thus we created a series of new variables, labeled BOSHIS50, 60, COPHIS50, 60 SELFHIS50, 60, etc. All these variables were dummies which took the value 1 if a certain event occurred in a given period of time. Thus, for instance, the value of BOSHIS50 is 1 if the respondent was promoted into a position of authority between 1950 and 1956, or the value of SELFHIS60 is 1 if the respondent gave up self-employment between 1960 and 1968. We tried to create such a variable for educational history too because we were particularly interested in understanding the historic timing of attendance at evening schools. But the EVNHIS variable did not perform particularly well in cross-tabulations, and we eventually included in the sample selection model only one such measure, EVNHIS57, a measure with a value of 1 if the respondent began to attend evening school between 1957 and 1959, when the pressure toward collectivization was at its lowest ebb. As we will see, EVNHIS57 does a respectable job as a measure of cadre status.

Besides fine-tuning and refining existing life history variables, we also created new ones based on the ethnographic story in Chapter 7. Earlier in the chapter we repeatedly claimed that people from particular backgrounds, who had acquired specific urban skills before they returned to the villages or to kolkhoz employment during the 1960s or 1970s, may have later played a key role in revitalizing entrepreneurship. From these insights we created three new life history variables: RETURN60, RETURN70, and INDAGR70. The value of the RETURN variable is 1 when the respondent, either between 1960 and 1968 or after 1968, returned from an urban to a rural job; INDAGR70 takes the value 1 when the respondent swapped a skilled industrial job for a kolkhoz job any time after 1968. All three variables performed well in cross-tabulations with income measures, and they do a reasonably good job in the sample selection models.

Entering these variables into our sample selection models proved to be problematic, for two reasons: (1) both the fine-tuned and the new variables usually captured a rather small population, and with small *N*s it was difficult to produce significant parameters for these very "fine" measures; (2) particularly the life event variables developed from COPYEARS, SELFYEARS, and BOSYEAR are highly correlated with the original "length of time" variables; thus as long as we keep the "parent variables" COPYEARS, SELFYEARS, and BOSYEAR in the model we cannot really get significant values for the new, fine-tuned variables.

In order to resolve this problem we built Models D″/FAPC, D″/FAPS1, and D″/FASP2 two ways. First, we violated the logic of nested model building and left COPYEARS, SELFYEARS, and BOSYEAR out of the models. Doing so produced quite a few significant parameters for several new life history event variables, but we are really unable to compare the goodness-of-fit statistics with the earlier set of models. Thus, in a second round, we built the models the "proper," nested way, with COPYEARS, SELFYEARS, and BOSYEAR included. Here we were unable to produce statistically meaningful parameters for the fine-tuned life history event variables, but we could assess the fit of the models and test the overall power of the life history hypotheses. In order to keep the text readable, we are presenting only the "proper," nested models, but before discussing each model I describe the results of the nonnested model building.

Results of fine-tuning the life history variables: statistical costs with some theoretical benefits

Statistically our fine-tuning of life history variables was not particularly successful. When we left the robust "length of years" variables out of the models, their overall fit deteriorated, although we gained a few interpretable parameters for the life history event variables that were meaingful for our theory. When we followed the rules of nested model building, only one of the fine-tuned models produced a better fit than the models without fine-tuning.

Model D″/FAPC

Nonnested version

In this version (without COPYEARS, SELFYEARS, BOSYEARS; results not presented) the fine-tuned and new life history variables perform by and large according to our expectations. They are not particularly important in explaining subsistence production; as in earlier models with FAPC as the dependent variable, the independent variables derived from the proletarianization theory are dominant. In the probit equation, 10 out of the 15 life history variables are significant; in the regression equation their power rapidly declines and only three variables are significant. As anticipated, COPHIS50, COPHIS57, and COPHIS60 are all positive and significant in the probit equation (only COPHIS60 remains so in the regression equation); SELFHIS50, SELFHIS57, and SELFHIS60 are also positive and significant in the probit equation but lose their explanatory power in the regression equation. The three COPHIS variables explain about as much of a family's production for its own consumption as COPYEARS did in the earlier model (see Table 6.3). This explains the overall deterioration in the fit of the model: the single, rough COPYEARS variable provides the same explanatory power as three COPHIS variables.

Generally, we gain little understanding of subsistence production from analyzing life histories. Those with a history of kolkhoz employment and particularly those who joined the kolkhozes as late as 1960 will be less likely to give up producing their own food. Similarly, those who remained self-employed until 1960 or beyond are more likely to produce their own food, but none of these indicators can compete with the explanatory power of the basic demographic variables.

Nested version (Table 7.1)

Even when we reentered the variables for length of time spent in different kinds of positions the properly nested new model did not improve its fit (in fact, the fit was worse, though not at a level of statistical significance!). With COPYEARS, SELFYEARS, and BOSYEAR back in the equation, the life history event variables lost their significance (SELFHIS60 in the probit and INDAGR70 in the regression equations being the only exceptions), but the fit of the model remained poor. This should not worry us much: as we have noted, we do not use life history variables to explain subsistence production, which is what FAPC measures. We do, however, need to improve the fit of the model when FAPS, the value of commodity production, is the dependent variable.

TABLE 7.1 *Nonstandardized (NS) and standardized (ST) parameters of the sample selection model for Model D″ with FAPC as the dependent variable (Model D″/FAPC; N = 7754/4389)*

	Probit			*Regression*		
	NS[a]	*ST*	*t values*	*NS*	*ST*	*t values*
AGE	.101	1.599	13.6	.005	.211	4.8
AGESQUARE	−0.001	−1.592	−13.4	−0.0001	−0.194	−4.3
ACTIVNO	.256	.275	10.5	.023	.071	9.4
HOMEDUTY	.267	.096	5.4	.014	.016	3.2
RETIRNO	.306	.215	9.2	.020	.042	6.2
CHILD	.075	.078	3.8	.007	.020	3.0
ONECOUPLE	.710	.321	15.3	.037	.043	5.4
MORECOUPLE	.774	.188	7.7	.041	.034	4.9
AGRAR	.315	.140	7.5	.011	.015	2.7
PFARM44	.104	.035	2.0	.017	.017	3.3
REFORMPW	.164	.060	3.7	.003	.003	0.6
MANORIAL	−0.076	−0.025	−1.5	.0003	.0003	0.1
NONAGR38	−0.411	−0.184	−10.6	−0.022	−0.025	−4.0
BOSYEAR	−0.005	−0.023	−1.1	.0002	.003	0.4
COPYEARS	.021	.169	6.9	.001	.022	3.4
SELFYEARS	.010	.067	3.2	.0003	.007	1.1
EVENING	−0.502	−0.156	−9.1	−0.011	−0.008	−1.2
FIFTHYEAR	−0.235	−0.084	−5.0	−0.024	−0.023	−4.1
BOSHIS50	.065	.008	0.4	−0.001	−0.0003	−0.1
BOSHIS60	−0.029	−0.004	−0.2	−0.012	−0.005	−0.9
COPHIS57	.084	.019	1.0	−0.011	−0.001	−1.4
COPHIS60	−0.033	−0.012	−0.5	.010	.011	1.7
SELFHIS50	.100	.019	1.1	−0.003	−0.002	−0.5
SELFHIS60	.269	.065	2.9	.0000	.001	0.1
EVNHIS57	−0.095	−0.007	−0.5	.030	.006	1.0
INDAGR70	.390	.087	1.2	.099	.063	2.7
Constant					9.129	1564.8
σ	.332		93.6			
ρ	0.1 (restricted)					
−2*loglikelihood	= 11,322					
DF	= 7,697					

Source: Our calculations from 1982–83 CSO Income, Social Mobility and Life History surveys.

[a] The nonstandardized parameters in this model were estimated from the standardized parameters with the formulae developed by Robert Mare of the University of Wisconsin–Madison. For details see note to Table 5.6.

Model D″/FAPS1

Nonnested version (results not presented)

Our fine-tuned life history variables are much more comfortable in this version of Model D″/FAPS1 than in the nonnested version of Model D″/FAPC. The relative success of our fine-tuning operation is particularly obvious in the regression equation. COPHIS60 comes forward as a very strong variable, almost as strong as COPYEARS in the similar rougher model (Table 6.4) and it tells us more about the larger of the large commodity producers than any of the mobility variables. SELFHIS60 is also highly significant in both equations but, interestingly, it cannot compete with COPHIS60. To have joined the kolkhoz in 1960 seems to be of vital importance in identifying the bigger, though not the biggest, commodity producers today.

BOSHIS variables do what we anticipated: BOSHIS50 and BOSHIS60 are negative or nonsignificant in the first equation and turn positive and at least marginally significant in the regression equation, whereas BOSHIS45 and BOSHIS57 remain negative or insignificant in both equations (but the *N* is very small in both cases!). Thus we have further evidence that becoming a boss during times when there are entrepreneurial alternatives is a sign that one is headed for permanent cadre status, whereas becoming a boss during collectivization drives proves to be a "parking orbit." People who went into supervisory positions in 1949–56 or 1960–68 are indeed more likely to be producing more commodities for sale by the 1980s.

One of the most exciting findings of this nonnested version of Model D″/FAPS1 is the powerful performance of INDAGR70. INDAGR70 produces higher coefficients in both equations than any other variable except AGE and AGESQUARE, but because its standard error is high, signifiance levels are moderate. In the models, INDAGR70 performs better than in the cross-tabulations, indicating that it adds something genuinely new to our understanding of commodity production. The claims made in the ethnographic discussion, that industrial skilled workers who returned to agriculture after 1968 were more inclined to turn entrepreneurial, are thus confirmed. At the same time, both RETURN60 and RETURN70 are negative, almost significantly so in the first equation. Thus we also have evidence to support our earlier speculations: some of the "return migrants" are indeed proletarianized losers, and the fact that they return does not make them into entrepreneurs. Among the "return migrants," the ones that reenter embourgeoisement are those who used urban or industrial jobs as parking orbits, acquiring skills and saving themselves for "better times."

Thus we gain several insights from this nonnested version of Model D″/FAPS1, but the overall fit of the model deteriorates when we compare it (inappropriately, because we violated the rule of nested model building) with Model D′/FAPS1. The −2*loglikelihood value of the nonnested Model D″/FAPS1 was 17,778, a significantly worse fit than Model D′/FAPS1, with a −2*loglikelihood value of 17,670.

Nested version (Table 7.2)
In this version of the model, unfortunately, virtually all the life history event variables lose their significance. Only INDAGR70 is robust enough to retain a statistically significant parameter in the probit equation. Despite the great number of nonsignificant new variables, however, the fit of this version of Model D″/FAPS1 improves modestly, but in a statistically significant way compared with Model D′/FAPS1 (the −2*loglikelihood value declines from 17,670 to 17,628).

Model D″/FAPS2

Nonnested version (results not presented)
In the regression equation of the version of Model D″/FAPS2 which was built without COPYEARS, SELFYEARS, and BOSYEAR, only two variables are significant: BOSHIS50 and SELFHIS60. Judging by rigorous statistical standards, then, we were not particularly successful in improving our understanding of the phenomenon which probably interests us the most: which biggest commodity producers are producing more and becoming "real" entrepreneurs?

One reason in particular for the rarity of significant values is that we have now sharply reduced the number of observations and thus increased the standard error. But if we look at the parameters and not at the *t* values, then the fine-tuned life history variables are performing quite well, better than ever before. If one adopts a more liberal attitude toward the level of significance and also interprets those parameters that appear to be quite large, then the behavior of our fine-tuned life history variables begins to make a lot of sense.

First, note the contrast in the performance of the COPHIS and SELFHIS variables in the nonnested versions of Models D″/FAPS1 and D″/FAPS2. In particular, COPHIS60 played a prominent role in Model D″/FAPS1 in characterizing market-oriented peasant-workers, protoentrepreneurs, and the bigger producers, but SELFHIS60 was significantly weaker. In the nonnested version of Model D″/FAPS2, their role is reversed: although COPHIS60 still leads SELFHIS60 in the probit equation, in the regression equation SELFHIS60 takes over from COPHIS60, which even ceases to be significant. Thus our most refined

TABLE 7.2 *Nonstandardized (NS) and standardized (ST) parameters of the sample selection model for Model D″ with FAPS as the dependent variable (Model D″/FAPS1; cutoff point 5000 Ft; N = 7754/3703)*

	Probit			*Regression*		
	NS[a]	*ST*	*t values*	*NS*	*ST*	*t values*
AGE	.056	.886	7.7	.015	.269	2.5
AGESQUARE	−0.001	−0.977	−8.4	−0.0002	−0.347	−3.2
ACTIVNO	.120	.129	5.2	.080	.107	5.6
HOMEDUTY	.106	.038	2.2	−0.025	−0.012	−0.9
RETIRNO	.141	.099	4.5	−0.007	−0.006	−0.4
CHILD	−0.002	−0.0002	−0.01	.014	.017	1.0
ONECOUPLE	.356	.161	7.7	.109	.057	3.1
MORECOUPLE	.407	.099	4.4	.006	.002	0.1
AGRAR	.427	.190	10.6	.129	.077	5.8
PFARM44	.259	.087	5.2	.090	.042	3.5
REFORMPW	.164	.060	3.8	.025	.012	1.0
MANORIAL	−0.043	−0.014	−0.8	−0.050	−0.021	−1.6
NONAGR38	−0.344	−0.154	−9.0	−0.076	−0.037	−2.3
BOSYEAR	−0.001	−0.007	−0.4	.005	.031	1.7
COPYEARS	.034	.269	11.7	.006	.069	4.4
SELFYEARS	.019	.128	6.4	.006	.058	3.9
EVENING	−0.077	−0.024	−1.4	.108	.037	2.4
FIFTHYEAR	−0.232	−0.083	−5.0	−0.038	−0.016	−1.1
BOSHIS50	.081	.010	0.6	.006	.001	0.1
BOSHIS60	−0.044	−0.006	−0.4	.039	.007	0.5
COPHIS57	−0.018	−0.004	−0.2	−0.045	−0.015	−1.2
COPHIS60	.094	.034	1.6	.032	.017	1.1
SELFHIS50	.005	.0001	0.01	−0.034	−0.009	−0.8
SELFHIS60	.123	.030	1.4	.062	.023	1.6
EVNHIS57	−0.270	−0.020	−1.3	−0.127	−0.001	−0.7
INDAGR70	1.139	.254	3.7	.245	.071	1.3
Constant					9.793	681.9
σ	.764		85.9			
ρ	−0.2 (restricted)					
−2*loglikelihood	= 17,628					
DF	= 7,697					

Source: Our calculations from 1982–83 CSO Income, Social Mobility and Life History surveys.

[a] The nonstandardized parameters in this model were estimated from the standardized parameters with the formulae developed by Robert Mare of the University of Wisconsin–Madison. For details see note to Table 5.6.

sample selection model also proves the hypothesis we stated in analyzing our cross-tabulations: that kolkhoz membership works against real entrepreneurship. Kolkhoz members are more likely to be peasant-workers; entrepreneurs to be made of that stuff which resisted "third serfdom." (The parameters published in Tables 7.2 and 7.3 for the nested models, although not statistically significant, also support this interpretation.)

This is, of course, a theoretically very important conclusion. János Juhász, for instance, argued eloquently (1980: p. 115) that the kolkhoz, by integrating the houseplots, made entrepreneurship possible.[13] Our figures seem to suggest that the opposite may be true. Those who became "real" entrepreneurs resisted collectivization the most vehemently, stayed self-employed as long as they could, and probably never joined the kolkhozes. The kolkhoz created new peasants; the new entrepreneurs are those who successfully resisted both industrial proletarianization and kolkhoz peasantization.

The BOSHIS variables also work splendidly in the nonnested version of Model D″/FAPS2. BOSHIS45 and BOSHIS57 both have negative values.[14] BOSHIS50 and BOSHIS60, as our theory predicted, are positive in both equations; BOSHIS50 even turns significant in the regression equation, and BOSHIS60 also becomes marginally significant. The performance of the BOSHIS variables throughout the nonnested version of the models in this chapter shows beautifully that there are two aspects to being in a position of authority; those who entered these positions "under duress," when embourgeoisement was blocked, are often among the most entrepreneurial types and reenter the embourgeoisement trajectory if and when the opportunity reopens.

Though the RETURN and INDAGR variables are not significant in the nonnested version of Model D″/FAPS2, their performance still deserves attention. INDAGR70 actually has a positive and significant parameter in the probit equation, and an impressive, though nonsignificant parameter in the regression equation. We have, then, further evidence that those who swapped skilled industrial jobs for agricultural employment during the 1970s may indeed enter the embourgeoisement trajectory.

Thus, we are inclined to read the substantive equation of the nonnested version of Model D″/FAPS2 as follows: in order to become a "real" family agricultural entrepreneur during the 1980s one had to resist collectivization as long as possible. When collectivization was

[13] We think this view is widely shared among those who usually praise the "integrative role" of the kolkhozes.

[14] Not one of the big producers had become a boss during 1945–49, and the variable was left out of the regression equation.

inevitable, those who wanted to preserve themselves for future entrepreneurship "hid" in the kolkhozes, often as bosses, or took up industrial jobs where they learned skills that could also be used for agricultural production.

Nested version (Table 7.3)
When we reentered the powerful COPYEARS, SELFYEARS, and BOSYEAR variables we lost all the significant parameters of the life history event variables. To make our lives even more difficult, we gained nothing, statistically, in the fit of our model. The value of the −2*loglikelihood was reduced by 1, which is less than the change in the degrees of freedom. This is the most disappointing result in our whole statistical exercise. In fine-tuning the mobility variables we could at least claim that we were most successful in explaining who the biggest entrepreneurs were, but fine-tuning our life history variables at this crucial point was not useful, although it added to our understanding of "protoentrepreneurs."

In general, we must conclude that although we have succeeded in contributing to our understanding of the broadly defined phenomenon of entrepreneurism, the more narrowly defined, biggest, most successful entrepreneurs remain outside the reach of our empirical research instruments. Perhaps they are not numerous enough, or we have not been particularly successful in defining the sociological determinants of entrepreneurial success. We will return briefly to this question in the Conclusions.

Our best models, with interaction terms

Although we were only moderately successful in our attempt to improve the goodness of fit in our sample selection models by fine-tuning the life history variables, we still gained theoretical insights and generated some evidence to support several of the hypotheses we developed from our ethnographic or statistical descriptions. In the following and very last step of our statistical analysis we likewise gain certain theoretical benefits at some cost to goodness-of-fit statistics (but because these models are not built in a nested way and are thus not comparable to the earlier models, this does not bother us particularly).

Our best model/FAPC (Table 7.4) contains mainly variables derived from the proletarianization theory, all the variables from our initial Models A and B in Chapter 5. Indeed, if our task is to explain subsistence production, our theory of reentry to an interrupted embourgeoisement trajectory is not particularly necessary; those who

TABLE 7.3 *Nonstandardized (NS) and standardized (ST) parameters of the sample selection model for Model D″ with FAPS as the dependent variable (Model D″/FAPS2; cutoff point 24,000 Ft; N = 7754/1254)*

	Probit			*Regression*		
	NS[a]	*ST*	*t values*	*NS*	*ST*	*t values*
AGE	.050	.785	4.9	.015	.399	2.5
AGESQUARE	−0.001	−0.972	−5.8	−0.0002	−0.505	−3.0
ACTIVNO	.172	.185	6.5	.041	.085	3.5
HOMEDUTY	.047	.017	0.8	−0.009	−0.007	−0.4
RETIRNO	.053	.037	1.4	−0.002	−0.003	−0.1
CHILD	−0.001	−0.001	−0.04	.005	.010	0.4
ONECOUPLE	.350	.158	5.4	.064	.049	1.6
MORECOUPLE	.269	.072	2.6	.034	.019	0.7
AGRAR	.440	.196	9.5	.096	.096	5.5
PFARM44	.286	.096	5.2	.062	.052	3.7
REFORMPW	.077	.028	1.5	.055	.042	2.5
MANORIAL	−0.095	−0.031	−1.6	−0.066	−0.044	−2.5
NONAGR38	−0.328	−0.147	−6.3	−0.093	−0.067	−2.8
BOSYEAR	.008	.037	1.4	.004	.037	1.6
COPYEARS	.025	.199	8.2	.003	.050	2.5
SELFYEARS	.019	.124	5.3	.004	.069	3.5
EVENING	.087	.027	1.3	.027	.016	0.8
FIFTHYEAR	−0.137	−0.049	−2.2	−0.031	−0.020	−0.9
BOSHIS50	.008	.001	0.1	.074	.019	1.0
BOSHIS60	−0.118	−0.016	−0.8	.003	.001	0.1
COPHIS57	−0.022	−0.005	−0.2	−0.028	−0.016	−1.0
COPHIS60	.118	.043	1.8	.005	.005	0.3
SELFHIS50	.058	.011	0.6	−0.040	−0.017	−1.1
SELFHIS60	.219	.053	2.4	.045	.032	2.1
EVNHIS57	−0.392	−0.029	−1.3	−0.221	−0.025	−1.1
INDAGR70	.924	.206	2.5	.149	.073	1.0
Constant					10.073	350.4
σ	.549		47.0			
ρ	.6 (restricted)					
−2*loglikelihood	= 7,505					
DF	= 7,697					

Source: Our calculations from 1982–83 CSO Income, Social Mobility and Life History surveys.

[a] The nonstandardized parameters were estimated from the standardized parameters with the formulae developed by Robert Mare of the University of Wisconsin–Madison. For details see note to Table 5.6.

TABLE 7.4 *Nonstandardized (NS) and standardized (ST) parameters of the sample selection model for the best model when FAPC is the dependent variable (with interaction terms; N = 7754/4389)*

	Probit			*Regression*		
	NS[a]	*ST*	*t values*	*NS*	*ST*	*t values*
AGE	.103	1.633	14.0	.005	.205	4.6
AGESQUARE	−0.001	−1.535	−13.1	−0.0000	−0.177	−4.0
ACTIVNO	.262	.281	10.8	.024	.073	9.4
HOMEDUTY	.275	.099	5.6	.014	.016	3.2
RETIRNO	.274	.192	8.4	.018	.038	5.5
CHILD	.078	.081	4.0	.007	.020	2.9
ONECOUPLE	.635	.287	12.3	.036	.042	5.0
MORECOUPLE	.424	.103	3.3	.032	.026	2.8
AGRAR	.515	.229	12.9	.017	.022	4.3
NONAGR38	−0.440	−0.197	−12.1	−0.025	−0.028	−4.7
FIFTHYEAR	−0.218	−0.078	−4.7	−0.025	−0.024	−4.3
COPHIS60	.278	.101	5.7	.023	.026	5.3
INDAGR70	.750	.167	2.3	.110	.070	3.0
xACTIVNO/ RETIRNO	−0.115	−0.114	−5.3	−0.002	−0.007	−0.9
xRETIRNO/ MORECOUPLE	.126	.042	2.6	.004	.005	1.2
xAGRAR/ AGESQUARE	−0.000	−0.038	−2.4	−0.000	−0.009	−1.8
Constant					9.13	1527.8
σ		.333	93.6			
ρ		−0.1 (restricted)				
−2*loglikelihood	= 11,558					
DF	= 7,719					

Source: Our calculations from 1982–83 CSO Income, Social Mobility and Life History surveys.

[a] The nonstandardized parameters in this model were estimated from the standardized parameters with the formulae developed by Robert Mare of the University of Wisconsin–Madison. For details see note to Table 5.6.

grow their own food are older, are working in kolkhozes, and have larger families. All that we can add is that people whose parents were not agriculturalists in 1938 are more likely to have completed their trajectory to proletarianization or cadre destinations, and that particularly prominent among the "new peasants" of the kolkhoz age are those who joined the kolkhozes only in 1960 and who gave up industrial jobs for agricultural ones after 1970.

In this best model we found three interaction terms that were significant, but only in the first equation. The interaction between ACTIVNO and RETIRNO produces a negative effect, whereas RETIRNO and MORECOUPLE interact positively. There is a negative interaction effect between AGRAR and AGESQUARE. None of these terms seems to offer much to our understanding of family agricultural production.

Our best model/FAPS1, in contrast (Table 7.5), summarizes the strength of our embourgeoisement theory. In explaining commodity production, the demographic variables lose their importance—only six out of the initial nine remain in the model—whereas the mobility and life history variables begin to play a significant role. Middle-peasant background, land grants to the family in 1945, delayed entry into the kolkhoz, and swapping skilled industrial jobs for agricultural ones in the 1970s seem to be the most important variables in explaining commodity production.

In our best model/FAPS1 we also found six statistically significant or theoretically interpretable interaction terms. Interestingly, COPHIS57 and AGRAR show a negative interaction, which should mean that people who joined the kolkhozes during 1957–59 are more likely to be entrepreneurial today if they later left the kolkhoz. This is an unanticipated, but meaningful result. Kolkhozes began to gain membership continuously after 1956, much before the official collectivization drive was launched during the fall of 1959. It is quite possible that the more aspiring among the small and poor peasants began to enter the kolkhozes before official collectivization began, only to be pushed aside by the middle peasants in 1960. These early kolkhozniks—at least the most ambitious among them—may well have left the kolkhoz and become entrepreneurs by the 1980s; thus we see a negative interaction between current kolkhoz membership and entry into the kolkhoz system between 1957 and 1959.

There is, as anticipated, a positive though not quite significant interaction in this model between COPHIS60 and BOSHIS60. In other words, among people who took management positions during the 1960s, those who joined the cooperatives are most likely to be entrepreneurs by the 1980s. Indeed, the most obvious option for those searching for a parking orbit in 1960, when they had to abandon family farming, was a position of authority in the kolkhoz. There is a similar positive interaction between COPHIS60 and SELFHIS60, again indicating that among new kolkhoz members in 1960, those who were previously self-employed are more likely to become entrepreneurs later. For the former poor peasants who joined the kolkhozes in 1960, entrepreneurial opportunities may not open up even in the 1980s.

TABLE 7.5 *Nonstandardized (NS) and standardized (ST) parameters of the sample selection model for the best model when FAPS is the dependent variable (with interaction terms; FAPS1, cutoff point 5000 Ft; N = 7754/3703)*

	Probit			*Regression*		
	NS[a]	*ST*	*t values*	*NS*	*ST*	*t values*
AGE	.065	1.019	9.3	.040	.716	6.2
AGESQUARE	−0.006	−1.051	− 9.4	−0.0001	−0.799	−7.2
ACTIVNO	.066	.071	3.5	.102	.137	7.7
ONECOUPLE	.504	.228	12.3	.343	.179	9.6
MORECOUPLE	.666	.162	8.8	.252	.085	5.2
AGRAR	.569	.253	15.0	.335	.200	14.0
PFARM44	.298	.100	6.1	.180	.084	6.2
REFORMPW	.191	.070	4.4	.093	.044	3.0
MANORIAL	−0.055	−0.018	−1.0	−0.060	−0.025	−1.6
NONAGR38	−0.371	−0.166	−9.7	−0.245	−0.119	−6.8
FIFTHYEAR	−0.212	−0.076	−4.7	−0.128	−0.054	−3.5
BOSHIS60	−0.074	−0.010	−0.7	.084	.015	1.0
COPHIS57	.590	.134	7.2	.256	.085	5.9
COPHIS60	.463	.168	9.2	.236	.122	8.2
RETURN60	−0.114	−0.028	−1.8	−0.069	−0.022	−1.6
INDAGR70	1.280	.285	4.2	.748	.217	3.5
xCOPHIS57/ AGRAR	−0.294	−0.052	− 3.7	−0.163	−0.042	−3.9
xCOPHIS60/ BOSHIS60	.232	.016	1.2	.134	.015	1.5
xCOPHIS60/ SELFHIS60	.142	.031	3.3	.087	.030	4.5
xREFORMPW/ MANORIAL	−0.057	−0.012	−1.0	.014	.004	0.4
xRETURN60/ MANORIAL	.130	.012	0.9	.129	.017	1.4
xINDAGR70/ MANORIAL	.676	.050	0.7	−0.571	−0.062	−1.1
Constant					9.120	536.8
σ	.888		83.9			
ρ	.7 (restricted)					
−2*loglikelihood	= 17,792					
DF	= 7,707					

Source: Our calculations from 1982–83 CSO Income, Social Mobility and Life History surveys.

[a] The nonstandardized parameters in this model were estimated from the standardized parameters with the formulae developed by Robert Mare of the University of Wisconsin–Madison. For details see note to Table 5.6.

We made a desperate effort to interpret our MANORIAL variable but were not particularly successful. We anticipated a strong positive interaction between MANORIAL and REFORMPW in models where the dependent variable is FAPS, but were unable to deliver this result. MANORIAL remains negatively associated with commodity production, and its interaction with REFORMPW in the first equation of best model/FAPS1 is also negative. This is disappointing, because earlier cross-tabulations with MANORIAL suggested that former manorial laborers who received land grants in 1945 might now be among entrepreneurially oriented peasant-workers or even protoentrepreneurs. Very distant support for such a hypothesis comes from the fact, that whereas the REFORMPW and MANORIAL interaction is negative in the probit equation of best model/FAPS1, it turns positive in the regression equation; none of these results is, however, statistically significant. Furthermore, MANORIAL shows a positive interaction with RETURN60; this should mean that people with a manorial-laborer family background are particularly unlikely to have become entrepreneurs if they returned about the time of collectivization. It is difficult to interpret the INDAGR70 and MANORIAL interaction, which is positive in the probit equation but turns negative in the regression equation (in both cases it remains nonsignificant). Our general conclusion is that no simple hypothesis will work if one wants to predict what has happened to people from a manorial-laborer or poor-peasant background. For some, the Márkus hypothesis may work effectively: not only did they become peasant-workers, but they even "jumped two steps ahead" and are now on an embourgeoisement trajectory. Others, however, just kept sliding down the slope to a proletarian destination.

Thus our best models confirmed the major statistical findings of this book: the proletarianization theory is useful and by and large is sufficient to explain subsistence production, but one must consider social background and life history, as the interrupted embourgeoisement theory suggests, in order to explain family agricultural entrepreneurship. We are confident that our best models have not made presentation of the earlier sample selection models unnecessary. The more detailed models of Chapters 5, 6, and 7, by including only marginally significant or even nonsignificant variables, have helped us to scrutinize many of the detailed hypotheses derived from ethnographic research. Thus they have proved to be useful in developing our theory and put more meat on the otherwise dry statistical bones.

In a final chapter, we turn to a general summary of both the empirical and theoretical findings of this book.

8
Conclusions

We are now at the end of our long tour of family agricultural production in socialist Hungary.

In this chapter we first summarize our major empirical findings, demonstrating that the interrupted embourgeoisement theory is supported by the analysis, but spelling out the limitations of the evidence. Next we return to the "metatheoretical implications" of the Introduction and elaborate our somewhat ironic view of the "Third Road." Finally, we comment upon the implications of our analysis for the study of East European class structure, briefly discussing how this book is related to our earlier work on state socialist class structure (Konrád and Szelényi, 1979) and, more specifically, how the rather unanticipated revolution from below which has occurred during the last decade and is described in this book alters our earlier analysis of a new, dominant class of intellectuals *in statu nascendi*.

EMPIRICAL FINDINGS: THE INTERRUPTED EMBOURGEOISEMENT THEORY SUPPORTED

Let us begin with the "dry bones"—the statistical findings. As our analysis progressed, the goodness-of-fit statistics for our models changed considerably. To what extent do these data justify the inclusion and gradual fine-tuning of variables derived from the interrupted embourgeoisement theory? We draw two main conclusions.

1. ***The fit of our sample selection models generally improved as we entered and fine-tuned variables derived from the interrupted embourgeoisement theory.***

With a few important exceptions, the goodness-of-fit statistics of our models gradually improved as we expanded and fine-tuned the sample selection models in this book. Table 8.1 summarizes the loglikelihood values of the different models.

Bear in mind that (a) in moving from Model B to Models C and D we included social background and life history variables, and (b) in fine-tuning the dependent variable we went from aggregate value of family agricultural production (FAP) to the value of production for consumption (FAPC) and the value of production for sale (FAPS). The results from these first steps are impressive and strongly support the hypotheses of the interrupted embourgeoisement theory.

TABLE 8.1 *Changes in the −2*loglikelihood values of the sample selection models in moving from Model A to Model D″*/FAPS2

		Changes in −2*loglikelihood values
A. Results of including new variables:[a]		
From Model	A to B	−602*
	B to C	−202*
	C to D	−470*
B. Results of fine-tuning dependent variable:[b]		
From Model	B/FAPC to D/FAPC	−436*
	B/FAPS1 to D/FAPS1	−817*
C. Results of fine-tuning social background variables:[c]		
From Model	D/FAPC to D′/FAPC	−82*
	D/FAPS1 to D′/FAPS1	+22*
	D/FAPS2 to D′/FAPS2	−44*
D. Results of fine-tuning life history variables:[d]		
From Model	D′/FAPC to D″/FAPC	+10
	D′/FAPS1 to D″/FAPS1	−42*
	D′/FAPS2 to D″/FAPS2	−1

Note: Negative values represent improvements in the fit; significantly better or worse values are marked with an asterisk.

[a] From Table 5.7.

[b] From Tables 5.8–5.11.

[c] From Tables 5.9, 5.11, 5.12, 6.3, 6.5.

[d] From Tables 6.3–6.5, 7.1–7.3.

(a) By adding social background variables we produced a model which fits better than the models based only on hypotheses from the proletarianization theory (by adding just two intergenerational mobility variables, we reduced the −2*loglikelihood value by 202). The inclusion of life history variables improves the fit even more dramatically (the five new life history variables cut the −2*loglikelihood value by 470).

(b) By fine-tuning the dependent variable we also demonstrated, in harmony with the hypotheses of the interrupted embourgeoisement theory, that the goodness-of-fit statistics are particularly improved by including family background and life history variables when the dependent variable is the value of production for sale. When we use consumption (FAPC) as a dependent variable in moving from Model B to Model D, the −2*loglikelihood value is reduced "only" by 436; when we use sales (FAPS), this value is reduced by 817.

So it pays off to add social background and life history variables to our models, particularly if we use the value of commodity production as the dependent variable.

It is less obvious that we spent our time usefully in fine-tuning the battery of family background and life history variables. In a strictly statistical sense, Chapters 6 and 7 are not particularly successful. Nonetheless, I hope I can justify including the models with fine-tuned independent variables.

In the first place, we kept producing improvements, no matter how miniscule, in half of the models of Chapters 6 and 7. Most important, Models D′/FAPS 2 and D″/FAPS1 are the best fitting models in the whole book! Second, lack of improvement in the fit is to some extent a technical problem. As we pushed ahead with fine-tuning, the impressive initial sample size evaporated and the *N*s behind the fine-tuned variables began to shrink, making the production of significant results difficult indeed. Finally, it is true that the fit of the models often did not improve at all, or as fast as we wanted, and that we had great difficulty in producing statistically significant parameters. But particularly when we violated the rules of nested model building to improve the relative power of the new, fine-tuned variables, as we did in Chapter 7, we could glean new theoretical insights from our statistical analysis. Even when the whole model did not perform particularly well, we produced individual parameters that supported important hypotheses derived from our ethnographic fieldwork or from theoretic elaborations.

The most general conclusion we can draw at this stage is this: On the one hand, we proved that the proletarianization and peasant-worker theories have only limited explanatory power; we demonstrated that we made significant gains by complementing them with hypotheses drawn from the embourgeoisement theory. On the other hand, this book should be read as a first attempt and not a last word in our effort to explain the social determinants of family entrepreneurship under state socialism. We will need more ethnographic work and better focused statistical analysis to work out the details, to identify more precisely, for instance, the jobs or job sequences that should be regarded as parking orbits at different historical times, or the mobility patterns of different cohorts from families that are not middle peasant in origin. With the present work we hope at the very least that we have succeeded in setting the agenda for such future investigations.

2. ***Many of the new entrepreneurs have a middle-peasant background, but family inheritance of entrepreneurship is not absolutely determinant.***

The most important substantive finding of this book is the discovery of a strong positive correlation between a family's presocialist entrepreneurial orientation and current entrepreneurship. People from a middle-peasant background are more likely to develop commodity-producing minifarms than people from other social strata.

Still, nothing can be further from our intent than to offer a "deterministic" view of social structure or historical change. If our most important "independent variable" is presocialist family background, we have treated the job history of our respondents as an "intervening variable," which significantly modifies the effects of family inheritance. I hope that we have proved to the satisfaction of our readers that occupational choices during the two or three decades of the "command economy" did affect individual opportunities for reentering the embourgeoisement trajectory by the 1980s. Those who succeeded in gaining a degree of autonomy in their jobs and acquiring certain skills during the years when private entrepreneurship was impossible are more likely than others to become entrepreneurs today, even if they are from the "wrong" family background—that is, if they are not children of former middle peasants.

People shape their own lives, under given circumstances: the family they were born into and the character of the social structure in which they live set limits to their actions, but within these limits they can and do make real choices; they can substantially alter the courses of their lives and the course of history.

But we must point out at least two important limitations to the evidence presented in this book.

First, when I emphasize the importance of life history in mediating the impact of family inheritance on the current structural position of individuals, I advocate a sort of Weberian culturalist theory of entrepreneurship (though a "weak version," since I do accept the idea of "limits set by structures"). One of the major puzzles of this research was this: How can entrepreneurship be "inherited" when neither land nor capital can be passed on from one generation to the next? The hypothetical answer is that inheritance of cultural capital may fill the role played by inheritance of material wealth in a developed capitalist society. In our research, occupational choices were treated as "indicators" of such cultural capital, and life history was used as a measure of the value that people attach to autonomy and to the acquisition of new skills, and as evidence that they are not seeking authority for its own sake.

I still think that this is a reasonable argument, but I must concede that in this project I had no direct "measures" of cultural capital and could not identify the precise mechanism by which such capital may have been passed from one generation to the next. Furthermore, I have really no explanation why certain people choose life trajectories that do not correspond to their family background. Why do people from entrepreneurial backgrounds often opt for either proletarian or cadre status? Why do some people from nonentrepreneurial families pursue "autonomous" employment, place themselves in parking orbits and, despite their "handicapped" social origin, enter upon an entrepreneurial career? In other words, I cannot account for the origin of values, which are of such importance for my theories.

Some of the inadequacies of the present analysis could be remedied relatively easily in future research. The absence of evidence about values is in part due to the nature of the data used in this book: the Central Statistical Office surveys did not gather information on values or political attitudes. Crunching numbers from sociological surveys using such "soft" variables may be useful, and I hope my book will stimulate those who believe in such data more than I do to conduct the analyses.

Second, although we can readily distinguish entrepreneurs, broadly defined, from peasant-workers, neither our social mobility nor our life history variables work particularly well when we narrow our analysis to entrepreneurs proper and try to identify the really successful ones. Here we are asking questions about a relatively small population, a few percent of rural families—a few hundred cases in our sample. But I must concede that our difficulties may not be merely technical. It is quite possible that entrepreneurial success may have little to do with an individual's social characteristics, but may be more closely linked to personality characteristics.[1] Is it possible that sociology may have little

[1] In our discussions, Robert Manchin repeatedly reminded me of this possibility.

to say about which entrepreneurs will become bigger and more successful? I don't think we should worry much about this as long as we have a decent explanation for the origin of the "class" or "category" of entrepreneurs. And, indeed, this book is not so much about entrepreneurial success as it is about the "making of entrepreneurs" or of the entrepreneurial class.

AN IRONIC VIEW OF THE THIRD ROAD

While writing this book, I most likely from time to time became too excited by the uniqueness of the phenomena I was analyzing and began to identify myself too much with the fate of my "heroes." It may at times seem that I see the "new model" of socialism currently emerging in Hungary as not only a possible but also a desirable or even inevitable future—that I am not simply analyzing but even advocating the Third Road, "socialist embourgeoisement."[2] So I want to conclude with two points: (1) the Third Road is not better, it is different; (2) the Third Road is only a "window of opportunity." Eastern Europe during the 1980s is once again at a crossroads: it may take the Third Road, but it may also restore a Stalinist model or convert to a Western style of development.

The Third Road is different

In the Introduction, while acknowledging my indebtedness to Bibó, the young Erdei, and other East European populists of the interwar years, I tried to distance myself somewhat from their vision of the Third Road. They were inclined to argue that backwardness might become an advantage, that Eastern Europe might have a special opportunity to create a system not only different from but also better than those its Eastern or Western neighbors had adopted. At this point (and only at this point) I accept György Lukács's criticism of Bibó. In an otherwise very controversial paper, Lukács accuses Bibó of trying to "picture our mistakes, weaknesses, and burdensome historical heritage as something positive, as an ideal" (Lukács, 1945 [1981], p. 302).

In pointing out the signs of an emergent Third Road in Hungarian development today, I have wished primarily to emphasize that it is far from restoration or adaption of "capitalism," although it is a substantial deviation from the Soviet model. The curious, mixed, dual social

[2] I am grateful to Gabor Kertesi for bringing this to my attention and to critiquing the manuscript along these lines.

structure and economic system emerging during these years in Eastern Europe has roots in the nearer or more distant East European past and may turn out to be a durable new form of social organization. Innovative theorizing will be necessary to grasp the unique features of this new socioeconomic system, in which the market already plays a significant role, though it is still subordinated to the dominant bureaucratic-redistributive institutions. If indeed a new "socialist mixed economy" is in the making, we need to create a political economy for this system, to reinterpret "entrepreneurship," "market," "labor market," or even "embourgeoisement" in this context.

In comparison with the Soviet type of socioeconomic organization, which was superimposed—to a significant extent by military and police force—on the countries of this region and which has proved increasingly unable to function efficiently, this emerging Third Road may appear as a "progressive" system, which is closer to national and regional traditions, is more likely to achieve legitimacy, and may more effectively regulate the economy. Still, I would not regard the socialist mixed economy as the best of all possible worlds. As we tried to indicate in the empirical analysis of this book, a fair degree of balkanization is occurring. As the market is articulated through the dominant bureaucratic-redistributive institutions, it adapts in curious ways to the paternalism of the state socialist economy (Kornai, 1980). At the point of articulation of the two systems a kind of networking emerges that may seem to observers operating with the values and within the rationality of bourgeois democracy and capitalist markets as corruption. Socialist embourgeoisement also produces entrepreneurs who, contrary to the expectations of dissident ideologues are more "bourgeois" and less "citoyen" than petty commodity producers in Western societies. These socialist entrepreneurs have much of the greediness of the capitalists and little of the civic consciousness of the urban burgher. Bibó hoped that embourgeoisement would create people dedicated to quality and craftsmanship, but the new entrepreneurs of the 1980s, operating within the uncertainties of the bureaucratic-redistributive environment, may be forced to rip off the system—and their customers—as often and as quickly as possible. Thus, to reiterate, I believe that this historically quite unique mixture of redistribution and market, state and society, rank order and class stratification, this "Third Way," is a viable and, for Eastern European societies, quite possible future, but not necessarily a desirable one.

Windows of opportunity

One important metatheoretical assumption behind this book is the idea that the Third Road in Hungary is to some extent a return to a past, "organic" trajectory. In observing changes in Hungarian society over the last decade I was struck by the increasing similarities between prewar and present-day Hungary.

But here again, as with the individual life histories, no simple historical or economic determinism is intended. I merely *predict* that if Hungary, or the rest of Eastern Europe, is left on its own by the superpowers, then it is most likely that it will continue to develop its own mix of statism and markets, rank order and class stratification, citizenship and clientelism. Thus, to use a counterfactual argument, if the Russians were to pull their troops out of Eastern Europe, Hungary or Poland would soon drift away from the Soviet model but might not turn into Switzerland, or even Austria—at least not for some time.

To predict a most likely outcome is not to make a statement about historical inevitability. Societies do change trajectories, and "windows of opportunity" open up particularly at historical points where an older trajectory is being blocked or proves to be a dead end (this appears to be currently the case with the Soviet model in Eastern Europe). To forecast a possible Third Road development for Hungary or for the rest of the region merely identifies one opportunity and in so doing implies that a similar opportunity to enter the developmental trajectory of Western European civilization may also exist. The last time such opportunities opened up, between 1945 and 1949, Stalinism, the Third Road kind of development, or a realignment with Western Europe were all perfectly possible futures. The most daring metatheoretical hypothesis of this book is that the 1980s may prove to be a similarly formative epoch for Eastern Europe.

THE SILENT REVOLUTION FROM BELOW: RECENT CHANGES IN EAST EUROPEAN CLASS STRUCTURE

We would like to end this analysis on an optimistic note. The most exciting lesson to be drawn from the recent history of rural Hungary is that the Hungarian peasant won after all. Around 1942–43, Erdei, the first theorist to identify rural embourgeoisement in Hungary as an alternative to proletarianization, gave up hope and accepted the wisdom of orthodox Marxism: in the last instance, proletarianization is inevitable. Particularly since the Russians would occupy this part of the world, he thought, Hungarian peasants were unlikely to have alternatives other than labor in government-owned factories or in kolkhozes. History has proved Erdei to be wrong. The Hungarian peasants were smarter than their ideologue Erdei. They figured out how to resist collectivization, how to force their bureaucratic rulers into concessions, and, after three decades of "class struggle," how to persuade them to reopen the embourgeoisement trajectory.

But this generally optimistic statement needs qualifications, the first to do with socialist embourgeoisement and the creation of a "petty bourgeois society," and the second to do with the politics of class alliances in the emergent new socialist mixed economy.

Petty-bourgeoisification

My own interest in family agricultural production in Hungary during the mid-1970s was influenced by the views of Ray Pahl, who around this time discovered for himself and for the new urban sociology the "informal economy." In his first publications on this topic (Pahl and Gershuny, 1979, 1980; Pahl, 1980), Pahl began to consider the informal sector or the "second economy" as a mechanism by which the poor could compensate for the decline of the social democratic welfare state, a way to fight back against leftist statism and neoconservative laissez-faire and create the conditions for their own survival. Pahl, unlike those who studied the informal economy in the Third World, was quite enthusiastic about the informal sector. Inspired by these ideas he began an empirical investigation on the Isle of Sheppey, then hit by unemployment, hoping to be able to document how successful the poor were in using the informal economy to counteract the problems of unemployment in an epoch when conservatives were dismantling the welfare state in Britain (Pahl, 1984). The research did not prove his initial hypothesis. Pahl now argues (1986), that the very poor are not really helped by the informal economy; the "fat middle" is the real beneficiary.

In linking Pahl's work to my own, I would suggest that the evolution of the informal or second economy in both the East and the West, but to some extent probably even in the Third World, may really imply a developing "petty bourgeoisification." "The fat middle," to use Pahl's term, may indeed benefit, may generate new sources of income and increase its autonomy from the bureaucratic-redistributive sector in the East and from corporate capitalism in the West.

This observation alerts us to be neither overenthusiastic nor too pessimistic about the second economy. The important qualification to my claim about the "successful revolution from below" in rural Hungary is that this is not a revolution from the very bottom of society, but yet another revolution carried out by agents from the "middle."

Bibó considered the possibility that his Third Road and the embourgeoisement he advocated might lead to a petty bourgeois society. He rejected this basically because he did not want to accept the "petty bourgeois" label, which he considered pejorative. My more ironic theory of the Third Road can probably live with this label. The new entrepreneurial class which is in the making in rural Hungary today is not composed of the ideal of "citoyens," the pure citizens that Bibó or Hungarian dissident theorists would like. But they are neither cadre nor proletarian; they are petty bourgeois—and what is wrong with that? I would even go a step further and ask: May not a society be better if under given circumstances it allows a larger proportion of its population to be petty bourgeois? Without subscribing to the Proudhonian utopia of an entirely petty bourgeois society, one may argue that even in the most complex postindustrial society there is quite a lot of room for petty bourgeois existence, more room than Marxists or bourgeois technocrats usually believe. Both state socialism, and corporate capitalism may have pushed their luck too far in eliminating the petty bourgeoisie. The resurgence of this class in East and West is possibly a correction of earlier distorted developments.

The politics of class alliances in the new socialist mixed economy

In 1974 George Konrád and I, in *The Intellectuals on the Road to Class Power*, argued that a new dominant class of intellectuals was being formed in the state socialist redistributive economy of Eastern Europe. Now, more than ten years later, here is a new book about embourgeoisement, the formation of a new socialist petty bourgeoisie or entrepreneurial class. To what extent do these two books complement or contradict each other?

In 1986 I wrote a postscript to the Japanese edition of *The Intellectuals on the Road to Class Power* (Szelényi, 1986–87). This postscript, which was by way of being a critique of our earlier work, does link that work in detail to my more recent studies of the latest transformations of East European social structure. Here I shall very briefly summarize its main argument.

I would still claim that the core of our book on the intellectuals was quite correct. That book expressed real social trends in the Soviet Union and in Eastern Europe during the 1960s, the post-Stalinist reform epoch. For a decade or so the Soviet bureaucracy, shaken in its legitimacy by the fall of Stalinism, considered entering upon social and economic reform, inviting the technocracy and even the ideological intelligentsia to share power. The scientific-technical revolution, scientific socialism, socialism as a rational, scientific transformation of social relationships were perceived as a joint agenda for an enlightened bureaucracy and a technocratic–ideological intelligentsia. *The Intellectuals on the Road to Class Power* was thus a friendly debate with Milovan Djilas, who had produced the class theory of state socialism for the Stalinist era, when the bureaucracy ruled. We, for our part, tried to describe the transformations in the nature of social domination and in the social composition of the dominant class after Stalinism. I must now concede (1987) that by the 1980s this new dominant class is still a class *in statu nascendi*. Furthermore, intellectuals today in Eastern Europe are further away from class power than they were in the late 1960s. Why? Because of unanticipated events of the last two decades:

1. The bureaucracy proved to be more stubborn than we anticipated. After some early concessions, it decided not to share power with the technocracy after all and was prepared to sabotage social and economic reform even at the risk of "sinking the boat" (Poland during the late 1970s and early 1980s illustrates such bureaucratic stubbornness);
2. If the bureaucracy was less inclined to make concessions in its dealings with the intelligentsia than we anticipated, it proved to be more flexible toward private business, particularly the petty bourgeoisie. The bureaucracy in Hungary appears to have realized that its own inefficient operation could be rescued by permitting the second economy to operate and allowing the formation of a new petty bourgeoisie. The Hungarian political and economic "miracle" is the result of this policy. During the early 1980s, while real wages stagnated or declined in the government sector, the second economy began to generate incomes to maintain living standards, keeping the economy afloat and creating political stability by distracting the working class from struggles at the "point of production." The Hungarian petty bourgeois dream suggests that one can create a good life if one works hard in the second economy. One should not worry much about unions, or about what happens in the state sector and in the state job. Life begins after working hours anyway!

The bottom line of my 1986 auto-critique was similar to the central hypothesis of this book: by the mid-1980s the earlier dichotomous social structure (cadre and proletarian) was transformed into a dual system of social stratification, with three basic structural positions: cadre, proletarian, and petty bourgeois. This new trichotomous social structure has opened new opportunities for class alliances, creating new political space, making it possible for the party bureaucracy to slow down or possibly even foreclose sharing of power with the technocracy.

History has perhaps produced a better scenario than the one we predicted in *The Intellectuals on the Road to Class Power*. We did not see the formation of the intellectual class as an unmixed blessing. We were critical of their class aspirations, but at the same time we believed that in comparison with the estate type of rule by the rather archaic Stalinist bureaucracy, the formation of a new dominant class of intellectuals was "progress," a move toward rationalization, change for the better. I now believe that the trichotomous social structure may be an alternative to a rationalized dichotomous structure, creating more political space for all actors, particularly for those who are subordinated to authority.

In a way, the emerging new socialist mixed economy is a *partial* restoration of capitalism: it creates an economic system in which there is an alternative to bureaucratic employment—self-employment or employment by small private entrepreneurs. For the powerless majority this means a system with two masters rather than one. Is this a change for better or worse?

The answer to this question is not obvious. One may argue, that the two masters will conspire to create a system of dual exploitation but I fail to see why that is inevitable. Cannot we envisage a scenario where the ruled can play off one master against another and increase their autonomy? That possibility, at least, lies at the heart of this book.

Appendices

References

Index

Appendix A
Methodological notes

Data in this book are all from the Hungarian Central Statistical Office (CSO), collected by different divisions at different times, with somewhat different methodologies. Some of the data we use here were published in official CSO reports, others are based on our own calculations from data tapes which were made accessible to us by courtesy of the CSO.[1] We use different data sources, despite the inevitable difficulties in establishing their comparability, first because we want to give our readers the fullest possible overview of the problem under investigation, and second because we want to test how well results from the data tapes, upon which our own calculations in this book will be based, compare with data from other sources.

A short description of the data sources used in this book is in order here. We also give the basic statistical definitions of family production that we use and reflect on some of the possible biases in the CSO Income Surveys, in particular the reliability of and problems connected with attaching monetary estimates to natural measures of agricultural production figures.

[1] Robert Manchin, who worked as my Research Associate on my National Science Foundation project, received permission from the Central Statistical Office to bring the data tapes of the 1982–83 Social Mobility Study and Income Survey to Madison, Wisconsin, and to analyze those with me. I am grateful to CSO for their generosity in making this project possible.

DATA SOURCES

We use three major data sources in this book.

1. Population census and current population estimates, produced by the CSO, are used whenever we are writing about the urban–rural population distribution.
2. The 1981–82 Agricultural Report of the Agricultural Statistics Division of the CSO (CSO, 1982, 1984, 1985). This report was based on a census of all families who, according to CSO criteria, were operating family "enterprises" and on a survey of a representative sample of this population conducted a few months later. Whenever in the tables or text we refer to "enterprises" in quotation marks we refer to data from this source, available to us in published form.
3. We also made calculations ourselves using data tapes from the 1982 Income Survey of the CSO and the 1982–83 CSO Social Mobility and Life History Survey. Both surveys were conducted using the same sample, and because the identification numbers for the families were the same we succeeded in merging them into one data base. Thus whatever we say about the 1982 Income Survey sample is also true for the 1982–83 Social Mobility and Life History Survey and is applicable to our merged data file.

The Income Survey was based on a national random sample. We analyzed different subsamples of the survey, so that *N* will vary in the different tables we present. A short summary of these subsamples (see Appendix Table A.1) may be helpful, to make it clear which population is being discussed in different tables or data sets.

DIFFERENT DEFINITIONS OF FAMILY AGRICULTURAL PRODUCTION

The Agricultural Report and the Income Survey collected data on agricultural family production quite differently. In the Agricultural Report the unit of observation was the "enterprise"; only those households which reached a certain level of agricultural production provided information on their production. The Income Survey, in contrast, asked all families, even those which did not meet the agricultural "enterprise" criteria, about income from all possible sources,

TABLE A.1 *Subsamples of the 1982 CSO Income Survey*

	No. in sample
Total urban and rural households	14,780
Subsamples	
All rural households	8,172
All rural households which produce agricultural goods	7,299
Rural households in our merged file[a]	7,754
Rural agricultural producer households in our merged file	7,000

[a] In merging the 1982–83 Income and the Social Mobility and Life History Survey, we were unable to find mobility information for 418 household heads, which became "missing values" for the purposes of further analysis.

including family agricultural production. The concepts we use throughout this book in presenting these data are set out below.

The Central Statistical Office defined as family agricultural "enterprises" all those units of production which cultivated at least 400 négyszögöls of land (1600 négyszögöl is one hold, or 1.422 acres). In order not to miss out "large" producers who cultivated little land, CSO accepted holdings between 200 and 400 négyszögöls as "enterprises" as long as they were vineyards, orchards, or gardens. CSO also regarded as "enterprises" family production units which did not cultivate land at all, but kept at least one large animal (cow, horse, etc.) or 50 chickens (Andorka and Harcsa, 1982, p. 205).

Whenever we use the term "enterprise," defined as outlined above by CSO, we want to distinguish it both from "family agricultural production" and from entrepreneurially oriented minifarms, or agricultural enterprises as we define them. First, family agricultural production is a broader concept than family agricultural "enterprise." As we will see, there are families who produce agricultural goods on holdings smaller than 400 or even 200 négyszögöls. Most of them are indeed very marginal agricultural producers, but a few, market-oriented gardeners, for instance, could achieve noticeable levels of production. The Income survey of the CSO gathered data on all agricultural producers, not only on the larger ones—those who had "enterprises"—and here we will often present data and theorize about all of these as family agricultural producers. We use the term "minifarms" or "minifundia" as a synonym for family agricultural production, that is, the most generic terms to encompass all family agricultural production units, not just "enterprises." Second, one of our main tasks is to identify those family producers who are entrepreneurially oriented, who have built up family enterprises proper. This is a concept which is much narrower than "enterprise" in the CSO definition. When in this book we write only about enterprises we will always mean an entrepreneurially oriented unit of production, which by the mid-1980s constituted only a small fraction of all "enterprises" as defined by the CSO.

For further conceptual clarification it is helpful to know that Hungarian statistics classify these family "enterprises" into two categories: houseplots and auxiliary farms. "Houseplots" are received by members of kolkhozes in exchange for their labor services on the latifundia. "Auxiliary farms" are the small farms or gardens owned or rented by people who are not kolkhoz members. The few full-time private farms are also registered as auxiliary farms in these statistics. The number of such private farms is very small, about 2 percent of all family "enterprises" by 1980 (Andorka and Harcsa, 1982, p. 205).

Thus the basic terms used in this book are:

Family agricultural production (or producers): all those producing agricultural goods within family production units, called minifarms or minifundia

Family agricultural "enterprises": minifarms which qualify as "enterprises" by CSO criteria

Family agricultural enterprises: minifarms which are entrepreneurially oriented

Houseplots: land allocated by the kolkhozes to their members

Auxiliary farms: "enterprises" owned or rented by people outside the kolkhoz, including the few remaining full-time private farms

METHODOLOGICAL PROBLEMS IN THE INCOME SURVEYS: TOWARD A "SOCIOLOGY OF OFFICIAL STATISTICS"

Here we would like to raise two methodological issues about CSO Income surveys: (1) the reliability of their results; (2) the construction of monetary measures for family agricultural production by CSO during the coding procedures.

I

Are income surveys reliable at all? Do people tell the truth when asked about their incomes? Don't they have sufficient motive to mislead the interviewers? Don't they try to hide their real incomes from the taxman in the West, and in a statist economy like the Hungarian one, will they tell us how much they really earn from a "suspect" private economic activity?

How much "peasants" earn has been the subject of controversy for quite some time in Hungary. When we completed our first rural survey in 1972 at the Institute of Sociology of the Hungarian Academy of Sciences and made the first family production figures public many of our colleagues did not want to believe us. They thought that the income figures we were reporting were too low and even began to question our sampling procedures. More than a decade later, with both the 1972 and 1982 CSO Income surveys at hand, we are confident that our data were on target, and that sociologists then (and probably also today), like most other urban people, significantly overestimated what one can earn from family production. A "well-informed" Budapest intellectual, relying on hearsay and impressions he gained from short visits to villages, would vehemently insist that most rural people earned from their minifarms more than, or at least as much as they got in their monthly paychecks. Figures we produced from our Institute of Sociology survey suggested that an average rural family was more likely to earn a third of the monthly income of one family member from its joint effort on the minifarm. The 1972 CSO Income Survey offered similar estimates and the 1982 Income Survey did not report much change in this. Who are right, the "well-informed" Budapest intellectuals or the surveys?

We have a great deal of faith in the agricultural income figures of these surveys. We would be quite skeptical about data on other second-economy activities, like incomes from tips, moonlighting jobs, and the like. But with agricultural production the situation is different. First, the motives to lie about agricultural production are not strong. Tax laws are relaxed; one has to be in the top 1–5 percent of producers in order to produce enough to be subject to taxes. Although many urban and industrial second-economy activities indeed belong to the gray if not to the black economy, there is nothing, or at least very little, illegal about agricultural production. The major illegality we can think of is cultivating—de facto owning—more land than allowed. Here legal limits are strict; they are broken, but probably very rarely, and only by the top 1–5 percent of the biggest producers. Second, we have sound control data for agricultural production figures. Agricultural production and marketing statistics give us the quantity of agricultural goods that has been produced in the country, and the Income Survey data should match these figures, which are generated by other methods. The CSO indeed compared the two sets of data and found that the Income Survey underestimates production figures by some 20 percent. Thus we have a sound approximation of the error caused by unreliable reporting. The CSO actually did multiply production figures by 20 percent. This is far from an unproblematic procedure, and we comment on some of its undesirable consequences, but it still enables us to state with some confidence that the level of production and incomes we report on the ground of the Income surveys is indeed a good approximation of reality (the same point was made by Tamás Kolosi, 1983, p. 150).

II

In this book we will for the most part use monetary measures, which are very convenient for the type of statistical analysis we offer. But we also owe the reader a word of warning about these measures. In the 1972 and 1982 Income surveys the CSO asked respondents to declare in natural measures—in kilograms, tons, liters—how much they produced from every imaginable product, how much of this they consumed, and how much they sold on the market. During the coding procedure the CSO experts attached monetary estimates to these figures. In doing so they used, for self-consumption, the retail sales price, and for commodity production, the wholesale price, and they deducted from those incomes an estimated cost of production (cost of fertilizers, fuel, etc., but not labor).

This procedure has some problems. The CSO assesses self-consumption and commodity production at different prices by arguing that, in the case of self-consumption, one should estimate how much these families would have had to spend on food if they were not producers and, in the case of marketed goods, one should assume, that all produce is sold through the kolkhozes or other intermediary agencies and provides cash income at the wholesale price only. This makes sense for CSO purposes, but at the same time it underestimates commodity production, and when a shift occurs within family production from subsistence to commodity production it underestimates the dynamism of the change over time.

There are further reasons that one should be very careful with all such CSO estimates. CSO does not operate in a political vacuum. According to informants who are familiar with internal CSO politics, CSO's "political line" changed from 1972 to 1982. In 1972 there was pressure on the CSO to produce statistics which would show how excessive the incomes of peasants and peasant-workers were. Around this time, there was a strong "ouvrierist opposition" within the Hungarian Communist Party and the central Trade Union bureaucracies to economic reform (Manchin and Szelényi, 1987). One of the main targets of these ouvrierists were the "Nepmen" of the 1968 economic reform. (In Russia during the 1920s, those small private businessmen who benefited from the more liberal and market-oriented reforms of the so-called New Economic Policy were called Nepmen.) They were the peasants, who, according to the ouvrierists, were beginning to earn unjustifiably high incomes. According to our informants, the ouvrierists were putting pressure on the CSO to produce figures showing that peasants earned more than workers.

By the early 1980s the political climate had changed. The ouvrierists suffered a major defeat around 1975–76. After 1978–79 there began a new wave of liberalism which showed even more tolerance toward small family business than the policies of the late 1960s. In the spirit of this "second reform," CSO was expected not to exaggerate the significance of the private sector. Hungarian reformers, who were now firmly in command of the internal politics, wanted to prove to their more conservative neighbors and particularly to the Soviet Union that they were in no sense of the word "out of line," that the private sector was under control and was not threatening state ownership and the principles of state socialism.

Thus in 1972 the CSO was under pressure to show how much peasants earned, but in 1982 they were expected to prove how little family agricultural production mattered. Under such circumstances the method of measuring the monetary value of production that we have just described was very useful indeed. In 1972, when most of production was subsistence, it overestimated income; in 1982, when most of production was sold on the market, it underestimated the significance of the private sector and also the dynamism of change during the decade.

Do not misunderstand: under no circumstances are we accusing the CSO of falsifying data. CSO is an excellent institution, and we greatly admire its operation. But of course it must respond to the political pressures of the times, and those who use CSO data had better do a little sociology of sociology—or sociology of official statistics—of the kind we were just elaborating.

There is another interesting feature of the CSO Income Survey data. As we have already mentioned, the Income Survey underestimated overall agricultural production by some 20 percent. CSO felt obliged to produce data from the Income Survey that were identical to data from its Agricultural Statistics Division. Thus they decided to multiply the Income Survey production figures by 20 percent. But how to allocate this extra 20 percent of production? In 1972 and 1982, CSO followed different guidelines. In 1972 the larger producers were assumed to have produced proportionally more, whereas in 1982 this extra 20 percent was equally distributed among all producers. Though the change in methodology probably was not—or at least not consciously—politically motivated, the results were again data which underestimated the concentration that may have occurred among the bigger producers during this decade.

All the biases we can detect in the way CSO statistics were constructed are, therefore, working against our hypothesis. We try to demonstrate how market orientation and commodity production are gaining ground, how an entrepreneurial group is reemerging, and how significant are the changes in this process during the last decade. If we find change in this direction *despite* these methodological biases, it speaks for the strength of our theory.

Appendix B

Variables, means, and standard deviations of variables used in regression models

VARIABLE LABELS AND DESCRIPTIONS[1]

Dependent variables

FAP: aggregate net value of family agricultural production, in Ft per month.

FAPC: net value of agricultural products produced and consumed by the respondent family, in Ft per month.

FAPS: net value of agricultural products produced and sold by the respondent families, in Ft per month.

Independent variables

In Model A

AGE: natural age of the head of household.

AGESQUARE: the square root of AGE.

ACTIVNO: number of active wage earners in the family.

HOMEDUTY: number of spouses and other adults in the household who are of an economically active age (women between 19 and 55, men between 19 and 60) but who are not gainfully employed.

RETIRNO: number of people of retirement age (women above 55, men above 60) in the family.

CHILD: number of dependent children under 19.

ONECOUPLE: dummy variable which takes the value 1 when the family contains a husband-and-wife couple and the value 0 otherwise.

[1] For means and standard deviations of dependent and independent variables, see the last section of this Appendix.

MORECOUPLE: dummy variable which takes the value 1 when the family contains more than one husband-and-wife couple and the value 0 otherwise.

In Model B

AGRAR: dummy variable which takes the value 1 when the head of household works in agriculture as a manual worker and the value 0 otherwise.

In Model C

OFARM44: a dummy variable which takes the value 1 if in 1944 the head of household or his father owned at least 10 hold of land; otherwise its value is 0.

REFORM: a dummy variable which takes the value 1 if the household under investigation had a larger landholding in 1948 than in 1944, indicating that they were recipients of land grants during the land reform of 1945. The value of the variable is 0 for households whose landholding remained unaltered or declined.

In Model D

BOSYEAR: number of years the head of household spent in a position of authority.

COPYEARS: number of years the head of household spent in cooperatives.

SELFYEARS: number of years the head of household was self-employed.

EVENING: a dummy variable which takes the value 1 if the head of household ever attended evening school at high-school level or above; otherwise its value is 0.

FIFTHYEAR: a dummy variable which takes the value 1 if the head of household had no more than 5 years of education; otherwise its value is 0.

In Model D′

Fine-tuned mobility variables

PFARM44: a dummy variable which takes the value 1 if the parents of the current head of household owned at least 10 hold of land in 1944; otherwise its value is 0.

REFORMPW: a dummy variable which takes the value 1 for households which had no land in 1944, but owned some in 1949.

MANORIAL: a dummy variable which takes the value 1 if the father of the current head of household was a manorial laborer in 1938; otherwise its value is 0.

NONAGR38: a dummy variable which takes the value 1 if the father of the current head of household had a nonagrarian occupation in 1938.

In Model D"

Fine-tuned life history variables in Model D"

BOSHIS45, 50, 57, 60: dummy variables which take the value 1 if the head of household was promoted to a position of authority during 1945–49, 1950–56, 1957–59, or 1960–68. If no such event happened during these times, the value of the variable is 0.

COPHIS50, 57, 60: dummy variables which take the value 1 if the head of household joined the cooperative in 1950–56, 1957–59,or 1960–68. If no such event happened during these times, the value of the variable is 0.

SELFHIS50, 57, 60: dummy variables which take the value 1 if the head of household gave up self-employment during 1950–56, 1957–59, or 1960–68. If no such event happened during these times, the value of the variable is 0.

EVNHIS57: a dummy variable which takes the value 1 if the head of household began to attend evening school in 1957–59. If no such event happened during these years, the value of the variable is 0.

RETURN60, 70: dummy variables which take the value 1 if the head of household returned from an urban to a rural job in 1960–68 or after 1968. If no such event happened during these years, the value of the variable is 0.

INDAGR70: a dummy variable which takes the value 1 if the head of household swapped a skilled job in industry for any job in agriculture after 1968. If no such event happened during these years, the value of the variable is 0.

In fine-tuning the life history variables in terms of the historical timing of life events, we distinguished five different "regimes," assuming that the same occupational or educational choice in different regimes may have the opposite meaning or consequence.

1. *Immediately after World War II (1945–1949)*. During this time new embourgeoisement opportunities opened up. Land reform dismantled the latifundia, and peasants, particularly middle and rich peasants, could enjoy relative prosperity. During this regime only those without embourgeoisement aspirations wanted to join the rank hierarchy and become bosses. Joining the kolkhozes so early was an indication of little entrepreneurial spirit and an inclination to be peasantized or proletarianized. Attendance at evening

schools could mean different things. Since the massive cadrefication of the Stalinist period had not yet begun, some people who were entering an embourgeoisement trajectory might then seek adult education unavailable to them before World War II. Evening education during those years could signal a propensity to embourgeoisement as much as it could signal a propensity to enter the cadre.

2. *Between 1949 and 1956*. These are the years of the first big push toward socialist proletarianization and cadrefication. Under such pressures it may have been reasonable for those on an embourgeoisement trajectory to join a kolkhoz and even to aspire to become a boss. Thus we anticipate a positive association between becoming a kolkhoz employee, a supervisor, or beginning evening school and family agricultural production during the 1980s.
3. *Between 1957 and 1959*. Following the 1956 insurrection, the Kádár regime adopted a dual strategy: it was brutally oppressive toward the urban proletariat and dissenting intelligentsia,[2] but it was reasonably liberal in the countryside, toward the peasantry. Though most people knew that this liberalism toward private farming would not last very long, little administrative pressure toward collectivization was applied until early 1959. Under such circumstances joining the kolkhoz, becoming a boss, giving up self-employment, or attending an evening school were signs of surrender to the dual pressure of proletarianization and cadrefication.
4. *Between 1960 and 1968*. This regime began with the second big push for collectivization. As we noted in our ethnographic account, further resistance to collectivization at this time was senseless. People on an embourgeoisement trajectory joined the kolkhozes and even accepted jobs as bosses, at least for a while. In order to use supervisory positions as parking orbits, they may have been willing to attend evening schools as well.

[2] It executed about a thousand people, mostly workers, during these years. The Hungarian regime is silent about the number of death penalties after 1956, but people imprisoned during those years report several executions every week for at least 18 months after the spring of 1958 in the Budapest jail alone. For instance, we interviewed Istvan Eörsi, who was a prisoner in the jail in which the executions took place. During the time he spent at this jail (Gyüjtöfogház), he says, there were executions about three times a week; each time about four people were killed. Eörsi and others reported that each time executions took place the condemned shouted their names as they were escorted to the scaffold. Thus one thousand dead is a modest estimate; it may not even count those murdered during the martial law imposed in December 1956.

5. *After 1968*. During these years the second economy gradually opened up. Embourgeoisement increasingly became an alternative to proletarianization or cadrefication. People who did not want to become cadres could find an alternative trajectory for upward mobility; they did not have to become bosses or attend evening schools. Thus we should anticipate that both attendance at evening schools and becoming a supervisor during these years will be negatively correlated to family entrepreneurship in the 1980s.

MEANS AND STANDARD DEVIATIONS FOR VARIABLES

Variable label	*Means*	*Standard deviation* ($N = 7754$)
	Dependent variables[3]	
FAP	1949.263	2239.885
FAPS	12981.312	23738.622
FAPC	6809.203	5167.104
LogFAP	6.584	2.326
LogFAPS	7.483	3.295
LogFAPC	7.782	2.768
	Independent variables	
AGE	52.650	15.783
AGESQUARE	3021.106	1699.947
ACTIVNO	1.339	1.074
HOMEDUTY	.135	.360
RETIRNO	.670	.720
CHILD	.783	1.044
ONECOUPLE	.713	.452
MORECOUPLE	.063	.243

[3] These are unweighted data. Whenever we refer to mean incomes, we present weighted data. The 1982–83 Income and Social Mobility and Life History surveys were conducted using a random sample, in which the selection rate varied according to the size of the communities. The CSO attached different weights to respondents from different communities in estimating values for the total population. Whenever we calculate descriptive statistics from these files, we report weighted values. The sample selection models and this table, in contrast, contain unweighted figures. In this table the figures for FAP are monthly income, whereas FAPS and FAPC represent yearly incomes, in Ft.

AGRAR	.273	.445
OFARM44	.176	.381
REFORM	.203	.402
BOSYEAR	1.148	4.753
COPYEARS	4.836	7.977
SELFYEARS	2.311	6.643
EVENING	.108	.311
FIFTHYEAR	.151	.358
PFARM44	.129	.336
REFORMPW	.160	.366
MANORIAL	.120	.325
NONAGR38	.278	.448
BOSHIS45	.002	.047
BOSHIS50	.016	.124
BOSHIS57	.007	.085
BOSHIS60	.019	.136
COPHIS50	.046	.210
COPHIS57	.054	.227
COPHIS60	.156	.363
SELFHIS50	.037	.190
SELFHIS57	.032	.176
SELFHIS60	.062	.242
EVNHIS57	.006	.074
RETURN60	.065	.242
RETURN70	.147	.352
INDAGR70	.052	.223

References

Andorka, Rudolf. 1979. *A Magyar Községek Társadalmának Átalakulása* [Transformation of Hungarian rural society]. Budapest: Magvető Kiadó.

Andorka, Rudolf. 1982. *A Társadalmi Mobilitás Változásai Magyarországon* [Social mobility in Hungary]. Budapest: Gondolat Kiadó.

Andorka, Rudolf, and Harcsa, István. 1982. A községi népesség társadalomstatisztikai leirása [A statistical description of the rural population]. *In* Vágvölgyi, A., ed., *A Falu a Mai Magyar Társadalomban* [The village in contemporary Hungarian society]. Budapest: Akadémiai Kiadó. Pp. 179–236.

Andorka, Rudolf, and Kolosi, Tamás, eds. 1984. *Stratification and Inequality*. Budapest: Institute for Social Sciences.

Bauer, Tamás. 1978. Investment cycles in planned economies. *Acta Oeconomica*, 21(3): 243–260.

Bauer, Tamás. 1981. *Tervgazdaság, Beruházás, Ciklusok* [Planned economy, investments, and cycles]. Budapest: Közgazdasági és Jogi Könyvkiadó.

Bell, D. Peter. 1984. *Peasants in Socialist Transition: Life in a Collectivized Hungarian Village*. Berkeley: University of California Press.

Bennholdt-Thomsen, Veronika. 1982. *Bauern in Mexico: Zwischen Subsistenz- und Warenproduktion*. Frankfurt: Campus Verlag.

Berend, T. Iván, and Ránki, György. 1972. *A Magyar Gazdaság Száz Éve* [One hundred years of the Hungarian economy]. Budapest: Kossuth Könyvkiadó.

Bettelheim, Charles. 1976. *Economic Calculations and the Forms of Property*. London: Routledge and Kegan Paul.

Bibó, István. 1940. Erdei Ferenc munkássága a magyar parasztság válságának irodalmában [Ferenc Erdei and the literature on the crisis of the Hungarian peasantry]. *In* Kemény, István, ed., *Bibó István Összegyüjtött Munkái* [Collected works of István Bibó]. Bern: Europai Protestáns Magyar Szabadegyetem, 1982. Vol. 2, pp. 327–337.

Bibó, István. 1945. A magyar demokrácia válsága [The crisis of Hungarian democracy]. *In* Kemény, István, ed., *Bibó István Összegyüjtött Munkái* [Collected works of István Bibó]. Bern: Europai Protestáns Magyar Szabadegyetem, 1981. Vol. 1, pp. 39–80.

Bibó, István. 1946a. A kelet-europai kisállamok nyomorúsága [The misery of the small East European countries]. *In* Kemény, István, ed., *Bibó István Összegyüjtött Munkái* [Collected works of István Bibó]. Bern: Europai Protestáns Magyar Szabadegyetem, 1981. Vol. 1, pp. 202–251.

Bibó, István. 1946b. A magyar társadalomfejlődés és az 1945. évi változás értelme [Hungarian social evolution and the meaning of the change in 1945]. *In* Kemény, István, ed., *Bibó István Összegyüjtött Munkái* [Collected works of István Bibó]. Bern: Europai Protestáns Magyar Szabadegyetem, 1982. Vol. 2, pp. 351–362.

Bibó, István. 1947. A Nemzeti Parasztpárt jellemzése [Characterization of the National Peasant Party]. *In* Kemény, István, ed., *Bibó István Összegyüjtött Munkái* [Collected works of István Bibó]. Bern: Europai Protestáns Magyar Szabadegyetem, 1983. Vol. 3, pp. 795–821.

Bibó, István. 1948. Eltorzult magyar alkat, zsákutcás magyar történelem [The distorted Hungarian character and the dead-end streets of Hungarian history]. *In* Kemény, István, ed., *Bibó István Összegyüjtött Munkái* [Collected works of István Bibó]. Bern: Europai Protestáns Magyar Szabadegyetem, 1981. Vol. 1, pp. 255–286.

Bibó, István. 1971–72. Az europai társadalomfejlődés értelme [The meaning of European social evolution]. *In* Kemény, István, ed., *Bibó István Összegyüjtött Munkái* [Collected works of István Bibó]. Bern: Europai Protestáns Magyar Szabadegyetem, 1982. Vol. 2, pp. 560–635.

Biró, Ferenc, Sós, Gábor, Szalai, Béla, and Szlamenczky, István. 1980. *Merre Tart a Magyar Mezőgazdaság?* [Recent trends in Hungarian agriculture?]. Budapest: Kossuth Kiadó.

Böhm, Antal, and Pál, László. 1985. *Társadalmunk Ingázoi—Az Ingázok Társadalma* [Commuters in our society and the society of commuters]. Budapest: Kossuth Kiadó.

Boros, Anna. 1982. Második gazdaság—rétegződés [Second economy and stratification]. *In* Kolosi, Tamás, ed., *Elméletek és Hipotézisek* [Theories and hypotheses]. Budapest: Társadalomtudományi Intézet.

Bourdieu, Pierre. 1979. *Outline of a Theory of Practice*. Cambridge: Cambridge University Press.

Braverman, Harry. 1974. *Labor and Monopoly Capital: The Degradation of Work in the Twentieth Century*. New York: Monthly Review Press.

Brenner, Robert, 1976. Agrarian class structure and economic development in pre-industrial Europe. *Past and Present*, No. 70: 30–75.

Brown, D. L., and Beale, C. L. 1981. Diversity in post-1970 population trends. *In* Hawley, A. H. and Mazie, S. M., eds., *Nonmetropolitan America in Transition*. Chapel Hill: University of North Carolina Press. Pp. 27–71.

Burawoy, Michael. 1979. *Manufacturing Consent*. Chicago: University of Chicago Press.

Burawoy, Michael. 1985a. Piece rates, Hungarian style. *Socialist Review*, 79: 42–69.

Burawoy, Michael. 1985b. *The Politics of Production*. London: New Left Books.

Burawoy, Michael, and Lukács, János. 1986. Mythologies of work: a comparison of firms in state socialism and advanced capitalism. *American Sociological Review*, 50(6): 723–737.

Buttel, Fred. 1980. Whither the family farm? Toward a sociological perspective on independent commodity production in U.S. agriculture. *Cornell Journal of Social Relations*, 15(1): 10–37.

Buttel, Fred, and Newby, Howard. 1980. *The Rural Sociology of the Advanced Societies*. Montclair, N.J.: Allanheld, Osum.

Cavazinni, A. 1979. *Part-time Farming in the Advanced Industrial Societies: Role and Characteristics in the United States*. New York State College of Agricultural and Life Sciences, Cornell University Agricultural Experiment Station, Department of Rural Sociology, Rural Sociology Bulletin No. 106.

Central Statistical Office, Hungary, 1982. *A Mezőgazdasági Kistermelés* [Family agricultural production]. Budapest: Központi Statisztikai Hivatal.

Central Statistical Office, Hungary, 1984 (Vol. 1), 1985 (Vol. 2). *Időfelhasználás a Mezőgazdasagi Kistermelésben* [Uses of time in family agricultural production]. Budapest: Központi Statisztikai Hivatal.

Cliff, Tony. 1979. *State Capitalism in Russia*. London: Pluto Press.

Coughenour, C. Milton and Wimberley, Ronald C. 1982. Small and part-time farmers. *In* Dillman, Don A., and Hobbs, Daryl J., eds, *Rural Society in the U.S.: Issues for the 1980's.* Boulder, Colorado: Westview Press. Pp. 347–356.

Csizmadia, Ernö. 1977. *Socialist Agriculture in Hungary*. Budapest: Akadémiai Kiadó.

Davis, K. and Golden, H. Hertz. 1954–55. Urbanization and the development of pre-industrial areas. *Economic Development and Cultural Change*, 3: 6–26.

Deppe, Rainer. 1984. Ungarns "Zweite" Wirtschaft—Das ungeliebte Kind der bürokratischen Planwirtschaft. *Osteuropawirtschaft*, No. 4: 285–305.

Dillman, Don A., and Hobbs, Daryl J. 1982. *Rural Society in the U.S.: Issues for the 1980s*. Boulder, Colorado: Westview Press.

Djilas, Milovan. 1966. *The New Class*. London: Unwin.

Donáth, Ferenc. 1969. *Demokratikus Földreform Magyarországon, 1945–47* [Democratic land reform in Hungary, 1945–47]. Budapest: Közgazdasági és Jogi Könyvkiadó.

Donáth, Ferenc. 1977. *Reform és Forradalom. A Magyar Mezőgazdaság Strukturális Átalakulása 1945–1975* [Reform and revolution. Structural changes in Hungarian agriculture, 1945–1975]. Budapest: Akadémiai Kiadó.

Donáth, Ferenc. 1982–83. Tulajdon és hatékonyság [Property and efficiency]. *Medvetánc*, No. 1: 161–190.

Dorner, Peter. 1976. *Economic and Social Change of Wisconsin Family Farms*. University of Wisconsin–Madison, The Research Division of the College of Agricultural and Life Sciences, Research Bulletin R3105.

Duchêne, G. 1981. La seconde économie. *In* Lavigne, M., ed., *Travail et Monnaie en Système Socialiste*. Paris: Economica.

Dupay, A., and Truchil, B. 1979. Problems in the theory of state capitalism. *Theory and Society*, 8(1): 1–38.

Eckart, Karl. 1983. Die Bedeutung der privaten Anbauflächen für die Versorgung der Bevölkerung in der DDR. *Deutschland Archiv*, No. 4: 415–420.

Enyedi, György, ed. 1976. *Rural Transformation in Hungary*. Budapest: Akadémiai Kiadó.

Enyedi, György. 1980. *Falvaink Sorsa* [The fate of our villages]. Budapest: Magvető.

Enyedi, György. 1983. *Földrajz és Társadalom* [Geography and society]. Budapest: Magvető.

Enyedi, György. 1984. *Az Urbanizácios Ciklus és a Magyar Településhálozat Átalakulása* [The cycle of urbanization and the changes of the Hungarian regional system]. Budapest: Akadémiai Kiadó.

Erdei, Ferenc. 1937. *Futóhomok* [Drifting sand]. 1977 ed. Budapest: Akadémiai Kiadó.

Erdei, Ferenc. 1939. *Magyar Város* [The Hungarian city]. 1974 ed. Budapest: Akadémiai Kiadó.

Erdei, Ferenc. 1938. *Parasztok* [Peasants]. 1973 ed. Budapest: Akadémiai Kiadó.

Erdei, Ferenc. 1940. *Magyar Falu* [The Hungarian village]. 1974 ed. Budapest: Akadémiai Kiadó.

Erdei, Ferenc. 1942. A magyar paraszttársadalom [The Hungarian peasantry]. *In* Kulcsár, Kálman, ed., *Erdei Ferenc a Magyar Társadalomrol* [Ferenc Erdei on Hungarian society]. Budapest: Akadémiai Kiadó, 1980. Pp. 188–209.

Erdei, Ferenc. 1943. A magyar társadalom [Hungarian society]. *In* Pintér, István, et al., eds., *Szárszó 1943*. Budapest: Kossuth Könyvkiadó. A lecture given at the Szárszó conference.

Erdei, Ferenc. 1976. A magyar társadalom a két világháború között [Hungarian society during the interwar years]. *In* Kulcsár, Kálman, ed., *Erdei Ferenc a Magyar Társadalomról* [Ferenc Erdei on Hungarian society]. Budapest: Akadémiai Kiadó, 1980.

Fazekas, Béla, Kovács, Imre, Molnár, István, et al. 1985. *Mezőgazdasági Szövetkezetek Magyarországon* [Agricultural cooperatives in Hungary]. Budapest: Termelőszövetkezetek Országos Tanácsa.

Featherman, David L., and Hauser, Robert M. 1978. *Opportunity and Change*. New York: Academic Press.

Fehér, Ferenc, Heller, Agnes, and Márkus, George. 1983. *Dictatorship over Needs*. London: Blackwell.

Fekete, Ferenc, and Sebestyén, Katalin. 1978. Organization and recent development in Hungarian agriculture. *Acta Oeconomica*, 21(1–2): 91–105.

Fél, E., and Hofer, T. *Proper Peasants*. New York: Viking Fund Press.

Ferge, Zsuzsa. 1979. *A Society in the Making*. White Plains, N.Y.: Sharpe.

Ferman, L. A., and Berndt, L. 1981. The irregular economy. *In* Henry, S., ed., *Informal Institutions*. New York: St. Martin's Press. Pp. 26–42.

Foster, John. 1974. *Class Struggle and the Industrial Revolution*. London: Weidenfeld and Nicolson.

Foster-Carter, Aidan. 1978. The modes of production controversy. *New Left Review*, No. 107: 47–77.

Franklin, S. H. 1969. *The European Peasantry: The Final Phase*. London: Methuen.

Friedmann, H. 1981. The family farm in advanced capitalism—outline of a theory of simple commodity production in agriculture. Paper prepared for the thematic panel "Rethinking Domestic Agriculture." American Sociological Association, Toronto, August 1981.

Gábor, I. R. 1979a. Második gazdaság és háztáji gasdálkodás [Second economy and production on household plots]. *Valóság*, No. 7: 101–103.

Gábor, I. R. 1979b. The second (secondary) economy. *Acta Oeconomica*, 22(3–4): 291–311.

Gábor. I. R., and Galasi, Péter. 1979. A második gazdaság módositó szerepe és a társadalmi struktura [The modifying effects of the second economy and social structure]. *In* Kolosi, Tamás, ed., *Társadalmi Strukturánk Fejlődése* [The evolution of social structure in Hungary]. Budapest: Társadalomtudományi Intézet.

Gaertner, Wulf, and Wenig, Alois. 1985. *The Economics of the Shadow Economy*. Berlin: Springer Verlag.

Galasi, Péter, and Gábor, I. R. 1981. *A "Második" Gazdaság* [The "second" economy]. Budapest: Közgazdasági és Jogi Könyvkiadó.

Galasi, Péter, and Sziráczki, György, eds. 1985. *Labor Market and Second Economy in Hungary*. Frankfurt: Campus Verlag.

Gershuny, J. I. 1978. *After Industrial Society*. London: Macmillan.

Gershuny, J. I., and Pahl, R.E. 1981. The future of the informal economy. *In* Henry, S., ed., *Informal Institutions*, New York: St. Martin's Press. Pp. 73–88.

Gilbert, Alan, and Gugler, Josef. 1982. *Cities, Poverty, and Development*. Oxford: Oxford University Press.

Gjerde, Jon. 1985. *From Peasants to Farmers*. Cambridge: Cambridge University Press.

Golachowski, S. 1967. Semi-urbanization? *Polish Perspectives*, 10(4): 22–30.

Gouldner, Alvin. 1979. *The Future of the Intellectuals and the Rise of the New Class*. Oxford: Oxford University Press.

Grossmann, G. 1977. The "second economy" of the USSR. *Problems of Communism*, No. 5: 25–40.

Gugler, Josef. 1982. Overurbanization reconsidered. *Economic Development and Cultural Change*, 31: 173–189.

Gunszt, Péter. 1974. Kelet-europa gazdasági-társadalmi fejlődésének néhány kérdése [Socioeconomic development in Eastern Europe]. *Valóság*, No. 3: 16–31.

Gyenes, Antal. 1968. Munkások és parasztok a mezőgazdasági termelőszövetkezetekben [Workers and peasants in agricultural cooperatives]. *Valóság*, No. 4: 26–36.

Hanák, Katalin. 1982. A falusi lakosság nemzedékek közötti mobilitásának néhány vonása [Rural intergenerational mobility]. *In* Vágvölgyi, A., ed., *A Falu a Mai Magyar Társadalomban* [The village in contemporary Hungarian society]. Budapest: Akadémai Kiadó. Pp. 237–288.

Hann, Chris M. 1983. Progress toward collectivized agriculture in Tázlár 1949–78. *In* Hollós, Marida, and Maday, Béla C., eds., *New Hungarian Peasants*. New York: Social Science Monographs—Brooklyn College Press. Pp. 69–92.

Haraszti, Miklós. 1977. *Workers in a Worker's State*. London: Penguin Books.

Hare, P. G., Radice, H. K., and Swain, N. 1981. *Hungary—A Decade of Economic Reform*. London: Allen and Unwin.

Haren, E. B., and Holling, R. W. 1979. Industrial development in nonmetro America. *In* Lonsdale, R. E., and Seyler, H. L., eds., *Non-Metropolitan Industrialization*. Washington D. C.: V. H. Winston and Sons. Pp. 13–45.

Harper, E. B., Fliegel, F. C., and van Es, J. C. 1980. Growing number of small farms. *Rural Sociology* 45(4): 608–620.

Hauser, Robert M. 1980. On "Stratification in a Dual Economy." Madison, Wis.: University of Wisconsin–Madison, Institute for Research on Poverty Discussion Papers, DP #592–79.

Hawley, A. H., and Mazie, S. M., eds. 1981. *Nonmetropolitan America in Transition*. Chapel Hill: University of North Carolina Press.

Heaton, T., and Fuguitt, G. 1979. Nonmetropolitan industrial growth and net migration. *In* Lonsdale, R. E., and Seyler, H. L., eds., *Non-Metropolitan Industrialization*. Washington, D. C.: V. H. Winston and Sons. Pp. 119–136.

Hegedűs, András. 1970. *Változó Világ* [The changing rural world in Hungary]. Budapest: Akadémiai Kiadó.

Henry, S., 1982. The working unemployed—perspectives on the informal economy and unemployment. *Sociological Review*, 30(3): 460–477.

Henry, S. ed. 1981. *Informal Institutions*. New York: St. Martin's Press.

Héthy, Lajos, and Makó, Csaba. 1972. *Munkásmagatartások és a gazdasági szervezet* [Workers' behavior and economic organization]. Budapest: Akadémiai Kiadó.

Hollós, Marida, and Maday, Béla C., eds. 1983. *New Hungarian Peasants: An East Central European Experience with Collectivization*. New York: Social Science Monographs—Brooklyn College Press.

Hoppál, Mihály. 1983. Proxemics, private and public—community and communication in a Hungarian village. *In* Hollós, Marida, and Maday, Béla C., eds., *New Hungarian Peasants*. New York: Social Science Monographs—Brooklyn College Press. Pp. 245–271.

Horkheimer, Max. 1972. Traditional and critical theory. *Critical Theory*. New York: Herder and Herder. Pp. 188–243.

Huszár, István. 1985. A társadalom szerkezetének átalakulásáról [Changes in social structure]. *Valóság*, 28(2): 1–7.

Jávor, Kata. 1983. Continuity and change in the social and value systems of a northern Hungarian village. *In* Hollós, Marida, and Maday, Béla C., eds., *New Hungarian Peasants*. New York: Social Science Monographs—Brooklyn College Press. Pp. 273–300.

Jerome, W., and Buick, A. 1967. Soviet state capitalism? The history of an idea. *Survey*, January: 58–71.

Juhász, János. 1980. *A Háztáji Gazdálkodás Mezőgazdaságunkban* [Domestic husbandry in our agriculture]. Budapest: Akadémiai Kiadó.

Juhász, Pál. 1973. A mezőgazdaság fejlődésében megjelenő tehetetlenségről [Continuities in the development of agriculture]. Budapest: Szövetkezeti Kutató Intézet. Közlemények [Working papers], No. 93.

Juhász, Pál. 1975. A mezőgazdasági szövetkezetek dolgozóinak rétegzödése munkahelycsoportok, származás és életút szerint [Stratification of workers of farming cooperatives according to types of work performed, social origins and life histories]. Budapest: Szövetkezeti Kutató Intézet. Evkönyv [Yearbook], pp. 241–278.

Juhász, Pál. 1976. Adalékok a háztáji és a kisegitő gazdaság elméletéhez [Contributions to the theory of family minifundia]. Budapest: Szövetkezeti Kutató Intézet. Manuscript. A version of this paper was published in 1982 as "Agrárpiac, kisüzem, nagyüzem" [Agrarian market, small enterprise, large enterprise]. *Medvetánc*, No. 1: 117–139.

Juhász, Pál. 1977. Miért nincsenek komplex brigádok? [Are the complex brigades irrelevant?]. Budapest: Szövetkezeti Kutató Intézet. Evkönyv [Yearbook].

Juhász, Pál. 1979. Lecture on the breakdown of the integrative function of the agricultural cooperatives. Conference paper. Published in conference proceedings, *30 Eves a Mezögazdasági Szövetkezet* [30 Years of the agricultural Cooperatives]. Szolnok: Történettudományi Társaság Kiadása.

Juhász, Pál. 1983a. Az agrárértelmiség szerepe és a mezőgazdasági szövetkezetek [The role of agricultural professionals in agricultural producers' cooperatives]. *Medvetánc*, No. 1: 191–213.

Juhász, Pál. 1983b. Medve Alfonz parasztpolgár és a magyar gazdasági csoda [Alfonz Medve, peasant-burgher, and the Hungarian economic miracle]. *Ne Sápadj* [Do not worry]. Budapest: Objektiv Filmstudio.

Juhász, Pál. 1984. The transformation of management, work organization and worker endeavors in Hungarian cooperative farms. Budapest: Cooperative Research Institute. (Manuscript.) Hungarian version was published in *Gazdaság, Társadalom, Értékrend: Előadások a MTA 1984 Tavaszi Tudományos Ulésszakán* [Economy, society, and value system: Lectures at the 1984 Spring Annual Meetings of the Hungarian Academy of Sciences]. Budapest: Magyar Tudományos Akadémia 2. Osztálya.

Juhász, Pál. 1985. A visszatorlódásról. Változások a falusi fiatalság életében [On the demographic turnaround. Changes in the life of rural youth]. *Kritika*, No. 2.

Juhász, Pál, and Magyar, Bálint. 1983. Néhány megjegyzés a lengyel és a magyar mezőgazdasagi kistermelő helyzetéről a hetvenes években [Some remarks on the position of Polish and Hungarian agricultural small-scale producers in the seventies]. Paper presented at the 12th Conference of the European Society for Rural Sociology. Published in Hungarian in *Medvetánc*, 1984, No. 2–3: 181–208.

Kada, R. 1980. *Part-time Family Farming*. Tokyo: Center for Academic Publications.

Kemény, István. 1972. A magyar munkásosztály rétegződése [Social stratification of the Hungarian working class]. *Szociológia*, 1(1): 36–48.

Kemény, István. 1982. The unregistered economy in Hungary. *Soviet Studies*, 34(3): 349–366.

Kerék, Mihály. 1939. *A Magyar Földkérdés* [The Hungarian land question]. Budapest: Egyetemi Nyomda.

Kolankiewicz, George. 1980. The new "awkward class"—the peasant-worker in Poland. *Sociologia Ruralis*, 20(1–2): 28–43.

Kolankiewicz, George. 1985. The peasant-worker in Poland—perspectives, prospects and prognosis. Paper presented at the III World Congress for Soviet and East European Studies, Washington, D.C., October 30–November 3, 1985.

Köllő, J. 1981. Taktikázás és alkudozás az ipari üzemben [Bargaining in industrial enterprises]. *Közgazdasági Szemle*, No. 7–8: 853–866.

Kolosi, Tamás. 1982a. A strukturális viszonyok körvonalai [On social structure]. *Valóság*, No. 11: 1–17.

Kolosi, Tamás. 1982b. Struktura, rétegzödés, metodologia [Structure, stratification, methodology]. *In* Kolosi, Tamás, ed., *Elméletek és Hipotézisek* [Theories and hypotheses]. Budapest: Társadalomtudományi Kutató Intézet.

Kolosi, Tamás. 1983. *Struktura és Egyenlötlenség.* [Structure and inequality]. Budapest: Kossuth Kiadó.

Konrád, George, and Szelényi, Iván. 1971. A késleltett városfejlődés társadalmi konfliktusai. *Valóság*. Eng. translation: Social conflicts of under-urbanization. *In* Harloe, Michael, ed., *The Captive City*. New York: John Wiley and Son. Pp. 157–174.

Konrád, George, and Szelényi, Iván. 1979. *The Intellectuals on the Road to Class Power*. New York: Harcourt, Brace, Jovanovich.

Kornai, János. 1980. *Economics of Shortage*. Amsterdam: North Holland.

Kornai, János. 1983. Bürokratikus és piaci koordináció [Bureaucratic and market coordination]. *Közgazdasági Szemle*, No. 9: 1025–1037.

Kovách, Imre, and Kuczi, Tibor. 1982. A gazdálkodási előnyök átváltási lehetőségei társadalmunkban [Cashing in the social benefits of agricultural entrepreneurial advantages in our society]. *Valóság*, No. 6: 45–55.

Kovách, Imre, and Kuczi, Tibor. 1983. Kisárutermelők gazdaságtörténetének kohorszonkénti elemzése [A cohort analysis of the history of small agricultural producers]. *Szociológia*, No. 3: 273–288.

Kovách, Imre, and Kuczi, Tibor. 1984. Agricultural small market producers. *In* Andorka, Rudolf, and Kolosi, Tamás, eds., *Stratification and Inequality*. Budapest: Institute of Social Sciences. Pp. 267–286.

Kovács, Imre, 1936. *A Néma Forradalom* [The Silent Revolution]. Budapest: Cserépfalvi.

Kövari, G., and Sziráczki, G. 1985. Old and new forms of wage bargaining on the shop floor. *In* Galasi, Péter, and Sziráczki, György, eds., *Labor Market and Second Economy in Hungary*. Frankfurt: Campus Verlag. Pp. 264–292.

Kulcsár, Kálmán. 1982. A magyar falu és a magyar parasztság [The Hungarian village and Hungarian peasants]. *In* Vágvölgyi, A., ed., *A Falu a Magyar Társadalomban* [The village in contemporary Hungarian society]. Budapest: Akadémiai Kiadó.

Kulcsár, László, and Szijjártó, András. 1980. *Iparosodás és Társadalmi Változások a Mezőgazdaságban* [Industrialization and social change in agriculture]. Budapest: Közgazdasági és Jogi Kiadó.

Kulcsár, Viktor, ed., 1976. *A Változó Falu* [The changing rural community]. Budapest: Gondolat Kiadó.

Lázár, István. 1976. The collective farm and the private plot. *New Hungarian Quarterly*, 17(63): 61–67.

Lenin, V. I. 1907. The agrarian programme of social-democracy in the first Russian Revolution 1905–1907. *Lenin Collected Works*. Moscow: Foreign Language Publishing House, 1961. Vol. 13, pp. 238–242.

Lenin, V. I. 1919. Economics and politics of the era of the dictatorship of the proletariat. *Lenin Collected Works*. Moscow: Progress Publishers. Vol. 3, pp. 288–297.

Long, Norman, and Roberts, Bryan. 1984. *Miners, Peasants and Entrepreneurs*. Cambridge: Cambridge University Press.

Lonsdale, R. E., and Seyler, H. L., eds. 1979. *Non-Metropolitan Industrialization*. Washington D.C.: V. H. Winston and Sons.

Losonczi, Ágnes. 1977. *Az Életmód and Időben, a Tárgyakban és az Ertékekben* [Ways of life, time, objects, and values]. Budapest: Gondolat Kiadó.

Lukács, György. 1945. A demokcrácia válsága, vagy jobboldali kritikája? [The crisis of democracy or its right-wing critique?]. *In* Kemény, István, ed., *Bibó István Összegyüjtött Munkái* [Collected works of István Bibó]. Bern: Europai Protestáns Magyar Szabadegyetem, 1981. Vol. 1, pp. 289–303.

Makó, Csaba. 1985. *Munkafolyamat: A Társadalmi Viszonyok Erőtere* [The labor process: an arena of social struggle]. Budapest: Közgazdasági és Jogi Könyvkiadó.

Mallet, Serge. 1975. *Essays on the New Working Class*. St. Louis: Telos Press.

Manchin, Robert, and Szelényi, Iván. 1985. Eastern Europe in the crisis of transition. *In* Misztal, B., ed., *Social Movements versus the State: Beyond Solidarity*. New Brunswick, N.J.: Transaction Books. Pp. 87–102.

Manchin, Robert, and Szelényi, Iván. 1987. Social policy under state socialism. *In* Esping-Anderson, G., Rainwater, L., and Rein, M., eds., *Stagnation and Renewal in Social Policy*. White Plains, N.Y.: Sharpe.

Mannheim, Karl. 1925. The problem of sociology of knowledge. *In* Wolff, Kurt, ed., *From Karl Mannheim*. New York: Oxford University Press, 1971. Pp. 59–115.

Márkus, István. 1972. *Kifelé a Feudalizmusból* [Moving out of feudalism]. Budapest: Szépirodalmi Könyvkiadó.

Márkus, István. 1973. Az utóparasztság arcképéhez [On the post-peasantry]. *Szociológia*, 2(1): 56–67.

Márkus, István. 1979. *Nagykőrös* [Ethnography of the city of Nagykőrös]. Budapest: Szépirodalmi Könyvkiadó.

Márkus, István. 1980. Az ismeretlen főszereplő—a szegényparasztság [The unrecognized driving force of history—the poor peasants]. *Valóság*, 23(4): 13–39.

Martin, Bill, and Szelényi, Iván. 1987. Theories of cultural capital and beyond. *In* Eyerman, Ron, and Sodequist, Thomas, eds., *Intellectuals, Universities, and the State*. Berkeley: University of California Press.

Marx, Karl. 1847. *The Poverty of Philosophy*. Moscow: Progress Publishers, 1973.

Marx, Karl. 1867. *Capital*. Moscow: Progress Publishers, 1977. Vol. 1.

Menchik, M. D. 1981. The service sector. *In* Hawley, A. H., and Mazie, S. M., eds., *Nonmetropolitan America in Transition*. Chapel Hill: University of North Carolina Press.

Mendras, Henri. 1967. *Le Fin des Paysans*. Paris: Librairie Armand Colin.

Miller, J. P. 1980. *Nonmetro Job Growth and Locational Change in Manufacturing Firms*. U. S. Department of Agriculture, Economic Development Division, Economics, Statistics and Cooperative Services, Rural Development Research Report No. 24.

Miller, S. M. 1964. The working class subculture. *In* Shostak, A. B., and Gomberg, W., eds., *Blue Collar World*. Englewood Cliffs, N.J.: Prentice Hall.

Moore, K. 1983. The household labor allocation of farm-based families in Wisconsin. The University of Wisconsin–Madison, Ph.D. dissertation.

Münch, Anne, and Nau, Hans. 1983. Zur Stellung, Bedeutung, und Organisation der individuellen Tierproduction unter sozialistischen Produktionsverhaltnissen. *Wirtschaftswissenschaft*, No. 5: 667–678.

Munslow, B., and Finch, H., eds. 1984. *Proletarianization in the Third World*. London: Croom Helm.

Murray, Pearse, and Szelényi, Iván. 1984. The city in the transition to socialism. *International Journal of Urban and Regional Research*, 8(1): 90–107.

Németh, László. 1943. Előadása [Lecture]. *In* Pintér, István, et al., eds., *Szárszó 1943*. Budapest: Kossuth Könyvkiadó. A lecture given at the Szárszó conference.

OECD. 1977. *Part-time Farming: Germany, Japan, Norway, United States*. Paris: OECD, Agricultural Policy Reports.

Orbán, Sándor. 1972. *Két Agrárforradalom Magyarországon* [Two agrarian revolutions in Hungary]. Budapest: Akadémiai Kiadó.

Oros, Iván. 1983. A mezőgazdasági kistermelés [Agricultural small producers]. *Statisztikai Szemle*, No. 12: 1216–1237.

Oros, Iván. 1984. Small scale agricultural production in Hungary. *Acta Oeconomica*, 32 (1–2): 65–90.

Őrszigeti, Erzsébet. 1985. *Asszonyok Férfisorban* [Women in male roles]. Budapest: Magvető Kiadó.

Ossowski, Stanislaw. 1963. *Class Structure in the Social Consciousness*. London: Routledge and Kegan Paul.

Pach, Zsigmond Pál. 1963. *Nyugat-europai és Magyarországi Agrárfejlődés a XV–XVII. században* [Agrarian development in Western Europe and in Hungary during the 16th–17th centuries]. Budapest: Akadémiai Kiadó.

Pahl, R. E. 1980. Employment, work and the domestic division of labor. *International Journal of Urban and Regional Research*, 4(1): 1–18.

Pahl, R. E. 1984. *Divisions of Labour*. Oxford: Basil Blackwell.

Pahl, R. E. 1986. Social polarization and the economic crisis. Paper presented at seminar organized by the Hungarian Academy of Sciences, ELTE University, and the Research Committee on the Sociology of Urban and Rural Development, Budapest, 25–28 March, 1986.

Pahl, R. E., and Gershuny, J. I. 1979. Work outside employment—some preliminary speculations. *New Universities Quarterly*, 34(1): 120–135.

Pahl, R. E., and Gershuny, J. I. 1980. Britain in the decade of the three economies. *New Society*, January 3, pp. 7–9.

Poulantzas, Nicos. 1973. *Political Power and Social Classes*. London: New Left Books.

Przeworski, Adam. 1986. *Capitalism and Social Democracy*. Cambridge: Cambridge University Press.

Radnóti, H. 1979. Háztáji gazdálkodás és a második gazdaság [Production on household plots and the second economy]. *Valóság*, No. 4: 92–94.

Richta, Radovan. 1969. *Civilization at the Crossroads*. White Plains, N.Y.: Sharpe.

Roseman, C. C., ed. 1981. *Population Redistribution in the Midwest*. Ames, Iowa: North Central Regional Center for Rural Development.

Rupp, Kálmán. 1983. *Entrepreneurs in Red: Structure and Organizational Innovation in the Centrally Planned Economy*. Albany: State University of New York Press.

Sabel, C. F., and Stark, David. 1982. Planning, politics, and shop-floor power: hidden forms of bargaining in state-socialist societies. *Politics and Society*, 11(4): 439–475.

Sárkány, Mihály. 1983. Economic changes in a northern Hungarian village. *In* Hollós, Marida, and Maday, Béla C., eds., *New Hungarian Peasants*. New York: Social Science Monographs—Brooklyn College Press. Pp. 25–56.

Schinke, E. 1983. *Der Anteil der Privaten Landwirtschaft und der Agrarproduktion in den RGW Landern*. Berlin: Duncker und Humblot.

Schmeljow, G., and Steksow, J. 1983. Die individuelle Nebenwirtschaft im Agrar-Industrie-Komplex. *Sowjetwissenschaft*, No. 6: 752–757.

Schumpeter, Joseph A. 1943. *Capitalism, Socialism and Democracy*. London: George Allen and Unwin, 1976.

Shmelev, G. 1981. Social production and personal household plots. *Problems of Economics*, No. 6: 840–849.

Simó, Tibor. 1983. *A Tardi Társadalom* [The society of Tard]. Budapest: Kossuth Könyvkiadó.

Sofranko, A. J., and Williams, J. D., eds. 1980. *Rebirth of Rural America*. Ames, Iowa: North Central Regional Center for Rural Development.

Sovani, N. V. 1964. The analysis of "over-urbanization." *Economic Development and Cultural Change*, 13(2): 113–122.

Sozan, Michael. 1983. Domestic husbandry and social stratification. *In* Hollós, Marida, and Maday, Béla C., eds., *New Hungarian Peasants*. New York: Social Science Monographs—Brooklyn College Press. Pp. 123–144.

Stark, David. 1985. The micropolitics of the firm and the macropolitics of reform—new forms of workplace bargaining in Hungarian enterprises. *In* Evans, Peter, Rueschemeyer, Dietrich, and Stephens, Evelyne Huber, eds., *States versus Markets in the World-System*. Beverly Hills: Sage. Pp. 257–273.

Stark, David. 1986. Rethinking internal labor markets—new insights from a comparative perspective. *American Sociological Review*, 51(4): 492–504.

Summers, G. F., Evans, Sharon D., Clemente, F., et al. 1976. *Industrial Invasion of Nonmetropolitan America: A Quarter Century of Experiences*. New York: Praeger.

Swain, Nigel. 1981. The evolution of Hungary's agricultural system. *In* Hare, P. G., Radice, H. K., and Swain, N., eds., *Hungary—A Decade of Economic Reform*. London: George Allen and Unwin.

Swain, Nigel. 1985. *Collective Farms Which Work?* Cambridge: Cambridge University Press.

Szabó, Lászlo. 1968. *Munkaszervezet és Termelékenység a Magyar Parasztságnál a XIX.–XX. században* [Labor organization and productivity in Hungarian agriculture in the 19th and 20th centuries]. Szolnok: A Damjanich János Muzeum Közleményei.

Szelényi, Iván. 1978. Social inequalities in state socialist redistributive economies. *International Journal of Comparative Sociology*, No. 1–2: 63–87.

Szelényi, Iván. 1981. Urban development and regional management in Eastern Europe. *Theory and Society*, No. 1: 169–205.

Szelényi, Iván. 1982. The intelligentsia in the class structure of state socialist societies. *In* Burawoy, M., and Skocpol, T., eds., *Marxist Inquiries—Studies of Labor, Class and States. American Journal of Sociology*, Vol. 88, Supplement. Pp. 287–326.

Szelényi, Iván. 1985. Recent contributions to the political economy of state socialism. *Contemporary Sociology*, No. 3: 284–287.

Szelényi, Iván. 1986–87. The prospects and limits of the East European new class project—auto-critical reflection on *The Intellectuals on the Road to Class Power*. *Politics and Society*, 15(2): 103–144.

Szelényi, Iván, Jenkins, Robert M., and Manchin, Robert. 1983. Part-time farming in contemporary Hungary: A research report. Final Report to National Council for Soviet and East European Research. Madison, Wis.: University of Wisconsin–Madison, Department of Sociology. (Manuscript)

Szücs, Jenő. 1981. Europa három történeti régionjárol [Three historical regions of Europe]. *Történelmi Szemle*, No. 3: 313–359.

Thompson, E. P. 1963. *The Making of the English Working Class*. London: Penguin Books.

Thompson, E. P. 1978. *The Poverty of Theory*. London: Merlin Press.

Thrift, N. J. and Forbes, D. K. 1985. Cities, socialism, and war—Hanoi, Saigon and the Vietnamese experience with urbanization. *Environment and Planning D: Society and Space*, 3: 279–308.

Till, T. E. 1981. Manufacturing industry—trends and impacts. *In* Hawley, A. H., and Mazie, S. M., eds., *Nonmetropolitan America in Transition*. Chapel Hill: University of North Carolina Press. Pp. 194–230.

Tóth, E. 1975. A háztáji és kisegitő gazdaságok szerepe az iparosodo mezőgazdaságban [The role of production on household plots and subsidiary farms in industrializing agriculture]. *Közgazdasági Szemle*, No. 1: 140–147.

Tóth, Tibor. 1981. *Ellentét vagy Kölcsönösség?* [Contradiction or Complementariness?] Budapest: Magvető Kiadó.

UNESCO. 1957. *Urbanization in Asia and the Far East*. Paris: UNESCO.

Unger, Jonathan. 1983. *The Chen Village*. Berkeley: University of California Press.

Vágvölgyi, András. 1976. A mezőgazdaság fejlődésének társadalmi hatásai [Social impacts of the evolution of agriculture]. *In* Kulcsár, V., ed., *A Változó Falu* [The changing rural community]. Budapest: Gondolat Kiadó. Pp. 152–161.

Vágvölgyi, Andras, ed. 1982. *A Falu a Mai Magyar Társadalomban* [The village in contemporary Hungarian society]. Budapest: Akadémiai Kiadó.

Voslensky, Michael. 1984. *Nomenklatura: The Soviet Ruling Class.* Garden City, N.Y.: Doubleday and Co.

Voss, P. R., and Fuguitt, G. 1979. Turnaround migration in the Upper Great Lakes region. Madison, Wis.: University of Wisconsin–Madison, Department of Rural Sociology, Applied Population Laboratory, research report.

Wadekin, K. E. 1973. *The Private Sector in the Soviet Agriculture*. Berkeley: University of California Press.

Wadekin, K. E. 1982. *Agrarian Policies in Communist Europe*. The Hague: Martinus Nijhoff.

Wallerstein, Immanuel. 1984. Cities in socialist theory and capitalist praxis. *International Journal of Urban and Regional Research*, No. 1: 64–72.

Weber, Max. 1921. *Economy and Society*. Berkeley: University of California Press, 1978.

Wesolowski, W. 1979. *Classes, Strata and Power*. London: Routledge and Kegan Paul.

Whyte, Martin K. 1985. Social trends in China—the triumph of inequality? Ann Arbor, Mich.: University of Michigan, Department of Sociology. (Manuscript)

Wilkening, E. A. 1981. Farm husbands and wives in Wisconsin: Work rules, decision-making and satisfactions, 1962 and 1979. Madison, Wis.: University of Wisconsin–Madison, Research Division of the College of Agriculture and Life Sciences, Research Bulletin R3147.

Williams, J. D. 1981. The nonchanging determinants of nonmetropolitan migration. *Rural Sociology*, 46(2): 183–202.

Wolf, Eric R. 1966. *Peasants*. Englewood Cliffs, N.J.: Prentice-Hall.

The World Bank. 1984. *Hungary—Economic Development and Reforms*. Washington, D. C.: The World Bank.

Wright, Erik O. 1978. *Class, Crisis, and the State*. London: New Left Books.

Wright, Erik O. 1985. *Classes*. London: New Left Books.

Index